We come [barcode] ...s why we
can't treat chil... ... They
can't articulate ... adults can;
their brains aren't fully formed; they don't
understand what's going on; they are prone
to be easily swayed too often; they're more
emotional than intellectual; etc.

TRANSFORMING KNOWLEDGE

Children & "other" from "man" &
                                    "woman"
Language
└ e.g. "primitive" or "folk" art vs.
  ~~modern~~ "the art of Europeans"

Children - why do we not seek out their
voices to tell us "their story". Why do we
feel that their voices, thoughts & feelings are
somehow 'lesser' than those of adults?
In this hierarchical political, social,
economic structure, we then assume the
position of "voice of the children" as we
advocate for the "best interests" of the
child, s̄ asking the children their
thoughts on the matter. Adult-child is
not a dualism but an inherent unequal
distribution of power/status not unlike
many of the 'perceived dualisms' mentione
in this book. (Part IV is good)

Transforming Knowledge

ELIZABETH KAMARCK MINNICH

Temple University Press 𝕋 Philadelphia

Temple University Press, Philadelphia 19122
Copyright © 1990 by Elizabeth Kamarck Minnich. All rights reserved
Published 1990
Printed in the United States of America

♾ The paper used in this publication meets the minimum
requirements of American National Standard for Information Sciences—
Permanence of Paper for Printed Library Materials, ANSI Z39.48-1984

Library of Congress Cataloging-in-Publication Data
Minnich, Elizabeth Kamarck.
Transforming knowledge/Elizabeth Kamarck Minnich.
p.   cm.
ISBN 0-87722-695-4 (alk. paper)
1. Critical thinking. 2. Methodology. 3. Feminism—Philosophy.
I. Title.
89-27302
CIP

For thirty years and more of unwavering friendship
that is the foundation of our home,
and for the work he does to make the world a safer,
fairer place for us all,
I dedicate this book to Si Kahn.
He joins me in recognizing here
that without those who started before us
and have never given up,
our work would be much harder:
to Jane Gould, Gerda Lerner, and Eve Merriam,
admiration, love, and gratitude.

It is not the intelligent woman vs. the ignorant woman, nor the white woman vs. the black, the brown, and the red,—it is not even the cause of woman vs. man. Nay, 'tis woman's strongest vindication for speaking that **the world needs to hear her voice.** . . . The world has had to limp along with the wobbling gait and the one-sided hesitancy of a man with one eye. Suddenly the bandage is removed from the other eye and the whole body is filled with light. It sees a circle where before it saw a segment. The darkened eye restored, every member rejoices with it.

—Anna Julia Cooper
A Voice From The South, 1892

CONTENTS

PREFACE AND
ACKNOWLEDGMENTS

A NOTE ON SOURCES

Books and articles are by no means the only or even the primary sources of ideas that change us. At least as often, and probably more so, such ideas come to us in conversation. But when it comes time to list sources, to give credit, to adduce examples, we turn to published works. I am sorry about that, although I understand it; we cannot offer introductions to all those with whom we have talked as we can list the works we have read and wish to recommend to others. Unfortunately, though, such listings can falsify the history of ideas by making it appear as if all Important Ideas are in texts, and only in texts. They also inaccurately and unfairly privilege those who write over those who think, talk, act, and teach with such involvement that they do not pause to produce the texts that, in a text-dominated culture, confer that peculiar thing, ownership of ideas.

Given all that, I have nevertheless settled on using endnotes to give basic bibliographic information as well as to surround what I say with generally accessible examples and sources of the thinking of others. I intend those notes to be evocative—no more, no less. They are in reality surrounded at every moment by memories I have that are recognized, if incompletely, in the listing of friends, colleagues, organizations, and institutions in the Acknowledgments that follow.

A NOTE ON USAGE

I am no more satisfied with some decisions I have made about usage, but I did the best I could when the time came to stop enjoying the complexities of language and *do* something.

"We"

Several of the readers of an early version of my manuscript commented on a confusing use of "we" throughout the text. They were right, and I made a lot of changes in accordance with their suggestions, but I could not find a way to clear up entirely the confusion caused by my membership in a number of different communities. I say "we" when I wish to stand with a group such as women that has been constituted as a *kind* of human despite serious and significant differences among its members. That seems to me the only response that recognizes some significant realities, whether they are chosen or desired realities or not (certainly they are neither constant nor immutable). I have little respect for those who disclaim or vigorously deny their membership in groups they fear it may be disadvantageous to belong to. Politically potent identifications are perpetuated and not changed by denial. I also believe that standing together is as important as recognizing differences. It is in part because both are important that my own use of "we" changes.

I also use "we" when it would be wrong, as well as ridiculous, to pretend I do not belong to a group such as white middle-class women that has participated in some power and privilege, whether or not I am always proud of that identification. Yet confusion unavoidably lurks here: I stand within the "we" of all women at the same time I know perfectly well that I am also a part of a very particular "we" within it. That is the way things are, and it is not up to me to pretend things are simpler or clearer than they are.

I also use "we" to claim my identification with feminism and feminists, again recognizing as I do so internal differences, even conflicts, within that group. I do not intend to slide into complicity with the efforts to divide and conquer that surround feminists today as they always have. At the same time, I refuse to renounce my participation in the "we" of academics, of teachers, of those who work within as well as on and against the dominant tradition. I, too, am a teacher; I, too, work in Academia. I participate in many of its privileges, so it would be, again, dishonest to dissociate myself from it. I also *choose* to be part of Academia, to struggle for as well as with it, to believe that at least sometimes the values that animate me are as basic to education as are those of others with whom I differ.

And sometimes I use "we" because I wish to speak with people on a basic level on which, despite all our differences, we live, love, work, and have our being. That I hold particular views does not mean that I *am* those views, that I have no common ground with people who disagree with me.

Underlying the use of "we" is the age-old tension of particularity with generality, even universality, as well as related political realities that both express and distort individuality and group membership. I have not found, and, in fact, neither expect nor desire to find, a simple way of resolving such conceptual/political tangles. They call for a life lived attentively and not for any kind of verbal 'solution.'

"Black"/"white"

As we all know, the terms by which groups of people are created and named *as* groups matter a great deal. Very few words, if any, are personally, intellectually, historically, culturally, politically neutral, and certainly such labels are not. They reflect the meanings of the times and situations in which they come into use, and they accrete multiple (even contradictory) meanings over time and across cultures and subcultures. Thus, they can wound and heal, liberate and entrap, threaten and promise, clarify and mystify, and do so differently for different people at different times and in different situations.

Even though I prefer to remain open to changing and multiple usages and try to follow the lead of those who have the right to name themselves and to expect that name to be honored, writing a book that will be with people when I am not necessitates that I make choices. I have most often chosen to use "Black" rather than "black," "Afro-American" or "African-American," on one level simply because it was most consistently used by many of the people I admire during the time in which I was doing the thinking that informs this book. I also chose it because it recalls the powerful anger and pride that burst forth in the Civil Rights Movement in the United States; "Black," in this country at least, is a term chosen within a liberation movement, not one imposed by oppressors. I use it to honor that choice.

I have not capitalized "white" because I do not believe or want to pretend that it is a parallel term. White people have not been oppressed in the United States *because* we are members of a racially defined group, whether or not we have suffered for other reasons. Quite the contrary: whiteness has been claimed as justification for dominance over others, and it is still the case that when we see "white" capitalized, we are often (not always) in the presence of white supremacists, neo-Nazis, the Ku Klux Klan, or others who feel aggrieved because their whiteness (and their Christianity—they are almost always anti-Semitic as well) does not grant them politically and legally protected dominance.

Scare Quotes

Another set of decisions I have made despite a lively sense of its difficulty involves my use of scare quotes. I could, for example, have used scare quotes around 'scare quotes' just as I could have used full quotation marks ("scare quotes"). I used neither here, because I want simply to refer to the marks in question, and neither to the words by which that reference is made nor to the popular sense of the meaning of the words. Elsewhere, I have tried to use quotation marks when I wish to refer to a word or words quite simply, *without* irony, self-consciousness, recognition or sensitivities, or desire to dissociate myself from a familiar usage. I have used scare quotes when I *do* want to indicate that I am using a word self-consciously, that I do want the reader to think a bit about the ways it is commonly—perhaps insensitively, perhaps wrongly, perhaps amusingly—used.

In other circumstances, I would have tried to reduce or eliminate such self-consciousness, such calling of words and usage to the reader's attention. But in a book in which I am thinking about the ways we think, including the words we use, it seemed important to ask the reader to join me in hearing language as it vibrates between levels and across situations and realms of meaning.

ACKNOWLEDGMENTS

When it came time to ask for help with my manuscript, I asked myself not only on whom I could bear to impose and whose perspectives would balance well, but also who would give me uncompromisingly honest responses. I realized then several things for which I remain profoundly grateful. I have friends who are remarkably generous with their time and attention, who would not even consider responding to a request for judgment of my work with evasions or polite lies, and whose differences from each other and from me extend and enrich my world incalculably.

For being such friends as well as for reading and commenting on an early version of my manuscript, I thank especially Nancy Barnes, Robert Dawidoff, Si Kahn, Gerda Lerner, Peggy McIntosh, and Sara Ruddick. Janet Francendese of Temple University Press, the three readers to whom she sent the manuscript at different stages, Mary Capouya, and Jane Barry also gave me very helpful suggestions at critical times. I am particularly grateful for the speed with which those suggestions were returned to me and the thorough reading upon which they were obviously based.

Because the 'research' for this book really took place through thousands of conversations, particularly those on campuses to which I was invited to speak and give workshops on the import and meaning of feminist scholarship, I thank all those who invited me, listened and responded so thoughtfully, and, in many cases, stayed in touch afterward. I cannot list all of the colleges, universities, independent schools, and professional and academic associations with which I have worked, nor name all the people with whom I have learned. Please know, then, that even if I have not listed you here, I do remember and thank you very warmly indeed.

I must, however, mention Peggy McIntosh here. For sharing with me the work of continuing thought about a special few of the curriculum projects from which I continue to learn, I owe her a great deal. The play of her precise, telling imagination has illumined many ideas for me, as her energy, courage, and humor have enlivened me—and many, many others.

The following people are among those with whom I have, over the years, stayed in touch, if too rarely and too often only by telephone or in passing at meetings. I have learned a great deal with and from them in various ways of which they themselves may not even be aware: Margaret Andersen, Barbara Ballard, Fontaine Belford, Harry Boyte, Johnella Butler, Douglas Davidson, Sara Evans, Berenice Fisher, Christina Greene, Gayle Greene, Gloria Joseph, Alice Kessler-Harris, Dorothy Helly, Elizabeth Higginbotham, Leslie Hill, Candice Hoke, Florence Howe, Marguerite Kiely, Rhoda Linton, Linda Koch Lorimer, Linda Marks, Chandra

Talpade Mohanty, Sandra Morgen, Joyce Parr, Carol Pearson, Karen Sacks, Betty Schmitz, Barbara Smith, Carol Stack, Catharine Stimpson, Barrie Thorne, Ruel Tyson, Mary Ruth Warner, Judith White, Margaret Wilkerson, Sandy Zagarell.

And then there are those whose work has so consistently overlapped with mine that I feel a special bond not only with them but with the organizations through and for which they have worked: Alison Bernstein (first at the Fund for the Improvement of Postsecondary Education, then at the Ford Foundation, which supported a major project on which I worked with Peggy McIntosh); Mary Ellen S. Capek (the National Council of Centers for Research on Women); Beth Reed, Kate Loring, Barbara Caruso, Jeanine Elliot, and Jon Fuller (the Great Lakes Colleges Association, and the National Women's Studies Institute, which the GLCA sponsored); Paula Goldsmid, Jean Walton, Jo Hartley, J'nan Morse Sellery, and other friends at the Claremont Colleges (especially Scripps College, which provided me with the Hartley Burr Alexander Chair in the spring of 1988 and so with new friendships as well as the time and support I needed to work on this book); Donna Shavlik and Judith Touchton (American Council on Education's Office of Women); Bernice Sandler (Project on the Status and Education of Women of the Association of American Colleges); Marcia Sharp (Women's Colleges Coalition); Adele Ervin (National Association of Independent Schools); Jean O'Barr, Mary Wyer, Anne Vilen, and editors of all sorts of *Signs;* Alice Barkley (the North Carolina Humanities Council); and, from the beginning of this work to now, many fine people at Sarah Lawrence College (where I was Director of Continuing Education), Hollins College (where I was Director of Studies), and Barnard College (where I was Associate Dean of Faculty and had the privilege of working closely with the Barnard Women's Center). I thank my present employer, the Union Graduate School, for the vision of genuinely empowering education it constantly tests and enriches, and the superb faculty and learners with which it allows me to associate. I cannot name the administrators of these institutions who have thoughtfully supported my work, the faculty members who have awakened insight, the learners whose work has complemented my own; I would have to list almost all of them. I thank them, then, collectively and personally.

For help in locating and thinking about materials that enrich this work as well as other projects, I thank Barbara Knuebuhl, Ellen Papadeas, and Virginia Walters Bryan. Their sense of responsibility, commitment to feminist scholarship, precision, and willingness to tell me what they thought as well as what information they found gave me not only help but pleasure.

Finally, I want to recognize four people who were, in the richest and fullest sense, *teachers*. Each left me, and many others, the gift of an inspiration we may receive only from lives well lived, work well done, commitments truly honored: Hannah Arendt, J. Glenn Gray, Joan Kelly, and Melissa Lewis Richter.

TRANSFORMING KNOWLEDGE

I

A View of Beginnings

Women's story begins—and begins again, and again, and again. The tellers of our tale have not had the advantage of "standing on the shoulders of giants" who preceded them. The tale is begun, developed among a courageous group that refuses to be silent, only to be erased from the "story of mankind." Discontinuity, disruption, loss mark our stories and so our self-perceptions just as surely as do discovery, achievement, and courage.

This is a book about transforming knowledge, about changing *what* and, just as important, *how* we think so that we no longer perpetuate the old exclusions and devaluations of the majority of humankind that have pervaded our informal as well as formal schooling. I take the curriculum that has been taught in institutions of 'higher' education, particularly those that concentrate on the liberal arts, as a focus. But to change the curriculum involves more than changing a text or two, a course or two. Behind, and within, the curriculum is a long, complex cultural, intellectual, and political tradition. We must consider the multiple contexts of the curriculum if we would understand what we wish to change in more than a narrow, superficial way.

Such changes are necessary, I believe, not only to transform what is accepted as knowledge by the dominant culture and what is passed on to new generations, but for the sake of thinking itself. We cannot think well as long as we are locked into old errors that are so familiar as to be virtually invisible. It is my particular purpose to

1

bring those errors to the surface, to characterize them *as* errors, to show how they have worked and still work to distort and limit our thinking, and so our knowledge, and so our selves and the world we share.

The culture and polity in which we live, and the educational institutions that contribute to and critique them, will not change just because some of us change our minds. But it is also true that unless we change our minds as well as our actions and our institutions, no lasting transformation will be possible.

STARTING AT THE CENTER

Let me say here, in highly condensed and abstract form, what I wish to suggest about *why* and *how* we need to change our minds— what the fundamental conceptual errors are. This sketch may seem both too simple, even simplistic, and too difficult because too abstract. Nevertheless, it states the conclusions I had come to when I began to write and that guided my thinking throughout. By the end of the book, I hope the basic insights I summarize here will be as clear and suggestive (not definitive—that is no more desirable than possible) as I can make them.

A single-sentence version of the theme of this book might go as follows:

> The problem we still have today in thinking well about the rich diversity of humankind is expressed by the observation that, at the beginning of the dominant Western tradition, a particular group of privileged men took themselves to be the *inclusive* term or kind, the *norm,* and the *ideal* for all, a 'mis-taking' that is locked into our thinking primarily in the form of faulty generalizations, circular reasoning, mystified concepts that result from the former errors, and the partial (in both senses of the term) knowledge that frames such concepts.

Or, unfolding that overpleated sentence a bit:

> There is a *root problem* underlying the dominant meaning system that informs our curricula. It is visible in the false universalization that has taken a very few privileged men from a particular tradition to be the inclusive term, the norm, and the ideal for all. The faultiness, or partiality, of that universalization has been hidden from us in part because we too often tend to express ourselves in singular terms

(especially "man" and "mankind," but also, for example, "the citizen," "the philosopher," "the poet," "the student"). Singular universals, even adequate ones, make thinking of plurality, let alone diversity, very difficult indeed. It is my task to locate and define the root problem as it has created errors in our thinking, to open it up so that we may become better at thinking about humankind in its vast and wonderful diversity as well as its commonalities. Basic to that effort is the location of four kinds of conceptual errors that derive from and continue the root problem: (1) errors of faulty generalization; (2) errors of circular reasoning; (3) mystified concepts even—or especially—on the highest levels of abstraction that result from (1) and (2); and, finally, (4) partial knowledge that is not recognized as such, but, indeed, sets the standard for 'sound' knowledge.

Thinking about what all that means, approaching it in different ways, setting it in different contexts, and then thinking it through specifically as it works within the curriculum will take the rest of this book. And thinking it through, thinking about it, entails, I believe, changing our minds. Minds are, of course, extraordinarily complex things, as are cultural and political systems. I do not pretend for a moment to have covered or even considered all the errors that are built into the dominant tradition, let alone to be in possession of some kind of underlying truth against which error can be seen as such. What I do believe is that, in the thousands of conversations about feminist scholarship I have had on campuses, with scholarly and professional associations, in communities across this country, I have found some of the central errors that have made it difficult for many to rethink what they know so that it can be opened to women in all our diversity. And I will suggest that the very same basic errors that have worked to perpetuate the exclusion of women do the same for the men of some groups as well, albeit without erasing gender hierarchy *within* those groups.

MORE PERSONAL BEGINNINGS

It has been working with faculty members, administrators, and students in our colleges and universities as well as with a wide variety of community groups (from women's projects of various sorts to humanities councils) that has led me to what I wish to say, and I am profoundly grateful to all those who have talked with me, argued with me, attacked and supported what I was trying to say. In particular, questions about the importance and the 'soundness' of works by and about women, questions raised by curious but unconvinced faculty members, forced me to rethink my own education, our culturally and professionally shared assumptions about knowledge, the curriculum, and education.

In the early 1970s, when I first discovered that a few women were beginning to think about what it means and has meant to live as a woman, to uncover and to create knowledge that speaks of and for us, I had a calm and uncomplicated reaction. Why not? I thought, that is very interesting. But, of course, I soon discovered that my reaction was by no means the norm, and that there was a great deal of work to be done persuading others that the effort was indeed interesting, significant, and important for those who were doing it, for their students and the readers of their work, for all of education. I began to speak publicly about the new scholarship on women, an effort that required me to think through why I found such scholarship interesting and so obviously important, and hence to think about *thinking* as well as scholarship and activism.

Initially, then, I thought in conversation with those who were raising new questions and doing new research on women (particularly Gerda Lerner, Joan Kelly, and Amy Swerdlow, who were at Sarah Lawrence College then, as was I), and also with those who were skeptical about, even hostile to, such work.

I began to give workshops for faculty members. It was through encountering their questions and exploring the ways they thought that I became deeply engaged in trying to understand what seemed to me a puzzle. Why was it not obvious that, if we do not know much about more than half of humankind, we do not know much about humankind? Why was it not obvious that this new (renewed, really) effort was intellectually as well as personally and politically exciting and necessary?

I wrote almost as many talks and papers as I gave workshops and presentations during those years because every time I left a conversation, on or off campus, I rethought what had seemed clear to me in order to take into account why and how some people had trouble understanding and accepting it. I became more conscious of the ways we tend to think, of the assumptions we make without knowing it, of the judgments that underlie what seems merely obvious. Slowly I began to realize that what I was finding was and is by no means restricted to scholarship or the thinking of faculty members. Through the problems faculty members have in rethinking their courses, and others have in rethinking their work, I was seeing the working of what I have come to call the *dominant meaning system*, which is a primary expression of the dominant culture. At first I simply referred to "the tradition," as did those with whom I talked. But that, of course, indicates precisely where the root problem lies: there are *many* traditions in this country, even though there is one that is most visible, most powerful, most defining.

In a different language, I realized that the curriculum, and the ways of thinking as well as forms of knowing that created, informed, and defended it, could be taken to be a 'text' from which one could read some of the critical conceptual constructions of a whole culture.

My work became an intellectual, political, and very personal crusade of sorts for me. I wanted to be able to reach and clear up what I increasingly saw as simple errors at the root of some very complex systems, intellectual and otherwise, errors I found within every discipline, in the very construction of the disciplines, and throughout the most influential thinking outside the Academy.

This kind of analysis, the search for why and how people think and construe knowledge, carried out by extensive and very careful listening to what they say, differs in some ways from that for which I was trained as a philosopher, but in other ways it is profoundly related. I draw constantly on my years of work with Hannah Arendt, and on Dewey, Kant, and Plato/Socrates, in particular. These are philosophers who thought about thinking, who wanted to know not only what we know but how and why we can know it, and *why it matters* that we know it this way, and not that. That is, they are all profoundly political and ethical philosophers whose lives as well as work reflect the intensity of their care not only for freedom of thought, but for freedom *for* thought.

If, as these philosophers held, we are thinking creatures in a way that is profoundly and intricately related to the fact that we are also creatures of speech, and so of society and politics, then education is of critical importance. It is in and through education that a culture, and polity, not only tries to perpetuate but enacts the kinds of thinking it welcomes, and discards and/or discredits the kinds it fears. Arendt, Dewey, Kant, and Plato/Socrates played often on the lines between what was considered acceptable and what was not. They were, in many senses of the term, critical thinkers who put the quest for freedom of and for thought before loyalty to any system of any kind. That, I believe, is not only one of the expressions of their greatness, but one of the reasons they may have understood how thinking is political in particularly acute and important ways.

As I began this work, I was, then, in direct and—it sometimes seemed—unending conversations with faculty members and community groups, and, at the same time, with philosophers who helped me think about why and how thinking is political and why it matters in the world. And, throughout, I talked with feminist thinkers and activists, sharing insights it would be impossible to disentangle any more. Thus, those who were curious about or even hostile to such work, a particular strain of philosophy, and feminist thought wove in and out of the writing, speaking, conversing, and rewriting I undertook. Still, the particularly sharp moments of focus, of illumination, came to me almost every time when I was suddenly asked a question in a faculty workshop, or after a public speech, for which I had no prepared response. I did not consider myself ready to write anything other than talks turned into papers until I found that it had been a good while since I had been asked anything new, anything for which I had no response at all. That, rather than a sense that I had read everything pertinent, indicated to me that I had done my 'research.'

It was an exhausting and largely very lonely time, for all that good talk. Such thinking takes one to one's own roots, surfaces assumptions, turns established beliefs inside out and upside down, and it must, finally, be done alone—if it is to make sense, to become coherent and consistent. I realized that the praise I sought—because one does listen carefully to praise when doing controversial work that often provokes highly personal as well as intellectual hostility—was, "That makes sense. Of course. It really is obvious, isn't it." *That* was what I wanted, not to be 'right,' but, simply, to be part of a common effort to make sense. Making sense meant that I had found and spoken *with* what people were thinking in a way that made even new thoughts their own.

That is the kind of thinking, the kind of relationship—political and moral as well as intellectual—in which I believe.

Transforming Knowledge is my report on the results of all that talk, all that thinking, all that effort to make sense. When I first wrote it, it contained no quotations at all. I simply reproduced the thinking that had crystallized in me in my own voice. But I do not want to present it that way now. I want the conversations to be more visible, even if it is somewhat artificial to introduce them in the form of quotations from books. But still more, I want you to know how much good work there is out there for all of us to draw on, to think with, to join, expand, and enrich. I have pillaged my library and the libraries of my friends to find sources to weave into this thinking, not to create an artificial synthesis out of all our differences, but to weave a multihued, multitextured tapestry that celebrates the work of many without losing the coherence of a single person's thinking. I accept responsibility for my own thinking without pretending for a moment that thinking ever proceeds without contexts much broader than even the thinker may know.

THE VOICES OF (TOO FEW) OTHERS

Let me, then, pause for a moment to introduce a few others whose presence I would like to invoke so that, as we begin thinking for ourselves in this complex area, we know that we do so in good and highly independent, diversified company from which many, many others could have been chosen.

Ann J. Lane writes of the American historian Mary Beard (1876–1958):

> Without much support from the woman's movement, without a large body of ideas upon which to build, without models of any kind to follow, virtually alone, she audaciously placed women at the centre of history and society, and then she insisted that the world look again from her perspective. . . . Beard's life and work embody her thesis: women are neglected in the writing of history, but the effect of their existence is a reality of history.[1]

"The effect of their existence is a reality of history"—the story is indeed there, as it has always been, and it is now being told. As Joan Kelly wrote in introducing her study of Christine de Pisan (1364–1430?):

> New work is now appearing that will give a fuller sense of the richness, coherence, and continuity of early feminist thought. . . . I hope to demonstrate a solid, four-hundred-year-old tradition of women thinking about women and sexual politics in European society before the French Revolution.[2]

There are many such efforts now, undertaken by feminist scholars with an inspiriting, renewing combination of passion and the most serious sense of responsibility. Paula Giddings says in her preface to *When and Where I Enter:*

For a Black woman to write about Black women is at once a personal and an objective undertaking. It is personal because the women whose blood runs through my veins breathe amidst the statistics. They struggled north during the Great Black Migration, endured separations, were domestics and schoolteachers, became pillars of their community, and remained ordinary folks. Writing such a book is also an objective enterprise, because one must put such experiences into historical context, find in them a rational meaning so that the forces that shape our own lives may be understood. *When and Where I Enter* attempts to strike a balance between the subjective and the objective. Although it is the product of extensive research, it is not without a point of view or a sense of mission. A mission to tell a story largely untold. For despite the range and significance of our history, we have been perceived as token women in Black texts and as token Blacks in feminist ones.[3]

In 1892, Anna Julia Cooper, recognizing the differences among us, chose nevertheless to speak of a singular "woman's voice,"[4] while Paula Giddings writes to claim her voice specifically as a Black woman. We come together intellectually, personally, politically—and we separate to think for ourselves, alone and with others whose voices we fear have also not been heard. Generative as well as divisive tensions continue—between the past and the present, the particular and the general, the individual and the group, the concrete and the universal, the historicized and the decontextualized, sameness and difference, research on specific groups and conclusions that might give us common ground. It has been a great struggle for women to speak with individual voices; it has also been a struggle to stand together.

To *remember* ourselves, our histories, separately and together, is more than to await a corrected scholarship, however crucial such an effort indeed is. In the strikingly personal yet simultaneously political and philosophical voice of feminist thought, Jeffner Allen explores remembering so that some of the richness of the term, now a central one to feminism, is revealed:

Touching, feeling, imagining, fighting, thinking, caressing, I remember myself. I remember the possibilities in my future, the actuality of my past, the openness of my present. I remember the members of my body, the actions that form my body as lived. In remembering, I am.

Remembering shapes my existence within a temporal horizon. The horizon of temporality is not neutral. Whenever the profiles of my memory, like the horizons of time, are erected by men, I cannot remember myself. At such moments, male domination not infrequently forces me to remember myself as essentially and "by nature"

the Other who "is" only in relation to men. I, dismembered, disappear into nonexistence.

   Yet, quite clearly, I am here. In everyday life I undergo and envision an experience of stopping the time and memories of patriarchy
and of unfolding a temporality in which I am myself.[5]

Such quests are more than corrective; they are in themselves transforming.

'LANGUAGES'

Listening to the voices of others, we also notice the easily forgotten
obvious: even when we are all speaking the same languages, there
are many other 'languages' at play behind and within what the
speakers mean and what we in turn understand. Becoming aware
of the levels and levels of different meanings in even the most
apparently simple and accessible utterance, we try to renounce the
hegemony of "the time and memories of patriarchy" so as to hear
better, comprehend better. But then we run the risk of finding
ourselves in no-time, with no place that is our own to stand, and no
tongue to speak that does not entrap us the minute we open our
mouths. It helps then to remember that women, very different
women, have indeed spoken, and if we do not wish, as I do not, to
write off all that they have said and are saying as irretrievably
infected by exclusive systems, we must listen carefully to them.
And, supported by voices that have spoken for themselves despite
the dominant systems, we can also proceed, if carefully, to make
use of the very systems we wish to change.

   In doing so, perhaps particularly if we are professional scholars
and teachers, we tend to adopt the conceptual language that seems
most promising. There are feminists who have worked within,
and always also on, most if not all of the established schools of
thought—including Marxism, Freudianism, object relations theory,
liberal democratic theory, literary criticism, and, increasingly, the
newer schools that are themselves attempting to undo much that
characterizes the dominant culture and curriculum, such as poststructuralism and deconstructionism.

   Emerging from the fear that we *must* misspeak ourselves if we
speak at all because of the power of the dominant 'language,' we
face the next problem, the co-existence of a veritable babble of
conceptual tongues.

   I have chosen no one of the available systems, or 'languages,' of
conceptual analysis/synthesis for my own work, although of course

I do to some extent speak culturally from my own background. I do not believe that one can make sense, or find it, in only one theoretical, conceptual frame at a time, however valuable such particular meaning constructions are. I do believe that we can speak sensibly to each other across disciplines, through theories, beyond technical languages, including those now developing within feminist scholarship itself (to the despair of those who fear the establishment of just one more fancy, élite, exclusive language where many had hoped to find their voices). If we could not speak to each other across these conceptual languages, intellectual work and achievement would be a great deal more alienated and alienating than they already are. If we give up on the effort to speak across fields, theories, systems, 'isms,' and to people in many different communities, we also give up our responsibility as thinkers who care about as we depend upon democracy, especially in today's highly specialized, technologized, fragmented world.

Choosing to try to speak to many people, feminist scholars as well as those curious about feminist scholarship, philosophers and those who love to think but are untrained in academic philosophy, people interested in and people worried about what is happening to higher education today, scholars and readers in all disciplines and many fields of work, I risk speaking a bit to all, adequately to none. I know that, of course, but the effort to keep up the conversation, to widen and deepen it, is too important to me to avoid the effort. I refuse to think I have only one tongue because I am a particular kind of woman, that I have only one tongue because of my academic training and predilections, that I must speak in only one voice—whichever that might be—even though I recognize that everyone will find some modes of talk and of writing more easily accommodating than others.

Thinking is political because it is an ability we all share, a need we all have, and a responsibility we can all accept or flee. To express thinking primarily and persistently in any one language is, in my view, a bit politically irresponsible, if sometimes forgivable, sometimes important, and sometimes even liberating, as when those who are regularly silenced in the dominant culture get together to speak their own language free of the incomprehension and uninformed judgment of those who stand guard over 'standard' English, 'proper' academic writing, 'good' public speaking.

I hope, then, that you will find ways to think with me through this prolonged essay in thought. To increase the openings to the center of what I want to say, I included the multiple and differing voices in the quotations above as well as a bit of my own story. Now I would like to offer several different ways to move into the conceptual center by exploring some of the contexts out of which Women's Studies, like African-American and other multicultural studies, arose. I do so because conceptual analysis always takes some, if not all, of its meaning from its real contexts, even when those contexts are not apparent because the language of the analysis is abstract. If we do not at least point toward those contexts, it is far too easy to misunderstand not so much what a conceptual conclusion states as what it *means*, and thus to be less able to make use of it in the immediate world in which action takes place.

As there are many beginnings for any realization that is of broad significance and use, there are many contexts. But there is no need for everyone to explore all of them; we think, as we act, differently. If none of what follows engages you, or if it is frustratingly familiar and introductory (though I hope it will at least be evocative), please feel free to move from the end of this introduction to Part III, "Conceptual Approaches: Thinking Through," where I begin the exploration of the basic conceptual errors I sketched above, or to Part IV, "Errors Basic to the Dominant Tradition," which focuses on them, although there, too, there will be circlings in and out: we are exploring a whole here, not tracing a line or making an argument or proving a point.

WHY FOCUS ON THE CURRICULUM?

Until very recently indeed, a quick way to lose the interest even of people who care about education was to announce that one was about to discuss the curriculum. The curriculum had become the purview of experts; specialists in curriculum or members of particular fields were held to be the only ones qualified to prescribe it (and were probably the only ones really interested in the topic, anyhow). Even scholars who make their salaries teaching usually think about curricular matters beyond their own courses only when they must, as a result of departmental planning and hiring needs, or when their institution draws them into discussion of, say, the desirability of a "core curriculum." But as long as we do not engage in critique and correction of the curriculum, the framework of meaning behind particular questions of what to teach to whom will continue to prove inhospitable to all those who have been excluded from knowledge and knowledge-making, and so also from effective participation in understanding and exercising power on a basic cultural level.

I believe that unless feminist scholarship is accompanied by on-going work on why and how the dominant liberal arts curriculum in all its varied expressions is not and, without fundamental reconception, *cannot be* receptive to the study of the majority of humankind, it remains at risk of disappearing as it has through the centuries before this wave of the Women's Movement. As we produce "the new knowledge of women," we must continue to work to understand why it is recurrently "new," rather than a further unfolding of all that has gone before. What is it, I ask through this book, that functions so effectively in the dominant meaning system to hold women and so knowledge of, by, and about women outside that which has been and is passed on, developed, taught?

This is a curricular matter. It is also more than that. The conceptual blocks to the comprehension and full inclusion of women that we find in familiar scholarly theories and arguments, as in their institutional expressions in organizations and systems, political and economic and legal, are at root the same blocks that are to be found within the curriculum. And if we do not remove them from the curriculum, much if not all that we achieve elsewhere may prove to be, once again, a passing moment. It is, after all, to a significant extent through what we teach to new generations that we bridge past, present, and future. That which is actively excluded from—or never makes it into—the curriculum is very likely to be forgotten and is almost certain to continue being devalued, seen as deviant and marginal at best.

Our educational institutions—those inspiring, impossible, frustrating, appealing, appalling systems within which we usually try simply to find the space and time to do our work of teaching and learning—are, not alone but preeminently, the shapers and guardians of cultural memory and hence of cultural meanings. Here too, then, we must do our work of critique, re-membering, creation.

As we do so, we also accept a number of risks. I am not referring only to the obvious risks of losing the privileges of participation in the Academy. As Linda Gordon puts it, "Existing in between a social movement and the academy, women's scholarship has a mistress and a master, and guess which one pays wages."[6] That these risks are complex and personally troubling does indeed need to be recognized. It is terribly difficult to work against the grain of what, after all, stands in our culture for "the life of the mind," particularly when one has had to struggle to achieve access to the institutions that have claimed to define it and have, indeed, succeeded all too well in professionalizing it, marking it as their own. I do not mean to trivialize even for a moment the struggle for access, the continuing difficulty of 'getting in.' But I want to point out here the risks that feminist scholars have warned one another about since the beginning of the curriculum change movement.

The dangers of such projects are indicated by the difference between the term "mainstreaming" and the phrase that, I am glad to say, has superseded it, "curriculum transformation projects." "Mainstreaming" implies that there is one main stream and what we want is to join it, that we are a tributary at best, and that our goal is to achieve the 'normalcy' of becoming invisible in the big river. "Transformation," on the other hand, puts the emphasis not on joining what is but on changing it.[7]

Teresa de Lauretis characterizes the problem, the risk, of "mainstreaming" as "the appropriation of feminist strategies and conceptual frameworks within 'legitimate' discourses or by other critical theories" in a way that "deflect[s] radical resistance and . . . recuperate[s] it as liberal opposition," which is "not just accommodated but in fact anticipated and so effectively neutralized."[8] That, indeed, would be the result of "mainstreaming." But it is something else again to work on transforming the curriculum with the full realization that women cannot be added to the present construction of knowledge because knowledge of, by, and for women is not simply more of the same; is not only knowledge of a subset of "mankind" that is conceptually compatible with that of which it is a subset; is not a category of exotica that can be tacked onto courses without implications for that which remains safely 'normal'; is not, indeed, neatly separable in any way from any knowledge that is adequate to human-kind.

The belief that knowledge about women *is* simply additive to, or a subset of, or a complement to, knowledge about men has been and is held both by nonfeminist scholars and educators and by some feminists involved with Women's Studies and curriculum-change projects. I understand those beliefs and know that some good work can indeed be done by those who hold them (just as valuable work is done in Women's Studies to find the women who did what women were not allowed to do so as to "prove that we can do it," that we "have been there"). But I do not believe such work is, by itself, adequate, because it remains within a system built on principles of exclusion and characterized by the conceptual errors those principles necessitate and perpetuate.

It is precisely to continue work on transforming the curriculum, not simply achieving access to it or joining its 'mainstream,' or providing it with an oppositional perspective that it can accommodate in the sense de Lauretis rightly fears, that this book is being written. Let me repeat here what I first wrote in 1979: what we are doing is as radical as undoing geocentrism, the notion that the earth is the center of the cosmos. If the earth—if Man—is not the center, then everything predicated on taking it/him to be so no longer stands as it has been formulated. This is not to say that there are no schools of thought with which we can join, or that there is nothing in the existing tradition we can draw on, use, and ourselves choose to perpetuate. It is not even to say that all feminist scholarship is or ought to be that radical, that it ought to work on that fundamental level. It *is* to say that as we do our work, we need to hold on to the radical critique, the effort to go to the root (*radix*) of the tradition that is premised on our exclusion, or we will watch helplessly as the tree of knowledge continues to grow exactly as it did before.[9]

But making the case for that position is what this book is about, so I will leave the point now with the statement that refusal to engage in, or at least support, work on transforming the curriculum leaves us not pure but vulnerable to being, once again, excluded, rendered marginal, or brought into and utterly lost within the mainstream that has through the ages flooded and washed away the recurrent spring growth of feminist scholarship and thought.

II

Contextual Approaches: Thinking About

It seems only right to recognize, however briefly and hence inadequately, that what we begin here, as we look at education and specifically at the curriculum, is itself another in a long history of beginnings. The struggles for women's education and for the study of women have their own histories. And it is also important to recognize at the same time, the parallels between and, still more important, the intimate intertwinings of, sex/gender, class, and race in the history of education as in all else. In a history of the curriculum in the United States, Frederick Rudolph reminds us that neither Black people nor white women have been included in the curricula even of institutions designed for us:

> By 1900 . . . the curricular directions of colleges and universities for blacks had been established basically in imitation of the institutions that served the dominant caste. Acceptance of segregation as the defining practice in the relations between the races required of the southern colleges for blacks the education of trained, vocationally prepared graduates in many diverse fields. The curriculum of the black colleges was shaped by a policy of apartheid in a society sufficiently democratic in the abstract to encourage the development of a

15

class of responsible professional leaders. . . . But the models for these institutions were those of the dominant caste: Fisk University's music department concentrated on classical European music to the exclusion of the music that expressed the black experience in America, and black history and sociology courses were rare and exceptional until after World War I.

Similarly:

Colleges for women were . . . founded . . . as an experiment in applied psychology, philosophy, and physiology. Vassar, Smith, and Wellesley, in quick succession, using the classical liberal arts curriculum that was on the brink of collapse in the old men's colleges, proved that women were mentally and physically equal to a demanding collegiate course of study. . . . As was true of the colleges for blacks, colleges for women were often colleges in name only; those that deserved the name, having survived the opposition of critics who sought to discredit them with accusations of having failed to live up to the curricular standards of men's colleges, soon found themselves criticized for imitating the men's colleges too well and for not providing a course of study appropriate to women's work.[1]

Women's work, in Rudolph's words, is "whatever men would not do."[2]

Thus, the majority of humankind was forced absurdly into proving that we were indeed fully human, that we could indeed think and learn, in curricula that either took no account whatsoever of us or were designed to keep us in our 'proper' place. The virtues (understood in a way that fluctuated oddly between the classical sense of *excellence of kind* and the Christian sense of *moral goodness*) of white middle- and upper-class women as of Black men and women, however different they were from each other, had in common being defined as different from the virtues of man-qua-citizen, or scholar. They were defined as virtues of service, not in the generalized Christian sense that calls all to act with *caritas*, but in a specific sense: those who were to serve the lives and interests of the small group of scholar–citizens were to develop the specific virtues of the 'naturally' servile.

This was the case even when some real pride and privilege went with fulfillment of the service role. For example, as Patricia Palmieri notes, "The American revolution made the entire society aware of the need to educate a populace capable of exercising democratic principles." Yet such civic arts and the virtue of their exercise were not to belong directly to all: "Women were to exert social influence through raising and educating sons. . . . Thus by 1800, while the vote was reserved for white men, white women could add to their domestic roles the role of 'Republican Mother.' "[3] Such provisions for influence—as distinct from power—were by no means extended to all those who served the dominant few. Even those who could proudly claim the mantle of "Republican Mother" did so through their relation to male citizens, their rearing of male children, the service they rendered the male order through those relations. Linda Kerber located for us the telling twist in such thinking, such provisions:

> A revolution in women's education had been underway in England and America when the Revolution began; in postwar America the ideology of female education came to be tied to ideas about the sort of woman who would be of greatest service to the Republic. Discussions of female education were apt to be highly ambivalent. On one hand, republican political theory called for a sensibly educated female citizenry [from the privileged groups] to educate future generations of sensible republicans; on the other, domestic tradition condemned highly educated women as perverse threats to family stability. Consequently, when American educators discussed the uses of the female intellect, much of their discussion was explicitly anti-intellectual.[4]

Black women, as always even more than privileged white women, have struggled continuously not only with the difficulty of achieving access to any education at all but with that of defining what Black people should be educated *for* even when slavery had been ended and some education could openly be sought and provided. They did so with great fortitude and ingenuity. Paula Giddings writes of the well-known debates about Black education around the turn of the century:

> Though in many instances there was accommodation to [Booker T.] Washington's ideas—and power—Black women also operated independently of his influence. The educators, for example, believed in industrial education, but they also believed that Blacks should attain the highest academic level possible. One foot was in Booker T. Washington's camp on this issue, the other with W. E. B. DuBois, who supported the concept of the "talented tenth," a well-educated cadre of Black leaders. Anna Julia Cooper, for example, may have believed in industrial education with all her heart, but as an educator, and principal of Washington, D.C.'s The M Street School, she was best known for her success in channeling Black students into the most

prestigious universities in the country. . . . Mary McLeod Bethune advocated "domestic science," but she also confronted (successfully) her White board members who wanted to maintain her school's curriculum below university status.[5]

Mere access to schooling has clearly never been enough, and cannot become so, as long as any remnants of the old assumptions that we are by nature inferior and ought to be educated to serve white men remain within the curriculum, however deeply hidden. Such assumptions, such curricula, serve not equality but maintenance of an inegalitarian status quo: those who can pass as similar to higher-class white men are allowed to partake of the crumbs of privilege, while all others are to continue to be trained not only to serve but to admire those they serve. The present status hierarchy among institutions of higher education reflects the continuation of an exclusive history, however well-intentioned are those who bemoan the difficulty of finding 'qualified' women of all groups for their faculties and administrations, the supposed rarity of 'qualified' Black, Hispanic, and other students to be admitted to make a more diverse student body. Old assumptions, built into our modes of thought, our standards of judgment, our institutions and systems, keep inappropriate discrimination functioning long after many have consciously and seriously renounced, even denounced, it.[6]

CONTEMPORARY MOVEMENTS FOR EQUALITY

In the 1950s and early 1960s in America, dissatisfaction with the distortions of human lives and spirits effected by blithely inegalitarian social, political, educational, and economic systems began once again to bubble and rise to the surface. The old ambivalences so well described recently by Giddings, Kerber, Palmieri, and others (as, earlier, by Jane Addams, Anna Julia Cooper, Mary McLeod Bethune, Mary Beard, and others) had by no means been resolved. As a participant in that time of ferment (I was in college between 1961 and 1965, and started graduate work at the University of California/Berkeley in 1966), it would disturb me not to remember the political roots of Women's Studies in the movements that arose then. From them came a great deal of the passion and vision of feminist scholarship; from them, too, came some of the tensions that remain with us.

Remember: the Montgomery bus boycott took place in 1956, the struggle to desegregate Little Rock High School in 1957, and the sit-in movement that triggered mass Civil Rights protests against the exclusion of Black Americans began in early 1960, revealing the ferment that had been working with intensity and intelligence and great creativity in Black communities, in particular, for some time.[7] Betty Friedan published *The Feminine Mystique* in 1963, providing a rallying point for middle-class white women suffering from "the problem without a name." Educators (for example, Melissa Richter, Esther Rauschenbush, and Jean Walton) tried to do something about the inadequacies of women's education even at élite colleges such as Sarah Lawrence, Barnard, and Pomona, which did not recognize the reality that many women did and would work outside their own homes for pay (by necessity as well as by choice). The (largely white male) Beatniks and their male and female successors, the hippies of the late 1960s and 1970s (who had their own peculiar notions about what was 'proper' to men and to women) defied conventionality to find some meaning in a culture that seemed obsessed with 'success,' war, and materialism.[8] And Black nationalism gained new political and cultural impetus, often apart from, even in opposition to, efforts to desegregate white America.[9]

These were complex, multivoiced movements that were sometimes at odds with each other even as they shared a sometimes rather abstract passion for justice and equality, for full recognition of those excluded from the dominant culture. They were all felt within the Academy, too. The long quest for educational equality in the United States had by no means ended with the entrance of a few members of the excluded groups into the established halls of 'higher' learning in the United States, any more than the quest for political equality had ended with the winning of the franchise, first by Black men and then by all women. The intertwined, though often separately (even oppositionally) defined struggles that exploded again in the Civil Rights Movement of the 1960s and 1970s were extraordinarily complicated, conflictual, creative.

By the mid-to-late 1960s, some women involved in the Civil Rights Movement were discovering something wrong even within the struggle itself. The awareness re-emerged that prevailing generalizations about 'equality,' about 'justice,' somehow did not hold for women. That seed of understanding germinated quietly but released an intense and unstoppable energy. Slender blades of grass began to crack through pavement:

> We've talked a lot, to each other and to some of you, about our own
> and other women's problems in trying to live in our personal lives
> and in our work as independent and creative people. In these conver-
> sations we've found what seem to be recurrent ideas or themes.
> Maybe we can look at these things many of us perceive, often as a
> result of insights learned from the movement.[10]

The "recurrent ideas or themes" that white women began to see
seemed at first not to speak to some of the Black women in the
movement. The Civil Rights Movement was, after all, for Black
women more 'their' movement, on the one hand, and, on the other,
they knew themselves to have some real power in it. However,
despite particular and by no means trivial differences in how it was
experienced, discrimination based on sex/gender affected Black
as well as white women. "Opposite ends of the spectrum" was
Cynthia Washington's metaphor for the relation of Black and white
women's experiences in the Movement: it described Black and
white women's complex and differing realities, but the "spectrum"
was indeed that of *women*. Many were beginning to realize that
there was a problem in some, at least, of the ways men perceived
and treated their female co-workers:

> During the fall of 1964, I had a conversation with Casey Hayden
> about the role of women in SNCC. She complained that all the
> women got to do was type, that their role was limited to office work
> no matter where they were. What she said didn't make any particular
> sense to me because, at the time, I had my own project in Bolivar
> County, Miss. A number of other black women also directed their
> own projects. . . . Certain differences result from the way in which
> black women grow up. We have been raised to function indepen-
> dently. The notion of *retiring* to housewifery someday is not even a
> reasonable fantasy. Therefore whether you want to or not, it is neces-
> sary to learn to do all of the things required to do to survive. It seemed
> to many of us, on the other hand, that white women were demand-
> ing a chance to be independent while we needed help and assistance
> that was not always forthcoming. We definitely started from opposite
> ends of the spectrum. . . . [Yet even though] we did the same work as
> men . . . usually *with* men, . . . when we finally got back to some
> town where we could relax and go out, the men went out with other
> women. Our skills and abilities were recognized and respected, but
> that seemed to place us in some category other than female.[11]

When some of the women in the Movement began to talk to each
other, to explore their experiences *as women*, white and Black, some-

times together but also separately, and to take those experiences and one another seriously, tensions increased, splits developed even between long-time co-workers—and change was on the way. Expressions of personal and then of social discontent became increasingly politicized as a Movement carried by strong convictions and courage encountered the need to deal not only with those who crudely, and sometimes violently, opposed civil rights for Black Americans but also with the contradictions and tensions we all internalize in a segregated, class-divided, gender-hierarchical culture.

Long, often agonizing debates developed out of the earlier quiet, more personal conversations, and were sometimes broken up by confrontations that led to stunned silence, to deep hurt and anger, between and among individuals and groups. Black women, white women, Black men, white men, southerners and northerners, Civil Rights workers and local residents, students and non-students, political sectarians and those with beliefs but almost no ideology at all, painfully discovered their differences, struggled to continue to work together, broke apart to work separately. The deep divisions of the 'melting pot' of America, hidden behind 'the American dream,' cracked open in the crucible of the Civil Rights Movement. And even within the Movement, the dream cracked as tensions, as well as profound commitments, were exaggerated by the high tension of real danger surrounding the Civil Rights workers.

Those of us who lived through those times remember them vividly, and some of the dreams and nightmares, divisions and alliances, that developed then remain with us today. Much as some might like to think it, the sixties and early seventies were not just an aberration that is now, thank goodness, entirely over and done with. As I have traveled around the country working with faculty members and community groups, I have again and again encountered people who are still struggling to understand and learn from what happened then, when a people's movement succeeded in undoing most legally enforceable segregationist practices, converted many people to a lasting commitment to equality, spawned hundreds of grassroots organizations, many of which continue today,[12] and ended a war that the majority of Americans had come to believe was morally wrong. Some who are today faculty members became teachers because they came to believe then that education is indeed where and how a culture creates itself, and they wanted to be part of and have an effect on that critical process.

I have also met many faculty members who are still hurt, still angry, still frightened, by what happened in the late sixties and early seventies. Among these are some of the major opponents of curriculum transformation. They seem still to be fighting with the ideas, the actions, the people who so challenged them twenty years ago, and they are finding a startling number of allies across the nation. Some of us were enlivened by dreams as well as struggles for equality and justice; others were traumatized and remain terrified of anything that seems even vaguely "like the sixties." There was indeed frightening violence and hatred then, as well as peace and love. The era saw the undermining of some beliefs and traditions and values that may be necessary to our culture right along with some that locked it into terrible injustices.

But I cannot here re-enter that time of dream and anger. What matters now is that when Women's Studies and Black Studies began to appear on campuses, their creators were often motivated primarily by the renewed dream of an equitable world that had emerged, with pain as well as hope, from the Civil Rights Movement as well as the growing movement of women—most visibly white middle-class women, but also, and very importantly, Black, Hispanic, and other women whose activities tended to be 'overlooked' by the media. There was a shared, if by no means fully articulated or understood, realization that equity requires more than access to unchanged structures. But that does not mean that equity itself was fully understood. The meaning of "equity" remained a stubborn conceptual and political issue. It is arguable, for example, that with the turn to consciousness-raising, the Women's Movement that had emerged from the Civil Rights Movement began to develop in ways that deepened divisions between white and Black women, just as the early emphasis of white 'women's liberationists' on finding fulfilling work outside the home continued to do.[13]

Still, those who became involved in Women's Studies saw that in the Academy, as elsewhere, all women were denied full and equal entrance and, even once 'inside,' were not well treated as students, workers, teachers, and administrators. Sometimes naively assuming that the emerging new knowledge would be as inclusive as the old was exclusive, we set out to make ourselves not just present but significantly so—to be *recognized* in the fullest sense.

While we, all of us, remained strangers to the Academy, even if some of us were present in it, we could expect no more than token efforts toward such recognition. And tokenism reveals not so much bad faith as a profound lack of understanding of the nature and depth of the problems to which it is an inadequate response. Tokenism, after all, assumes that exclusion, which is an effect of complex hegemonic systems, is itself the problem. In this view, adding a few of those who have been excluded solves the problem, even though it actually leaves untouched the systems that produced (and, if left unfixed, will go on producing) exclusion and devaluation, both of which reflect also incomprehension. That is why tokens, even those included in (uncomprehending) good faith, even those who themselves fully intend otherwise, become available to play the role of "exceptions that prove the rule."

We added to our work toward political and professional equity efforts to bring full representation of our half of humankind into the body of what is taught. Many white women worked for Women's Studies without adequate efforts to learn from and with Black and other women, but not without awareness of the importance of doing so—a statement that is intended to be neither an excuse nor a judgment. Undoing racism in the Women's Movement—not just as exclusion perpetuated by bad feelings of whites toward Blacks but as an expression of the overarching oppressive system that benefits whites and exploits Blacks—is as complex as undoing it anywhere else. This is an acknowledgment that must be made and remade however painful it is, lest the pain block what must be done.[14]

It is in the direct feminist challenge to the knowledge the Academy preserves, enriches, and passes on that I locate one important context for the extraordinary explosion of thinking and new knowledge that no one should ignore any longer. Much has indeed changed, but the commitment to education that genuinely serves egalitarian democracy remains.[15]

EARLY—AND CONTINUING—QUESTIONS

There is also another way to move into the subject of transforming knowledge, and the ways we think. We can change our perspective from the dramatic, stirring, inspiring, and troubling history of the times in which this commitment re-emerged, and focus on the unfolding thinking itself. To do so, it may be helpful to return to some of the early questions. We could start with the conclusions reached after much thought, making them as clear and accessible as possible, but some may find it more helpful to start where the thinking started, to move into the thinking as it actually developed rather than, or in addition to, focusing on its historical *or* its purely conceptual contexts. There are always lots of ways to begin, different contexts within which to locate that which we wish to understand, many perspectives on what we are trying to see.[16]

Scholarship vs. Politics?

From the beginning, the commitments of feminist scholars have been complex and often in creative, demanding tension with each other. For example, an early conference in a continuing series run by the Barnard College Women's Center took on the question of the relation of scholarship to politics (the conferences, led by Jane Gould as director of the center, were in the late 1980s still called "The Scholar and the Feminist"). Were we, as many of those opposed to Women's Studies held, threatening to 'politicize' scholarship and the Academy in some new and dangerous way? Is it true that formal scholarship as traditionally conceived and practiced is disinterested, objective, removed from the interested, subjectively grounded advocacy efforts of the political realm? Are knowledge and action two separate human activities, and ought they to be so? Can one serve both equity and excellence, or does commitment to one threaten to undermine the other? To respond to such questions, we were faced with the need to rethink what scholarship has meant and should mean, and that effort led us to undertake an analysis and critique of the construction of knowledge.

The Disciplines

Among the most evident characteristics of the prevailing construction of knowledge is its disciplinary nature, a characteristic that is given power by the discipline-based departments that are at the heart of academic institutions. Hence, we were faced with an obvious intellectual and institutional problem. Women's Studies put the study of women at the center of concern as no then-existing discipline did. In what discipline–department were we to work? Women as authors–scholars and as subject matter were largely or wholly invisible in all of them. Furthermore, the search for any *one* disciplinary–departmental 'home' quickly came to seem peculiar, since it is quite obvious that women cannot be studied adequately in only one discipline any more than men can. That is in part why Florence Howe issued her well-known call to "break the disciplines," and why we early claimed that Women's Studies must be "interdisciplinary."

But then we had also to ask whether even interdisciplinary work would suffice. Were *any* of the standing disciplines adequate to the study of women? Obviously not. How, then, could an amalgam of fields, none of which had proved open or adequate to the subject, transcend its component parts? It seemed clear that we would have to create a new field, not a pastiche of old ones, in order to be free to locate and when necessary create the theoretical frameworks, the methods and techniques of research and of teaching, that we might need to illuminate our complex subject.

A new debate arose. Should the goal of Women's Studies be the creation of a new discipline, and a new department, rather than the transformation of all the other standing disciplines? But the scholars who worked on Women's Studies were themselves trained in those disciplines, and the students who might take Women's Studies would also take other courses that would continue to exclude and/or devalue women. Our task seemed to require us not 'only' to create a whole new field, but also to rethink each discipline and all disciplines—separately, in relation to each other, and as they reflected and perpetuated this culture's understanding of knowledge. We realized that scholarship that refuses old exclusions and invidious hierarchies not only does not fit into any of the old fields, but, for that very reason, potentially transforms them all.

Therefore, we have worked to establish a new discipline, Women's Studies, and, simultaneously, to support that work with efforts to spread "the new scholarship on women" (as Catharine Stimpson early named it) to all fields through curriculum-transformation work. Despite the concern of some feminist activists and scholars that woman-focused work would be lessened by curriculum-transformation work, both undertakings have flourished side by side, one often leading to the other. The Academy has been changed by the burgeoning of feminist scholarship in general, its fostering in Women's Studies programs in particular, and its effects on all disciplines. The decision as to which kind of work to undertake has in fact usually been the result of realistic assessments of what is most possible and likely to succeed in a particular institutional setting at a particular time.[17]

"Lost Women"

Both projects—the creation of Women's Studies programs and work toward the transformation of courses in and across all disciplines—depend, of course, on the availability of works by and about women. At first it seemed that, whatever anyone's intentions, it might be impossible to include knowledge of women in any courses at all until generations of dedicated scholars had produced enough sound new knowledge. Across the country some women and a very few men (notably, William Chafe and Joseph Pleck), while teaching what they had been hired to teach and struggling to continue the research on which jobs, promotions, and tenure depended, turned to finding the "lost women" whose lives, works, and perspectives could be brought into the curriculum. There was a sense that we had to prove that women and women's works really did exist, but—more important—there was an urgent desire to find our history. Stunning works of retrieval emerged with equally stunning speed: for example, Ann Sutherland Harris and Linda Nochlin's work locating, documenting, and studying women artists resulted in the ground-breaking show of women artists at the Brooklyn Museum of Art. The catalogue, later *Women Artists: 1550–1950*, was immediately picked up and used as a text. Also enriching our sense of continuity, culture, and complexity in women's lives were (and are) Gerda Lerner's anthology, *Black Women in White America*, and Rayna Rapp Reiter's anthology, *Toward an Anthropology of Women*, among many others, as well as Dorothy B. Porter's monumentally inspiring long-term work collecting, commenting on, and making available the story of Black women and men through the Moorland Spingarn Research Center at Howard University.[18]

As such work appeared, it allowed us to deepen the critique of the construction of knowledge, to question more concretely the notion that what had been taught was the product of disinterested, nonpolitical, objective scholars. Nochlin's early essay, "Why Are There No Great Women Artists?" that uncovered and analyzed the historical realities of discrimination faced by women began questioning of the very definitions of art that reflected and appeared to legitimize that discrimination.

The search for 'lost' women again pushed our quest for knowledge about women deeper than some had expected. We began to realize the full, complex implications of the obvious statement, "Women have always been here." We refined our understanding of the intellectual problems we faced when we realized that we have always been here *and* that we have been largely invisible in the body of knowledge passed on by the educational and research institutions whose purview is supposed to be the preservation, transmission, and enrichment of humankind's knowledge.

"Add Women and Stir"

In a now-famous line, Charlotte Bunch characterized the problem: "You can't," she said, "just add women and stir."[19] It was an apt observation, crystallizing what many had learned in their own efforts to find 'lost' women and add them to their courses. The women could, in fact, be found. There have been women mathematicians, women physicists, women philosophers, women writers, women musicians. There have been women in history, in classical Greece and Rome, and women in politics. But, once found, they often didn't *fit*, couldn't just be dropped into standing courses. Why not? In looking for individual women who had done what men had done, we had not, after all, shifted anything very radically (as we would, and by now have). The problem was that although the now-found 'lost' women seemed to prove something that needed proving yet again—that women are by no means and in no ways inferior to men—we had not, in fact, learned much about *women*. In fact, we had not even proved anything about female abilities: exceptions, as we know, can easily be used simply to prove the rule. If some women were mathematicians, why were not more mathematicians women? There must be something about most if not absolutely all females that disqualifies us. That was not, of course, a reasonable conclusion. In finding the 'lost' women, we had also found more about why and how they were 'lost.' We began to know more about the practices of exclusion exercised against our sex.

But was the point of all our efforts to document that women had not performed as well as men in all the 'important' areas of life because we were discriminated against and actively excluded? Yes, of course that needed, and needs, to be acknowledged, studied, comprehended. But it leaves untouched some other critically important questions. What were women who led the lives prescribed for women doing in the past? What were *those* lives like? What do we all, women and men, need to learn from as well as about them? Those were the questions we could not ask within the constraints of the familiar courses and fields on our campuses. We realized that we did not need only to find the few women who did what men did, but to ask, Where were the women? What can we know about *women?* We needed to undo the established centrality of men.

What was required was a complete rethinking, first of the basic models of reality, truth, and meaning in the dominant tradition, and then of all the knowledge predicated on them. *If it is an intellectual, moral, and political error to think that Man has been, is, and should be the center of the human system, then we must rethink not only the basic models but all knowledge that reflects and perpetuates them.*

To be additive, knowledge must rest on the same basic premises, be of the same basic sort, as that to which it is to be added. But, in the language most often used in the earlier days of Women's Studies work, knowledge about women cannot be added to knowledge about men, because the center of the system has shifted radically when women are moved from "margin to center" (to use the phrase adopted by Bell Hooks for her second book).

That apprehension is sound, but it was not yet adequate to explain, or at least help us begin to explore fruitfully, the challenge of Women's Studies to the old male-centered curriculum. The basic errors that put some men (in their falsely universalized, singular representation as Man) at the center needed to be explored directly and in depth along with at least some of their conceptual consequences. Those errors began to appear as we realized that problems in each field were by no means unique, that there were striking commonalities on a deep level across all fields and outside the Academy as well.

There were many more issues debated and questions raised as we moved further into the effort to rethink a tradition that had excluded so many for so long, but perhaps those I have discussed will suffice to introduce that effort for now. What is important is to think through for oneself, as well as with others, how scholarship and politics are related, why the new scholarship on women did not become simply a subspecialty within the standing disciplines, why finding things that women had done that were as similar as possible to men's achievements did not tell us anything about the lives of *women,* and why, then, it would not suffice—was not even possible—just to add women on to scholarship that was premised on our devaluation and exclusion.

Clearly, we had to consider not just what was already known and how women could be added to it, but how knowledge was constructed, and what kind of thinking the dominant tradition has privileged. We need not give up all that has come to be known, or all the ways and forms and techniques of thinking that have been developed. Quite the contrary: we need to make use of whatever can help us think not only within but also about the dominant tradition. There is no articulable, communicable stance *utterly* outside the tradition for us to take. Should we try to find such a position, we risk falling back into silence just as surely as we do if we speak only within and in the established terms of the dominant culture.

Fortunately, humans are creatures of translation, transitive creatures able to understand more than one language and to move between languages without losing either what is unique to each or what is common enough to make translation possible. We are able to apprehend more than can be spoken in any one language, and can stretch that language in ways that change and enrich it. There are many ways to be both within and without our own cultures.

CRITIQUE AND REFLEXIVE THINKING

In addition to the personal, historical, political, and intellectual contexts within which efforts to change the curriculum developed, there is also what must, I suppose, be called a philosophical context. No one undertakes an effort to understand anything without bringing to that effort some more or less formulated, more or less conscious, philosophical assumptions, tools, frameworks, values. Certainly I do not; in fact, as I have said, some of the primary conversations that have informed my work have been with philosophers. *Furthermore, even more now than when I began, I believe that the effort to find out why and how our thinking carries the past within it is part of an on-going philosophical critique essential to freedom, and to democracy.* As we work on the curriculum, and so on understanding the dominant tradition, maintaining a critical stance will allow us to avoid tripping ourselves up precisely when we most need to think creatively and, often, in radically new ways.

Thinking With and Without the Tradition

I found my thinking in this book on a commitment to critique in a generally Kantian sense, asking, What is *behind* this knowledge, this mode of thought? What were and are the conditions of its possibility? What makes, and keeps, it what, and as, it is? And I take the ground for the possibility of critique to be the human gift of reflexive thought, which is, I believe, not only a given possibility for us all but one of the primary bases of both the idea and the personal experience of freedom. Neither critique nor reflexive thinking is enough to give us freedom, but they help us comprehend and experience it in ways that help us know and value it as a necessity for full human be-ing.

Still, I must note that I am well aware that there is some irony in the project of thinking ourselves free, of transforming knowledge. The tradition to be critiqued is being used against itself. I count on some familiarity with the dominant tradition as part of the common ground we share as we communicate with each other about what needs to be changed, and I draw, to a large extent, on established forms and methods and rules of thought to try to speak with and persuade people. However, I believe in the liberatory quality of reflexive thinking. In thinking about thinking, we are not simply running around in circles like a squirrel in a cage, trapped despite all its frantic activity. We are working to see the thought displayed in particular ways of thinking from a standpoint that is relatively, not absolutely, outside them. I claim no 'higher' or more privileged—let alone absolute or definitive or 'pure'—perspective. I simply claim that it is possible for humans to think as and about ourselves, to think reflexively, self-consciously as we do when we observe ourselves becoming angry, or notice how we see something, or pay attention to how we learn and make discoveries. In what follows, I will discuss patterns of thought and of knowledge I have found in all disciplines as well as in the broader culture in the belief and hope that, having seen them, we may choose to use, vary, or discard them more freely.

That is, I do not believe that we are trapped by the fact that we learned to think in particular ways in this particular culture and in the Academy, nor do I believe that we can simply decide to be free of our formal and informal education. There is no either/or here, no "We are free *or* we are determined." Such dilemmas, created by abstracting two possible positions from all that grounds them in real experience and placing them artificially in opposition to each other, are part of a pattern of thought by which we may refuse to be coerced. In fact, we all know perfectly well that while we can and too often do think in ways that reflect a trap, we can also think about any specific trap and how it works to limit our thought in such a way that the problems it seemed to pose simply dissolve. We can think about our thinking as well as that of others and, in so doing, actualize a specific mode of human freedom that never suffices unto itself to effect genuine liberation but, as I have said, underlies and supports all other efforts—except, of course, those that are animated by a desire to replace one hegemonic system and ideology with another that is equally absolutized; and I, at least, do not consider those to be genuinely liberatory even if the new system seems in many ways better than the old.

Effects of Exclusion

Analyzing the conceptual errors that lock the dominant meaning system shaping liberal arts curricula into exclusive, invidiously hierarchical sets of structures, values, principles, beliefs, and feelings is the basic task and challenge of this book. More, much more, will be said about the errors I introduced earlier. Here, I will simply summarize a major problem in including women and the excluded groups of men in the dominant meaning system by repeating that some conceptual errors are so fundamental to the dominant Western tradition that an additive approach to change simply cannot work. For example, work by and about women is not just missing from the academic curriculum; it is to a remarkable extent incompatible with it. That is, *knowledge that is claimed to be inclusive—claimed to be both about and significant for all humankind—but that is in fact exclusive must be transformed, not just corrected or supplemented.* Discoveries indicating that the world is round do not merely supplement knowledge shaped by and supportive of the theory that the world is flat. Similarly, feminist work by and about women is not just missing from the academic canon: it is incompatible with some of the canon's basic, founding assumptions. And that means *not* that feminist scholarship is 'out of order' but that whatever makes noninclusive knowledge unable to open to the subjects and perspectives so long devalued and/or excluded must itself be changed.[20]

I had the notion behind this idea for quite some time, but, as with many such flashes of understanding, it illuminated my thought only fitfully. I had not allowed it to stay, had not let myself think it through. But one day, after I had given my talk at a conference opening a curriculum-transformation project, it came to me. I was listening to other speakers on changes taking place in specific disciplines when suddenly I found myself whispering to the sociologist

Margaret Andersen, who was sitting next to me, "We weren't *omitted. We were *excluded.*"

As I have said, that is obvious. But it remains hard to say. It sounds as if constant evil intent was involved, and so it threatens to move the attention of both speaker and audience from the *effects* of the intent to exclude that remain in the curriculum to the *motivation* of the excluders. And that shift is almost certain to make those who have not changed their courses, or their way of thinking about their work, suddenly feel attacked rather than included in an exciting effort to think about our thinking. But if I and others do not say, "We/women were excluded," we cannot get to the critical observation that *the reasons why it was considered right and proper to exclude the majority of humankind were and are built into the very foundations of what was established as knowledge.*

That is, women were not overlooked through a prolonged fit of the famous academic absentmindedness (much like that attributed to the British to 'explain' how they ended up with an empire), as the use of the word "omitted" tends to imply. Women were excluded from lives of scholarship, as from 'significant' subject matter, as from positions of authority and power, when the basic ideas, definitions, principles, and facts of the dominant tradition were being formulated. But does that mean that *all* the creators and guardians and transmitters of the dominant tradition were and are personally animated by a consistent, purposeful intent to think consciously about excluding women, and many men, every moment? No, it does not (although it does not preclude the observation that some, indeed, were and, I fear, still are so animated). It reminds us that *the principles that require and justify the exclusion of women, and the results of those principles appearing throughout the complex artifices of knowledge and culture, are so locked into the dominant meaning system that it has for a very long time been utterly irrelevant whether or not any particular person intended to exclude women.* The exclusion was and is effected by the forms and structures within which we *all* try to live, work, and find meaning.

Thus, although it at first sounds as if using the strong term "excluded" might divide us radically from each other, such that all who are not part of the solution are seen as actively, consciously, and willfully part of the problem, in fact it reminds us of something quite different. We are all, albeit to varying degrees that matter a great deal, a part of the problem. Insofar as we speak and think and act in ways that make sense to other people within the dominant meaning system, we cannot avoid participating (again to varying degrees) in precisely that which we wish to change. We have all at times thought, said, and done things that, as our consciousness grew through the use of our ability to think reflexively, we wish we could disavow or at least hope we have outgrown. And that "we" includes (again in critically different ways, and with critically different results) not only those who benefit but also those who suffer from the dominant system. One of the struggles of the oppressed, excluded, and colonized is always to break free of internalized oppression—which does *not* mean that "women are their own worst enemies," a ridiculous exaggeration of the reasonable insight that we tend to learn what the dominant culture teaches us, and reteaches us, sometimes harshly, when we begin to struggle free.

This is, of course, only another way of saying that prejudices such as sexism and the deeply related homophobia, racism, and classism are not just personal problems, sets of peculiar and troubling beliefs. Exclusions and devaluations of whole groups of people on the scale and of the range, tenacity, and depth of racism and sexism and classism are systemic and shape the world within which we all struggle to live and find meaning. I and other white women benefit to varying degrees from the system of racism, however strongly we oppose it, just as all men benefit to varying degrees from the sex/gender system. And those of us who work in various ways within and with the Academy benefit from it, too, however much our work is designed to change it. That all these systems also, and profoundly, damage in some ways those who benefit from them can be recognized without thereby excusing them/us from responsibility for their perpetuation.

Men and women sometimes say to me, "But men suffer, too. They aren't allowed to cry or be nurturant, and they die younger than women on the average because they carry an inordinate amount of responsibility." I recognize the problem and am very pleased to see men join in dismantling the systems that give them burdens related to their privileges. However, it must be noted that while some of the privileged of all groups understand and feel the harm done to them, most seem to want to get rid of the harm without giving up the privilege. The movements of many, many people we have come to associate with Mahatma Gandhi, Martin Luther King, and Susan B. Anthony provide striking examples of how the harm done to those in power as a result of their holding that power can indeed be brought to consciousness, and that consciousness can be enlisted in support of a collective (if by no means inclusively egalitarian) political movement. Each of these movements developed important methods of persuasion as well as coercion, of what we might call consciousness-raising, not only among movement activists but among those against whom they were protesting. They did not simply take up guns and try to force agreement; they used what Gandhi called *satyagraha,* soul-force, to convert others to the view that a *system* must be changed, a system that was unjust and so harmful for all.

But by itself consciousness of the costs of systems that also give privileges often does no more than make those in power a bit guilty and grumpy—harder, not easier, to live with.

The questions of 'harm' and 'benefit,' of 'consciousness' and 'false consciousness,' of 'oppression' and 'internalized oppression' are extraordinarily complex. Such complexities are important. They serve to hold us to the level of systemic analysis without allowing us to forget that it is individuals who participate in and rebel against systems. We can critique these systems from within, often using their own abstract principles against them. In the case of the Academy, it is clear that knowledge that is claimed to be objective and inclusive yet reflects and perpetuates societal discrimination and prejudices fails even on its own terms. Knowledge that was created and has been passed on within a culture that, until very recently indeed, excluded the majority of humankind from the activities, positions, and thinking that were considered most important can hardly be disinterested and politically neutral, as it is claimed to be. It replicates in what it covers, how it treats its subjects, how it explains and judges, the most basic assumptions of the dominant culture—not entirely, not absolutely, but consistently enough so that it remains related to the culture from which it arose. Such knowledge is almost certainly blind to some of its own basic assumptions and methods, but they are there to be found.

Consider the example of geocentrism. Copernicus's move to put the sun at the center of the cosmos was greeted as what it indeed was, a challenge to many of the most deeply held beliefs of his culture, and more—a challenge to a remarkable range of systems of explanation, of knowledge, even of mores and morals. Darwin's theory of evolution had, and for some still has, the same devastating effects. It dethrones Man, suggesting that he is *not* the center, is not a unique creation that is discontinuous with and superior in kind to all else. Shifting from an invidiously hierarchical view of humankind entailed then, and entails now, a concomitant shift in all areas of knowledge, of ethics, of politics. Consider, too, the deep differences between the knowledge of the English and Europeans who colonized this country and the knowledge of the Native Americans. One set of cultures saw the land as given to Man to tame, to use, to make his own so that thinking about the earth tended to be instrumental. The other saw the land as sacred; thinking about it tended to be descriptive, celebratory, mythic, with the instrumental entering in the mode of propitiation, not mastery.

Centering attention on women rather than on a particular group of men involves a shift in focus, a reconfiguration of the whole, that is just as profound and suggestive. To take only one example for now, we can return to one of the initial insights of the Women's Movement, the realization that the personal is political. The full implications of that simple statement are still unfolding, but from the start it reminds us that everything that appears in public needs to be seen in relation to the private, and vice versa, so the terms "public" and "private" themselves cease to be firmly distinct. Thus, among other effects, the whole panoply of 'women's virtues' is released from containment within the functions relegated to women to reveal its significance and value in and for everyone, rather than being shunned by the 'Real Man' who must, above all, display no 'effeminate' qualities, whether 'virtuous' or not. Heroism can then cease to be a singular individual quality expressed in highly visible deeds and become a quality of character developed in a whole life, a life led in relation to many others that expresses care, honesty, integrity, intimacy, constancy, as well as (even instead of) the ability to 'win' through dramatic confrontations and adventures. And leadership can then be understood not in terms of dominance but as an ability to empower others.

Consider the 'conquest' of the West in the United States. Was it really the work of single scouts, of brave men 'penetrating' the wilderness, of lone individuals developing a culture based primarily on an individualistic notion of self-reliance? What about women struggling to establish homes, to care for families, to find and build the community that was essential to efforts to survive? What about the sexual and physical abuse of women, which, while it remains an untold story, makes all other frontier stories not just incomplete but dangerously falsifying? What about the terrible dangers of childbirth in situations where little or no care was available?[21]

When we remember women, the story and its interpretation change, become much more complex; context and community re-enter; the exigencies and heroism of everyday life, of reproducing and caring for life itself, take on the importance they really have.

Most basically, perhaps, we can say that when we focus on women the peculiarly abstract versions of the dominant Story of Mankind are undone so that the logics of connection, concreteness, context, and community can emerge. Such modes of relation cannot simply be added to a logic of externally related monads, of abstract individualism, of singular Great Deeds, of public life apparently ungrounded in and distinct from 'private' life. The coherence in many of the stories we have inherited was manufactured after the fact to make sense of characters, events, and motivations that had been removed from their real contexts. To uncover what women were doing and undergoing is to locate and ground a different and more truthful coherence, and that means, again, that we are not merely adding information but fundamentally reconceiving what we thought we knew.

Examples could be multiplied, but let us just note here the basic point: the shaping assumptions on which influential knowledge—which is always knowledge-accepted-as-such by a particular group in a particular culture—continues to be based are influential not *despite* but *because of* the fact that most people are unaware of them.

Thus knowledge and the whole culture and accepted process of knowledge-making need to be changed in their congruent basic claims and assumptions before that which has been defined as out of order, as rightly to be excluded, can be heard, seen, studied—comprehended. Old knots and tangles that are in all our minds and practices must be located and untied if there are to be threads available with which to weave the new into anything like a whole cloth, a coherent but by no means homogeneous pattern.[22]

III

Conceptual Approaches: Thinking Through

CONCEPTUAL ERRORS: THE ROOT PROBLEM

This is where all these beginnings, these different ways 'in' through our quick exploration of various contexts—personal, political, historical, philosophical—began, and arrive. We begin again, now circling toward the central root problem, discovering it, circling out again to see it differently, returning to reconsider it. Throughout what follows, I will continue to follow that kind of spiraling logic. I do so in part because, as I have said, my thinking has from the beginning been in conversation with many people, and I want to continue trying to keep open as many doors as possible. I do not want to argue anyone into agreement; that kind of agreement is entirely unstable, and rightly so. Argument by certain prevailing rules of logic is a kind of force; a good argument "compels agreement." I do not wish to compel agreement. I wish to invite it, and I would like the reasons for it to belong genuinely to each of those with whom I think. The whole point of this exploration is to try to think ourselves free, to free our own thinking.

The *root problem* reappears in different guises in all fields and throughout the dominant tradition. It is, simply, that while the majority of humankind was excluded from education and the mak-

37

ing of what has been called knowledge, *the dominant few not only defined themselves as the inclusive kind of human but also as the norm and the ideal*. A few privileged men defined themselves as constituting mankind/humankind and simultaneously saw themselves as akin to what mankind/humankind ought to be in fundamental ways that distinguished them from all others. Thus, at the same time they removed women and nonprivileged men within their culture and other cultures from "mankind," they justified that exclusion on the grounds that the excluded were by nature and culture 'lesser' people (if they even thought of the others as having 'cultures'). Their notion of who was properly human was *both* exclusive *and* hierarchical with regard to those they took to be properly subject to them—women in all roles; men who worked with their hands; male servants and slaves; women and men of many other cultures.

Thus, they created root definitions of what it means to be human that, with the concepts and theories that flowed from and reinforced those definitions, made it difficult to think well about, or in the mode of, anyone other than themselves, just as they made it difficult to think honestly about the defining few.

"Know thyself," said the few ancient Greek men who had the leisure for and took the privilege of exploring "the life of the mind" and the "free life of the citizen"—and who are still mistakenly called "The Greeks" as if they were *all* the Greeks. Thus, they also created (indubitably *not* for the first time in human history) a haunting not-self that was essential to the admitted, recognized, claimed self. The not-self—the Barbarian (who was originally simply one who did not speak Greek), women, slaves, men who worked with their hands—surrounded the self they sought to know, setting its boundaries by constituting some activities, some feelings, some human functions, some deep desires, as forbidden because projected onto lesser others whom they must not be like.

This deep construction of a self inextricably tied to a not-self was, much later, brilliantly characterized in the concept of the Other that Simone de Beauvoir took up and transformed. *The Other* catches an existential reality as well as a conceptual trait that remains at the very heart of the Western tradition in a way that is particularly potent because it is far too often unrecognized. But it seems profoundly familiar once introduced:

> In actuality the relation of the two sexes is not quite like that of two electrical poles, for man represents both the positive and the neutral, as is indicated by the common use of *man* to designate human beings

in general; whereas woman represents only the negative, defined by limiting criteria, without reciprocity. . . . She is defined and differentiated with reference to man and not he with reference to her; she is the incidental, the inessential as opposed to the essential. He is the Subject, he is the Absolute—she is the Other.[1]

The concept of the Other is a clue to the difficult conceptual tangles we must undo. It is very strange to maintain that one small group of people is simultaneously the essence, the inclusive term, the norm, *and* the ideal for all. Yet that is what we hear: "Man is a generic term," and, at the same time, *"Vive la différence,"* which positively celebrates the notion that "men and women are by no means the same." What, then, are we to do about the differences that mark women as not-men yet give no substantive, positive identity, no reality of their own? Those differences must be the marks of non-humans—if "man" is to be generic. Women then become beasts or gods (whores or virgins in the not-unfamiliar sexualized construction imposed on women), and/or non-entities, non-selves.

We hit absurdity fairly fast on this level. Consider the famous syllogism: "Man is mortal. Socrates is a man. Therefore, Socrates is mortal." Try it with a woman: "Man is mortal. Alice is——" what? A man? No one says that, not even philosophers. "Man," the supposedly generic term, does not allow us to say, "Alice is a man." So we say, "Alice is a woman." Then what are we to deduce? "Therefore, Alice is——" what? It is man, a supposedly universal category that is simultaneously neutral and masculine but *not* feminine ("masculine" is defined in contradistinction to "feminine"), who "is mortal." Is Alice, who is female and hence not in a category that is either neutral or masculine, then *immortal?* Is she mortal insofar as, for the purposes of such reasoning, she may be subsumed under the category *man,* but not insofar as she is, specifically, female? Are women, then, immortal insofar as we are female? Alice ends up in the peculiar position of being a somewhat mortal, somewhat immortal, creature. Or, we must admit, we cannot thus reason about Alice while thinking of her as female at all. We can think of Socrates as a man without derailing the syllogism; we cannot think of Alice as a woman. Reason flounders; the center holds, with Man in it, but it is an exclusive, not a universal or neutral, center. Alice disappears through the looking glass.

The fact is that "man" does not include (or "embrace," as witty grammarians used to like to say) women or all humans, any more than qualities derived from man as he has been understood represent either the norm or the ideal for all humankind.

That kind of tangle, and the errors it produces, is starkly evident in the curriculum.

SOME EXAMPLES FROM THE CURRICULUM

To begin on common ground, we can consider the following familiar examples (which I have made up but which derive from a large collection of syllabi gathered from around the country and my work on many campuses).[2] They contain clues to basic conceptual errors that make a change to more inclusive thinking improbable if not impossible as long as they are still unrecognized, unquestioned.

| An introductory course in Art History requires one basic text. In that long text generically titled, let us say, *The History of Art* (not, you notice, "*A* History of Art"), the works of no more than four women are discussed. None of the supplemental materials introduced in this course mentions women at all. There are few references in the text or other materials to the art of cultures other than those that like to trace their origins to Greece. Asian art, for example, is 'covered' in a short unit at the end of the text. The art of nonprivileged peoples of all sorts is not mentioned, except in a couple of short sections under the label "folk" and/or "primitive" art.

| An Introduction to Music course addresses the work of twenty European, British, Scandinavian, and American male composers who worked within, and/or created, a specific set of musical forms. All other kinds of music are, if not entirely ignored, presented as less serious than the small sampling of the world's music written and performed by these men from certain groups, places, eras, and social classes. The music of others is, students are told, properly considered only under some subhead such as "ethnomusicology," a specialty that is interesting but less serious because not committed to the study of 'serious' music.

| Students in a History course are taught that Europe had an Enlightenment and a Renaissance. These terms—"Enlightenment" and "Renaissance"—focus attention on the activities, creations, and meanings important in particular ways for a particular group of men, who were then studied and written about by those trained to be professional historians. The Renaissance and the Enlightenment become, in students' minds, thing–events that contain, that *were*, an era's most significant and interesting reality. That the majority of

the population—women and significant groups of men in Europe and in what have been called "the less developed countries"—experienced and understood these times in radically different ways is not considered worthy of much if any discussion.

I In a Literature course, the development of the study of literature as a profession is never discussed. Judgments of what is significant and 'good' in literature appear, then, to have been made without any admixture of professional ambitions, rivalries, or exclusions resulting from inherited prejudices. Students are left with the impression—or are directly told—that significant works "emerge over time" and are "recognized," as if greatness is an essential quality (like the wetness of water) that is simply there to be experienced.

I In an Economics course, no mention is made of the role of gender in economic systems, nor is there any attempt to discuss or think about the implications of unpaid and underpaid labor, productive and reproductive, upon which paid labor—not to mention the whole society—so intricately and intimately depends. Thus, the degree to which gender, intertwined with race as with class, has provided categories of workers persistently locked into particular kinds of jobs, which are overwhelmingly among the lowest-paid, never surfaces for attention. Students are left with the implication that such things do not matter, are not real—or are, perhaps, mere aberrations in an otherwise 'rational' system, or, worse, the fault of those who are trapped in dead-end, low-paid jobs.

I In a Physics class, no mention is made of the history and politics of the development of the presently prevalent knowledge. Names of great physicists who made recognized and influential discoveries are mentioned, but none among them are women's; Lise Meitner, who had the insight that ultimately made it possible to release atomic energy, is not mentioned, although Otto Hahn, her research partner, is.[3] Furthermore, students in such a class are led to believe that a 'real' scientist does work that is in no way involved in political realities, because 'real' science is ahistorical, apolitical. Thus, some become able, in later life, to contemplate with equanimity employment in laboratories that give them 'excellent' colleagues and equipment no matter where their funding comes from, no matter what the final purpose of projects to which their specific research contributes. Those are matters for others to worry about; they are "just doing good science."

We are so familiar with such examples that sometimes, when we begin to critique them, they seem to reflect specific instances of unfairness and/or thoughtlessness rather than fundamental errors and confusions. But we can see the underlying errors clearly when we think in terms of groups we are not used to thinking of either as central or as victimized. Imagine a course on the art of North Carolina that was called, simply, "Introduction to Art," in which any other art (if mentioned at all) was carefully prefixed, or marked: for example, "New York art" or "Roman art." Imagine discussing North Carolinian art, called simply "art," in such a way that it became not only the defining but also the criterion-setting kind of art. Florentine art, because it was from Florence and differed from "art," could then be considered only as a *kind* of art, and, insofar as it differed from the (North Carolinian) art that set the standard for art studies, would also be judged "less good" or "less significant" than (North Carolinian) art. The official story of the development of art, Art History, would then also exclude what was going on in Italy, in France, or in Germany, except insofar as it could be seen as having influenced or been influenced by (North Carolinian) art. If North Carolinian artists believed it right and proper to exclude Italian, French, and German people from participating in what was (in North Carolina) considered 'real' and 'significant' art, then one could count on the fact that almost no Italian, French, or German art would ever appear in the (North Carolinian) Art History texts. And that would be explained, perhaps sadly, by saying, "Those people just haven't yet produced anything worthy of inclusion."

Ridiculous. Yet if North Carolina had been the home of the development of the profession of Art History, that might be what art historians taught. More to the point, "ridiculous" is a reaction that those who would teach about women have indeed encountered. Why? On a basic level, because *the tradition has prepared us to consider it absurd to teach particular kinds of art, literature, religious practices, cultures, and the rest as the thing-itself, except in the case of those particular kinds that stand at the defining center of the fields.* That which does not carry a prefix seems to be, is assumed to be, universal: literature as it has been taught by professional scholars is the thing-itself, while women's literature is a kind of literature. Black women's literature is a still more narrow kind, and Third World Black women's literature is even further removed from generality and definitional centrality. The more prefixes, the further from the real, the significant, the best.

We also do not say, in speaking about our experiences in our communities, "my wonderful heterosexual white male banker," or lawyer, or doctor (at least we do not do so when we are speaking with and/or in the language of the dominant culture). These adjectives—"heterosexual," "white," "Euro-American," "male"—go against the grain of the hegemonic discourse. Why? Because they are not used there to mark *kinds* of people or works. They are used, if and when they are used at all, to indicate attributes it is not usually necessary (or appropriate) to notice. A picture of a white male physician will be called "a picture of a doctor" by most; a picture of a Black female physician will be noted to be not just a picture of an *unusual* doctor but of a *kind* of doctor, a Black female one.

It is, in fact, very easy to locate some of the key instances of false universalization in the dominant meaning system. One need only note where prefixes, or markers, are not used *and would be startling:* "the white male philosopher Kant."

The point is that when we do not say "white men's literature" and *do* say "Black women's literature," we are reflecting and perpetuating a kind of knowledge in which white men's literature is seen as literature-itself, the inclusive term, the norm, and the ideal. Other literatures are relegated to subcategories or, if brought into the 'mainstream' category, are improperly judged because they are placed against standards, closed within contexts and discourses, that not only did not include them in the first place but were founded by people who thought they *ought* to be excluded. At present, only the works and lives of the few are regularly discussed in the curricular canon *within their own contexts,* such that the meanings that emerge from analyses of intertextuality are coherent and mutually illuminating. Works from other traditions, other discourses, cannot make much sense, cannot seem very good, when they are removed from their own and forced into someone else's conversation. Like all of us, they can then only fall silent, imitate rather poorly those in whose company they are suddenly dropped, stammer, or seem distastefully defiant or ignorant when they inadvertently break the rules.

CONCEPTUAL CONTEXT: THE TRADITIONAL STORY

When we speak of the development of the disciplines that dominate our curricula, of the knowledge we teach within them, we are indeed speaking of a very particular tradition, a particular if multi-voiced discourse, the one taught in "Western Civ" courses. Those educated in the United States are familiar with historical, intellectual, social, political, and economic forms, systems, and structures that are said to participate in a story that started in Greece, moved to Rome, spread through Europe and Great Britain (but mostly England), and then arrived on the shores of the United States. Knowing something of this story—it is a kind of culture-binding and celebratory story told and retold as such stories are—has been considered the mark of one who has a 'sound' liberal arts education. We could trace the story again, watching this time for how the few achieved and maintained not just their dominance but their defining and standard-setting centrality. But that, of course, is a monstrous task unto itself and one well begun elsewhere (for example, in Gerda Lerner's important *Creation of Patriarchy*). Let us, then, consider briefly some moments in the development of the root problem in notions of and about education in the dominant tradition in the United States. As always, we need at least some clues to the contexts that inform any subject we pick out to consider, to study.

Paideia

Werner Jaeger, in *Paideia: The Ideals of Greek Culture*, once a highly influential book and one that has given educators a by no means neutral term with which to conjure, writes, "The formative influence of the community on its members is most constantly active in its deliberate endeavour to educate each new generation of individuals so as to make them in its own image. . . . Therefore, education in any human community . . . is the direct expression of its active awareness of a *standard*."[4] Note that there is here no location of the "community" that is deciding on what standards to use in educating new generations into its own image. We know, of course, since Jaeger is writing of "the Greeks," that the community making such decisions did not include women, slaves, barbarians, or men who worked with their hands. "The community" is the few who held power, the few who had relegated all the work that provided for their freedom to those they considered less fully human than themselves.

Such education, Jaeger continues, "starts from the ideal, not from the individual. Above man as a member of the horde, and man as a supposedly independent personality, stands man as an ideal . . . the universally valid model of humanity which all individuals are bound to imitate."[5] "Man" is not to be considered as a member of the community—now called "the horde," and so perhaps including all the excluded others—or as an individual, but as "an ideal." And that ideal, developed, as Jaeger has said, by a specific community with a view to perpetuating the values, knowledge, ethics, of those who take themselves to *be* "the community," is then to be taken to be a "universally valid model of humanity." This, precisely, is the origin and unabashed announcement of the basic tangle of conceptual errors we are trying to unknot.

Such exclusivity, mystified and raised to the highest power through universalization, was not a temporary aberration on the part of a few Greeks. It was present also in the great medieval universities, not only in their exclusion of all but the few who qualified as those-to-be-educated, but also in their distinction between the liberal and the servile arts. The liberal arts were for those who could indulge in study of the 'higher' things; the servile arts, for those whose knowledge would be put to some direct use. The old privileged male Athenian notion remained—the idea that that which is of no use (that is, is an end in itself) is higher than anything that is involved intimately with the maintenance of life. And, as in Athens, that hierarchy of value was applied to people, not just ideas or works. Liberal arts were for "the free man," meaning not the man who had political freedom but he who need not take care of himself or his own 'natural,' that is, necessary needs in any way. Those—women, male slaves and servants—who made that freedom possible were 'lower' beings, conditions for the existence of the proper, genuine, and ideal man.

In the Italian male Renaissance, the use of formalized education to separate the privileged few males from all others continued. For example, the teaching of Latin was taken more, not less, seriously as Latin was superseded by Italian as the medium for educated public discourse. Privileged boys left their homes to learn a language few women or uneducated males learned. With Latin, they marked themselves as grown up—meaning grown away from the home and those whose work was care-taking. The educated man was he who need not lower himself to the pursuit of useful knowledge, or the work of caring for others, or even to taking care of himself.[6]

Novus Ordo Seclorum: Ideals and Practices
in the 'New' World

That peculiar hierarchy, in which the dominance of the few reflected and helped perpetuate abstract philosophical schemes of worth, carried over into the so-called New World. Not until the middle of the 1800s in this country were women, Black men, and the children of those who worked with their hands recognized as belonging in 'higher' education. Oberlin College's motto, "To work and to learn," and its admission of the historic outsiders, Black and white women and Black men, constituted a radical break in the tradition that has yet to be fully realized there or elsewhere.

It is nevertheless true that, despite the formative and persistent influence of the root problem, education in the United States has meant something different from education in Europe and Great Britain. Invoking the culturally entrenched and inspirational aura of the ideal of *paideia* even as he attempts to alter its meaning, Lawrence Cremin has suggested that the United States has developed a "national *paideia*" that unites "the symbols of Protestantism, the values of the New Testament, *Poor Richard's Almanac,* and the *Federalist Papers,* and the aspirations asserted on the Great Seal."[7] Different, then, but by no means wholly open, adequately democratic. That the ideal of education in the United States called for more democratic forms and practices in which to realize itself *and* has not often been successfully served has long been recognized.

Walt Whitman, in his 1871 essay "Democratic Vistas," wrote that this country would continue to fail its own noble—and necessary—vision "until it founds and luxuriantly grows its own forms of art, poems, schools, theology, displacing all that exists or that has been produced anywhere in the past, under opposite influence."[8] Challenging the *paideia* inherited from Greece via Europe and England, Whitman envisioned "a programme of culture, drawn out, not for a single class alone, or for the parlors or lecture rooms, but with an eye to practical life, the west, the workingmen, the facts of farms and jackplanes and engineers, and of the broad range of women also."[9] Whitman, like other visionary educator–philosophers such as Anna Julia Cooper, Mary McLeod Bethune, W. E. B. DuBois, John Dewey, William James, Maria Montessori, and Alexander Meiklejohn, recognized the need for change in the hierarchical system of supposedly egalitarian America. That need had also been tellingly enunciated by Frederick Douglass, who observed "that the day of rejoicing for a white majority celebrating independence constituted a time of mourning for the blacks they oppressed."[10]

The work of many other Black and white women, the creators of land grant universities, the early proponents of women's formal education who founded such schools as Mount Holyoke, Bennett, Bryn Mawr, Spellman, and Vassar, speaks eloquently to the continuing vitality of an American vision of *paideia* that transcends in some ways, but by no means all, not only the privileged male Athenian concept caught so well in Jaeger's description but that of early America as described by Cremin.

About forty years ago Gunnar Myrdal caught the tension between ideals and realities that so profoundly characterizes the experience of education in the United States. He noted that America has "the *most explicitly* expressed system of general ideals in reference to human interrelationships. This body of ideals is more widely understood and appreciated than similar ideals are anywhere else. . . . To be sure, the Creed . . . is not very satisfactorily effectuated in actual social life. But as principles which *ought* to rule, the Creed has been made conscious to everyone in American society."[11] Myrdal, of course, also documented what he called "the American dilemma"—racism—which revealed the stubbornly failed promise of the Creed.

Where ideals persist and yet persistently fail, we need more than renewed invocation of that to which we all supposedly aspire. Many superb works have been dedicated to helping us understand what is wrong and what we might do about it. Here, I am concerned primarily with the conceptual knots, the basic errors, that keep us from thinking clearly within—and about—the ideals and the practices of the dominant meaning system.

It goes without saying that we cannot finally and completely untie or cut through the conceptual knots that keep us from understanding exclusions that are not just omissions, that reflect and reinforce complex power hierarchies. I have attempted a sketch of the situation simply to indicate its persistent challenge to feminist and democratic efforts to call it on its own ideals, and to continue the effort to rethink the ideals themselves. However, locating and clarifying the root problem and some key conceptual errors that persist can help us and coming generations of thinker–activists free ourselves to think more effectively. That is an important step in the right direction.

Having explored a few moments of its history in education, let us turn to four more specific manifestations of the conceptual tangle resulting from the root problem of taking a dominant few as the inclusive group, the norm, and the ideal for humankind.

The forms of the root problem I will discuss are deeply inter-related. I distinguish among them here so that we can see them more readily and because the root problem appears more sharply in some areas and at some times in one or the other of its guises.

IV

Errors Basic to
the Dominant Tradition

The four basic kinds of errors that derive from and express the root problem of taking a particular few to be simultaneously the inclusive term, the norm, and the ideal are (1) *faulty generalization*, abstraction, or universalization; (2) *circular reasoning;* and, resulting from the first two, (3) *mystified concepts;* and (4) *partial knowledge*.

In what follows, I will introduce these errors, exploring different ways of approaching and thinking about them, selecting examples both of the errors and of some correctives to them, and reflecting about some of their consequences—thinking them through.

The *contextual* and *conceptual* approaches that preceded give us some frameworks for the errors that have developed over time in the dominant Western tradition and are expressed in a wide variety of political and institutional structures, including, of course, educational institutions. These conceptual errors are both expressions of the meaning and institutional systems that shape our worlds and causes of their perpetuation insofar as those systems are based on old exclusivities.

Sometimes it seems possible to locate an error in thinking and/or its expression in speech and/or a particular institutional practice and then, simply, change it. For example, it is quite rare to hear an adult Black man referred to as "boy" these days, although that inaccurate and belittling term was common in white speech until the time of the Civil Rights Movement. But the errors that produced what it appears we have corrected are so deeply rooted within systems that they cannot really be changed without fundamental redesign of the systems themselves. Similarly, where we find in the economy a sector dependent upon underpaid labor that is and has for a long time been defined as "women's work" (such as "pink-collar" workers, nurses, daycare workers, housecleaners), change will depend on a lot more than revised nomenclature. Here we see conceptual errors expressed systematically in ways that depend on and affect how we think (for example, the assumption that it is 'appropriate' for women to be in service professions that have to do with caring for the needs of men and children) as well as how systems depend on and reinforce each other (for example, white families needing two incomes and hence affordable daycare and housecleaning services that cannot be found unless others—often Black and immigrant women—are forced to work for very low wages). Changing the mystified concept of "women's work" entails more than a change in our thinking, speaking, and writing.

Thus, because the errors have so many different expressions even though the errors themselves are quite simple, the discussion of each that follows is long and sometimes rather intricate. Once seen, the errors are, I believe, obvious (although it is easy enough to make them seem very complex if one wants to get into the trickier philosophical questions, such as what "generalization" and "mystification" 'really' mean). I want them to be obvious and, most of all, to make sense on a useful level. To achieve that would mean that, having located, understood, and become used to working with them, we can proceed to uncover old ways of thinking and knowing that would otherwise continue to shape our thought despite our best efforts to think, and also to act, more adequately, truthfully, freely. What we are looking for are, in a sense, touchstones, not conclusions. As many different examples and issues as I have raised here, I could have raised many more. The coherence in the discussion that follows does not depend on comprehensiveness, nor derive from any elaborate undergirding theory. It rests on the constancy of the errors, which, thought about and used as touchstones, reveal the root problem in many different expressions.

It may help, then, to review the four kinds of errors and to keep this brief guide in mind as you explore what they reveal and suggest:

| *Faulty generalization* and/or universalization is the result of faulty abstraction, of taking humans of a particular kind to be the only ones who are significant, the only ones who can represent or set the standard for all humans. For example, it is faulty generalization when someone learns that many white middle-class housewives suffer from a sense of meaninglessness, frustration, and boredom— and then writes about those problems as the problems of *women*, with no restrictive prefixes.

| *Circular reasoning* may be most clearly seen when standards of what is 'good' work are derived from the study of a particular kind of works by a particular group but are then used as if they were generally, even universally, appropriate. For example, when notions of what makes 'good' music *good* are derived—as they were— from close study of a very particular tradition of music, and then those notions are themselves cited as neutral grounds of judgment appropriate for the evaluation of *all* music, circular reasoning is in play. American jazz, which was not around when the criteria for 'good' music were derived from English and European classical music, is then judged not different, but less good.

| *Mystified concepts* result at least in part from the first two errors. In this context, they are ideas, notions, categories, and the like that are so deeply familiar they are rarely questioned. Their complex cultural meanings not only perpetuate old exclusivities but involve us in them. Often such concepts even lead us to think and act against our own interests and commitments without our being able to see why or how we got so tangled up. For example, the dominant American idea of individualism carries within it a set of connotations centered on a positive valuation of 'rugged' independence expressed as a radical lack of strong ties to or mutual interdependence with other people, with tradition, with place. The concept can thus make it seem as if many American women, and the people of some other cultures, are inadequately—by those particular standards—'individualized.' More than one American has said, observing news reports of suffering in Third World countries torn by war or drought, "It *is* tragic, but those people simply don't care about the individual the way we do"—as if that made the suffering less real, less significant, less of a claim on us to respond. Mystified concepts have very real consequences, as do all the errors.

| *Partial knowledge* comes from posing and resolving questions within a tradition in which thinking is persistently shaped and expressed by the first three errors. It is partial in both sense of the

term; it is actually about, and therefore tends strongly to work for, a part and not the whole. For example, the elaborate sets of theories as well as all that derives from them that we can group under studies of "Western Civilization" tend very strongly to be partial insofar as they do not seriously take into account other civilizations except as they have been encountered by and then defined in relation to the dominant few in the West.

The discussion of mystified concepts and partial knowledge differs in some ways from that of the first two kinds of errors. I thought it important to explore some central concepts that are mystified and yet, rethought through a feminist analysis, can help us demystify our thinking and our knowledge. No such survey of central concepts can be exhaustive or even adequate, but I wanted it to be rich enough to engage your interest, and long enough to familiarize you with some interesting aspects of feminist scholarship. The thinking and ideas I introduce here are also in flux; there is little consensus even among feminist scholars on these concepts and all that surrounds and informs them. I simply wish, here, to engage you in thinking with me about them. Thus, describing what mystified concepts are does not constitute a touchstone in quite the same way that describing the other kinds of errors in reasoning does. Each concept unfolds differently, and it takes exploration of a fair number of them to recognize for oneself the patterns that emerge in what is revealed.

The final section, on partial knowledge, explores some conceptions of knowledge that have resulted from as they have informed the other, more particular (if always overlapping and mutually implicated) areas of error. Because discussion of knowledge *per se* moves into the territory of epistemology, I have had to (actually, I have enjoyed) raising some feminist considerations about epistemology as it, too, has been constructed.

FAULTY GENERALIZATION

The Error of Faulty Generalization, or noninclusive universalization, resulting from abstraction from an inadequate sample is often expressed conceptually in *hierarchically invidious monism* and politically in an *articulated hierarchy* of power. It is characteristic of the dominant tradition that one kind of human has been and continues to be studied both intensively and extensively. That restriction of subject matter expresses the lingering belief that only that one kind is fully, properly, or ideally human. It follows from that root problem that only one group is generalized from, or taken to speak for, of, and to all of us. When abstractions about 'mankind' have been made within the dominant tradition, they have far too often been distilled not from knowledge gathered from the study of humankind but from knowledge about one group within it. That is faulty abstraction—it is rather like creating "abstract of vanilla" but labeling it "flavor."

Let us remember that, in the span of human history, the inclusion of the majority of humankind in 'higher' education is a very recent event indeed. In what has been called the "Western tradition" or "Western civilization," women were not in the centers of learning, and our exclusion from every aspect of the 'higher' learning was considered right and proper. That is worth emphasizing again because it reminds us that, however mystifying language such as that quoted from Jaeger is, the majority of humankind was not left out either inadvertently or unconsciously. *The universalization of the definitions and values of the few entailed universalizing once purposefully exclusive notions.* We deal here not with the presently popular postmodern attack on universals *per se*, but with faulty generalizations, faulty abstractions, that have too often been universalized.

Hierarchically Invidious Monism: Difference

What developed in the form of noninclusive constructs still persists unquestioned and can be characterized as a kind of *hierarchically invidious monism*. Here, I mean by that a system in which one category is taken to be not literally all there is, but the highest, most significant, most valuable, and, critically, *most real* category—which sets up all others to be defined and judged solely with reference to that hegemonic category. Eventually, that one category/kind comes to function almost as if it were the *only* kind, because it occupies the defining center of power, either casting all others outside the circle of the 'real' or holding them on the margins, penned into sub-categories. Thus, some men became Man, and all other people were relegated to some degree of 'outsider' status, some kind of 'deviant' subcategory of Man. This is not the same as dualism, in which there are two primary principles that are equal and opposite, as in Good and Evil, God and the Devil, Man and Woman (and within the category of Woman, virgin and whore, 'good' woman and 'bad' woman). Although there certainly are influential strains of dualism in the dominant tradition, I believe hierarchical monism is more deeply embedded.

For example, Augustine (one of the "Church Fathers") found his 'solution' to the dualism of Manicheanism in the Neo-Platonic view that takes evil to be not God's equal opposite, but the *absence* of Good. That solution was satisfactory to him, and to many after him, in particular because it established that evil has no being, and hence no power, of its own. Plato, whose work influenced Augustine via the Neo-Platonists, not only drew a line (expressed literally as such in the famous "divided line" section of *The Republic*) between the realm of Being and the realm of Appearance, which by itself might suggest a true dualism, but also held that the lower realm was *less real* than the higher.

In dualisms of the equal-but-opposite sort, it is possible to achieve a nonhierarchical view of mutually complementary opposites, such as Yin and Yang. Some dualisms, that is, may give us the possibility of conceiving and even establishing socially and politically an equality of being, a being split in half but fully and carefully balanced. Some feminist anthropologists debate whether societies that construct two distinct and radically different sex/genders can nevertheless properly be called "egalitarian" because difference, while institutionalized, is not ranked invidiously.[1] But in the West, as de Beauvoir noted, the terms "woman" and "man" are not parallel, equal terms: man is what it means to be human; woman is his Other (as, in different but related ways, slave is Other to master, and the 'primitive' is Other to 'civilized man').

In the meaning systems we are considering, there were at the beginning the few privileged men who generalized from themselves to Man, thus privileging certain of their qualities that, they asserted, distinguished them from "the horde." From then on, differences from those few were seen as marks of inferiority. Woman was, as we see in the profoundly influential works of Aristotle, not the equal opposite of man but a failed version of the supposedly defining type, higher than animals but lower than men. Woman was seen by those in power, by those setting the terms of what has become the dominant meaning system in the West, only in inferior relation to Man. Thus, differences from men were, for women, encoded as failures, not merely as distinctions. And that meant that, whereas the qualities picked out to be defining of men's humanity were taken to be universally human, women's qualities were seen as particularities and hence not to be generalized about or abstracted from in the quest for knowledge about humankind.

There is no idea of universal Woman, then, any more than there is an adequate idea of universal Man that was genuinely abstracted from knowledge about all men, let alone all humankind. The "Eternal Feminine," a curious notion that has made a few appearances, is not quite a stand-in for universal Woman. "Feminine" is a term that has no meaning without its paired supposed opposite, "masculine," but, more important, "feminine" and "masculine" are both terms for attributes, for qualities, and as such are not normally used in place of Man or Woman, the creatures who are supposed to display such qualities. The popular usage of these terms, translated a bit, goes something like this: there are by nature females and males who live within human culture as women and men, among whom some enact their roles more intensely and successfully than others, so that we can say of a man that he is "masculine," of a woman that she is "feminine," without tautology. "Feminine" *adds* something to the idea of woman; it doesn't just restate it. It tells us that a woman enacts her gender in obvious ways (for example, she "enjoys being a girl" and may not even mind being called one when she is well past adolescence because "feminine" has been defined in ways that entail enactment of weakness and dependency). When feminine and masculine qualities *are* thought about other than in the stereotypic sense, they sometimes lift off and become universalized principles, as when some Jungians speak of "the feminine principle" and the "masculine principle"—the anima and the animus—that "we all have in us, and need to recognize."

In such constructions, inessential attributes that the dominant culture has established as appropriate either to women or to men turn around and reappear as *essential characteristics* of humankind. Here it is not Nature that is usually invoked to explain, and justify, differences between women and men, but something spiritual, mythic, unconscious. In some versions of this view, the old unequal hierarchy is thereby re-expressed on a spiritual level so that an unfeminine woman becomes not so much socially as spiritually suspect. In others, an effort is made to establish a complementary dualism, a view of humankind that says a healthy person balances both the feminine and the masculine principles—although even here it is usually held, on some level, that a female person ought to express more of the feminine, a male person more of the masculine principle, which recognizes the present state of society (and perhaps smuggles the primacy of the biological back in). Thus, the present nondualistic hierarchy is recognized: the complementary dualism of the mythic construction may be desirable, but it is not (yet) actual.

It is no wonder that the whole issue of difference has become so central to feminist thought. It is extremely hard to think coherently or consistently about differences within a system based on faulty generalizations because distinctions keep slipping and blurring precisely where we most need them.

Thus, when we first began again to struggle to gain access to the institutions, systems, and curricula that excluded us, many of us wanted to be included in the universal Man, to end all recognition of difference because *our* differences had been construed as inferiorities. Some among us began to hold what amounts to an egalitarian dualism: women are different from *and* equal to men (or, in some constructions, different and, in some critical respects at least, superior). Today, still others *start* with acceptance of the idea that woman has been constructed as Other (that is, as radically lacking in positive, real identity) by a phallocentric logos, and then proceed to use precisely that lack of meaning to de-center the hegemonic system. This view embraces what many have seen as the problem, claiming that as women we can crack the hegemonic logos, the ruling system, precisely because, by its terms, women exist *only as* a problem. Thus, if and as we speak ourselves, what was established itself becomes problemmatized, particularized, unstable.

Each of these approaches[2] has some merit and brings to the surface some important questions and considerations. But we can, and I think should, also think about redoing prevalent notions of universality (including that of Woman-as-Problem), and all notions of particularity (which are not universalized but *are* abstracted, as are all ideas for which we have common words), because both universals and particulars can and do reflect faulty past generalizations and abstractions. That is, I think it very important that we not become so bemused by the heady postmodern attack on universals *per se* that we overlook the fact that it may not be universals that are the problem but, simply and profoundly, *faulty* universals and the particularities they frame.

We may not want to do away with the idea of universals. It

reminds us that humans are capable of thinking ideas that cannot be known and so may be useful in recalling the free powers of thought that can illuminate and play around the limitations of knowledge. A universal idea of humankind, for example, is useful, perhaps particularly on a moral level, as long as we remember that no content it has yet had is adequately inclusive, on the one hand, and that even much more inclusive thinking cannot 'fill' an idea that is inspirational, regulative, evocative—that raises rather than answers questions.

With regard to particulars, while I do not think we can confront any phenomenon directly in some way that would allow us to start all over again with no preconceptions at all, I do think we can locate and remove some conceptual lenses that we know to be harmful in their consequences. As part of that effort, we can particularize what has seemed universal and, conversely, universalize what has seemed particular to see what happens. We can also historicize what has been formulated as if it had no reference to history, and contextualize that which has been falsely presented as if context were irrelevant. We can also travel abroad, imaginatively if not actually, in order to immerse ourselves in systems of meaning so different from ours that, when we return, we can see what was once so obvious as to be invisible. We can become, in a double sense, expatriates. As we do so, we do not risk reducing everything to some particular time in some particular culture as if it had no implications for any other time, place, or people. We simply prepare the material, as it were, from which to risk generalizing again, now with a great deal more before us.

That is, by thinking critically, reflexively, imaginatively, we can perform thought experiments that surface and vary what has been so deeply buried as to be invisible, and thus open up all kinds of new possibilities without mistaking *faulty* generalizations, and/or universals, for universals-themselves. Thus, we can also begin to rethink what universals are *for*, and when and how we wish to use rather than submit to them. As we do so, we prepare ourselves to think better about the differences that do indeed characterize us as individuals, in our groups and kinds, our times and cultures, without unthinkingly ranking them along a sliding scale that moves downward from the centrally defining kind. Turning the divisions among us back into distinctions and then considering whether or how those distinctions are useful—and to whom they have been and are useful, whose purposes they serve—frees us from having to be suspicious of distinctions *per se,* allowing us to make new ones with more care.

Articulating the Hierarchy: Sex/Gender, Class, Race

Sex/gender, class, and race are mutually implicated on a deep level; here I wish to explore in a preliminary way how each looks when, for the moment, it becomes the figure against the ground of the others—the figure that would not be as it is without that ground, or without the shaping force of hierarchically invidious monism. In what follows I am simply changing focus as I move from one topic to the next within the whole complex, articulated system about which we are trying to think.

Sex/Gender ≕

In the hierarchical monism that results from faulty generalization, the sex/gender order that is central is not simply a dualism of Man and Woman (or Man vs. Woman, as in the old "battle of the sexes" construction). Man has been established as the inclusive term at the same time and in such a way that men have been reinforced as the kind of human who ought to be dominant. That dominance has been supported intellectually, politically, economically, culturally, socially. In the resulting belief systems, men are supposed to be superior to women in almost all respects that reflect and/or confer power. And not only men generally, but each particular man: boys grow up in the dominant culture thinking they each *ought* to be and become, to achieve 'manhood,' smarter, stronger, faster, taller, more responsible than girls. More than one boy child has been told that, in the temporary or permanent absence of a father, he is to be "the man of the house," meaning that he is to be responsible for and to protect the females, however much older and more capable the females may be. In heterosexual couples, the male is still expected to be older, more highly educated, taller, more 'worldly,' more highly paid. That sometimes the male is *not* in all these ways 'more' than the female does not disprove the cultural prescriptions masquerading as descriptions. It simply means that the couple must find ways between themselves and in public to explain or otherwise compensate for their 'abnormality.' And not just heterosexual couples, but whole populations in which females are just as or even more likely to receive, say, 'higher' education or jobs (as in some Black communities), tend to bear the burden of analyses from the dominant culture that depict them as 'dysfunctional.' Thus, the dominant culture maintains the sex/gender hierarchy, perpetuating the twisted idea that the few are the norm and the ideal, so that generalizations about them, generalizations that serve their priority, hit and hurt us all (including the boys and men who also benefit from them—it is difficult to live a lie).

But things are more complicated still; the sex/gender hierarchy by which males/men become the central category of humankind does not exist all by itself. Women, who were, of course, always present at all levels of a society also stratified by class and race, were in the past invidiously distinguished not only from Man, and so from men, but also from each other. There were noblewomen who, in some regards, were considered 'higher' than peasant women *and* peasant men, just as the wives of slave-owning men in the antebellum United States were considerably 'higher' than slave men as well as women. But that does not mean that class or condition of servitude or race overrode the sex/gender hierarchy to the point at which differences between women and men of the same 'level' or condition were erased. The sex/gender system is always also there, and critically so.

Thus, there were and are different questions to be raised to sort out the tangled systems of sex/gender, race, and class, but some are particularly useful when we wish to focus on the first. "Who controls women's sexuality and how is that control effected?" is such a question, as feminist historians Joan Kelly, Gerda Lerner, Linda Gordon, and many others have pointed out. For women, it can be argued, that question is at least a necessary complement to "Who controls the means of production?" or, simply, "Who holds power over whom?" Once it was asked and taken seriously by feminist thinkers, the first simple but suggestive response became apparent: in the dominant tradition, men have in many ways taken control of women's sexuality. Their systems of thought defined it, their laws regulated it, their morals constrained it, their mores shaped it. That is, in the prevailing sex/gender system created and controlled by men, females are constrained to enact gender, to 'be' women, in a way that overdetermines us sexually so that we are devalued as human beings precisely as we are distinguished from males.

But noting and taking very seriously that women's sexuality has been controlled by men, by male-dominated and defined institutions and systems, does not mean that *all* real, historical women have been entirely controlled, sexually or otherwise, by particular real, historical men. The sex/gender hierarchy is more complex than that. As we have noted, some women have had real power over real men as well as some other women in some respects within the hierarchy. Moreover, no system/structure absolutely determines the meaning and full experience of any real individual lives. There have always been women who lived independently, for example, and there have been men who have had virtually no social, political, or economic power. But it remains necessary to take seriously the fact that, as Gerda Lerner notes, even when we look at brothers and sisters of the same family, of the same race, of the same class, the relation of the siblings to the power hierarchy is *not* the same. Gender constructs them differently and keeps them different in important ways.[3]

Even when a woman, by not marrying, avoided one of the primary institutions by which the profoundly heterosexist sex/gender system is maintained, and so held on to such supports for independence as the right to own property, the question of who controlled her sexuality remains pertinent. She might have chosen to retain control by not marrying, but the terms within which she made that choice were set by her sex/gender. Her brother, after all, faced quite different consequences from marrying (or not marrying) than did she. In some historical periods upper-class men also had their sexuality controlled by their fathers and lords, as in arranged political/economic marriages. For them, however, marriage entailed *gaining* the property and power the women they married *lost*. And regardless of whether a man's sexuality was controlled to his benefit or loss, men's sexuality has never been controlled *by woman-run systems*. A man's sexuality, even if controlled (or, more usually, directed but not entirely restricted), was controlled by a system that functioned to keep power in the hands of men—by the hierarchically invidious sex/gender system.

It is still the case today that a woman's relation to her sexuality is profoundly mediated by the hierarchy in a way that breaks through any neat divisions between women constructed in terms of class or race, however influential those *also* are. Consider that sexual abuse and violence, and harassment of all sorts, affect all women, as threat all the time, as actuality with stunning frequency. As Susan Brownmiller, Catharine MacKinnon, Andrea Dworkin, and others have pointed out, rape may be violent, but it is not explained by saying that it is a violent, as distinct from a sexual, act. Women have been and are beaten by men; that may or may not be as horrifying as rape, but it is not *the same*. Sexual harassment and abuse in many ways express specificities of the gender hierarchy, as exploitation and alienation do that of class, and de facto and de jure segregation do that of race. Sexual abuse is almost always male power inflicted on females in a way that, in the prevailing hierarchy, reduces a person to a woman, a woman to a female, and a female to an object for the sexual use of men. It reveals the horror of the sexual over-determination of the gender, woman—of the still-common notion and reality that women, unlike men, are primarily defined by sex. In this sense, the sex/gender system locks in a hierarchy of power that is encoded sexually, and then turns around and, in circular fashion, 'explains' gender in terms of sex, which is itself 'explained' in terms of a mystified Nature.

There is also sexual abuse of males by males, of males by females, and of females by females, of course, but most men do not live with the fear of sexual abuse by men, and women do not characteristically live in fear of abuse by women. That such situations do exist is painful in ways compounded by their 'abnormality,' as male abuse of females is by its exaggerated 'normality.' The realistic (usually repressed but constantly constraining) fear with which girls and women live is the real consequence of power defined, signified, and enacted in terms of gender, of gender 'explained' in terms of sex and reproduction, of sex constructed in heterosexual terms that are themselves prescribed by a phallocentric system within which females/women are lesser human beings. This complex tangle is the sex/gender system.

But that is not to say that the hierarchy confers no privileges on those who abide by the sex/gender system in its particularized forms. It does, although they are double-edged and costly ones. Any woman (whatever her race or class) who chooses to direct her sexuality toward relations with women makes herself vulnerable to loss of some gender privilege, regardless of what other privilege she may have (although such losses may be cushioned, for example, by wealth, which can buy mobility and increase privacy). Women who affiliate with men, accepting the terms of the sex/gender heterosexual hierarchy, can find themselves treated significantly better in some ways than they would be if they 'belonged' to no one man, or to no male-defined group or profession (as long as they 'behave' themselves). And there are female-specific privileges built into the gender system too, primarily in the form of rights to 'protection.' I have a hard time describing these as "privileges," however; as more than one feminist has pointed out, such 'privileges' granted within patriarchy are the result of a protection racket: first we threaten you and then we 'protect' you, if you submit to the terms we set for that 'protection.' (Ask yourself against whom, and from whose systems, do women need protecting, after all? And what is being protected— remember, for example, when we used to be 'protected' from better-paying jobs that involved perfectly manageable physical labor?) Still, those who refuse the norms of the heterosexual hierarchy know very well that there is indeed a penalty for doing so.

Without trying to take on the enormously complex issue of male as well as female suffering from the heterosexism that is deeply complicit in the gender hierarchy, we can recognize that 'deviance' is a structural aspect of the system in particular ways for women and for men. As Adrienne Rich puts it, "The lesbian trapped in the 'closet,' the woman imprisoned in prescriptive ideas of the 'normal,' share the pain of blocked options, broken connections, lost access to self-definition freely and powerfully assumed."[4] So, of course, do gay men and heterosexual men constrained by "prescriptive ideas of the 'normal.'" There are indeed common grounds to be found and claimed here—but they do not obliterate the hierarchical differences that privilege men over women, and they do not make relations between us any less twisted and complex. As Eve Sedgwick writes with regard to the strange inclusion/exclusion of male relations with males:

> "Homosocial" is a word occasionally used in history and the social sciences, where it describes social bonds between persons of the same sex; it is a neologism, obviously formed by analogy with "homosexual," and just as obviously meant to be distinguished from "homosexual." In fact, it is applied to such activities as "male bonding," which may, as in our society, be characterized by intense homophobia, fear and hatred of homosexuality. To draw the "homosocial" back into the orbit of "desire," of the potentially erotic, then, is to hypothesize the potential unbrokenness of a continuum between homosocial and homosexual—a continuum whose visibility, for men, in our society, is radically disrupted.[5]

Homosexual men in this period of the dominant history have been cast out of the category Man with so much vehemence that in some ways—but not all—they have become as marginal as women. But the male "homosocial/homosexual" continuum is not the same as the "woman/lesbian" continuum. For one thing, the continuum of men includes those who are dominant in our culture, polity, and economy at the same time that it includes those who are subject to extremes of hatred and violence for expressing sexually the bonding that maintains the system.

Generalizations about Man and about Woman, cast in the falsely abstracted singular terms that characterize the whole dominant meaning system (and certainly the sex/gender system), hide the old exclusions, but do not erase them. Quite the contrary. All that is closed out of the category of the central, the real, the ideal, persists in categories branded as lesser and/or deviant. The sex/gender system, pulled out for analysis, brings with it the whole tortuous system by which human sexuality is constructed. And that system is primary, not peripheral: male and female created he them, and still the first question asked about a newborn is, "Is it a boy or a girl?"—a question whose answer announces crucial parameters of a whole life. Whereas once feminist scholars defined gender as the cultural enactment of what is given by biology—that is, sex—today many would claim with me that things are just the opposite, that sexuality (and even sex) are constructions and enactments of gender. In any case, while we continue to struggle with this enormously fraught and complex set of issues, it is helpful to use the term "sex/gender" to refer to what is, undeniably, one of the primary power, identity, and meaning systems of the dominant culture.

Class =

Suppose one started instead with class and tried to sketch some semblance of the power relations justified by the hierarchical monism that rests on faulty generalizations. The sketch might start with levels defined by the varying material conditions and possibilities of men. Women's 'places' would then be indicated as mediated through relations to men, as men's relations either to material conditions or to each other are not mediated through women. On the hierarchy chart, the lines between levels of men separated by class could perhaps be drawn directly, while those between levels of women would connect them only through the men or would not connect them openly at all.

Perhaps each stratum of men on such a chart should have not one but two appended, lower groups of women: one group that is in critical if not all-inclusive ways 'dependent,' whose members achieve their place through relation to a man as mother, wife, daughter, and one group that is not dependent directly on such a relation with a male but whose situation is nevertheless not parallel and equal to that of otherwise similarly placed male groups. The first category would be of women as men have defined and delimited us in the sex/gender system, which turns us far too often into dependents, hanging from/onto a man's class, status, power. The second would be of women who, by choice, chance, or necessity, have lived independent of men and so lost a major route of access to direct participation in defining material conditions.

Still, women can also be recognized as a major socioeconomic category, albeit not in the same way as men. The idea that women as a whole constitute in some senses a class has been widely debated, but I believe it is safe to say that it has real usefulness in revealing the differential ways in which women and men as categories are created by *economic* systems. That woman *is* an economic and class category with its own varying levels is starkly revealed in any study or chart of categories of work and of pay. Women are to be found overwhelmingly in a very few job categories (service professions, teaching on the primary school level, secretarial work, nursing). Those categories have consistently been poorly paid. It is noteworthy that, historically, the change of a hitherto male-dominated profession to one defined as "women's work" marks the point at which power, status, and money decrease, as when teaching became "women's work." Conversely, pay and status increased when health care became 'professionalized' as men took over.

That woman was for so long not seen as at least a class-related category, and "women's work" was not studied as such by economists, is the result in part of faulty abstraction and generalization—and then universalization. Consider "Economic Man," who, whatever else can be said about him, was certainly *not* involved in what Marxist and socialist feminists call "reproductive labor" in their analyses of the historical socioeconomic roles of women. But without analysis of women's work, underpaid and unpaid, productive and reproductive, there is no possibility that adequate analyses of economic systems can be carried out. The availability of cheap female labor, cheap because female as well as immigrant, or Black, or some other 'low' category, has sustained the economy, and the underpaid and unpaid labor of women on all levels of the male and female class hierarchies has underwritten much more than has ever been acknowledged. Consider the volunteer work in their communities of women of all groups and the unpaid home work of many that made it possible for men to go out to work without renouncing the possibility of home and family, as well as the paid domestic work that allowed privileged women to pass their prescribed function 'down' to other women. To bring to the surface the socioeconomic centrality of women's work, and to realize how entirely ignored it has been in studies of the economy (faultily generalized about with regard to men alone), it may suffice simply to try to compute the essential economic value—not just the 'replacement cost' figured by insurance companies—of home-makers (who are cleaners, gardeners, shoppers, entertainers, protectors, schedulers, drivers, decorators, nurses, teachers, counselors, and more), house-workers, and volunteers. That we still have no really good tools to do so indicates, also, the degree to which whole fields, and their 'neutral' methodologies, have been based on faulty generalizations.

Today we know how deeply embedded the socioeconomic construction of woman as a category has been, in part because women have challenged and in some instances changed it. As Alice Kessler-Harris writes:

> As it turned out, moving toward, even achieving, equality at work proved to be the beginning, not the end, of the battle. Each step on the road to equality—equal pay, an end to discrimination in hiring and training, access to promotion—exposed a deeply rooted set of social attitudes that tried to preserve women's attachment to the home. . . . To work freely, women required control over their own reproduction and sexuality. They felt entitled to sexual gratification, as men had always been, and to access to birth control and to abortion if necessary. Economic independence encouraged freer life styles, reducing the dependence of women on men and permitting a genuine choice of life partners—male or female. Women who earned adequate incomes could choose not to have children or among a variety of child-care arrangements if they had them. Freedom for women to live without men, to live with them without benefit of legal marriage, to create two-career families, or to live without families at all posed staggering challenges to traditional values.[6]

The sex/gender system, the patriarchal system of heterosexuality that both necessitates and viciously suppresses the homosocial/ homosexual and woman/lesbian continua, is so tightly bound with the socioeconomic system that one cannot vary one without revealing the other as suddenly in jeopardy. Both assume a particular group of men faultily universalized as Man, as the real, 'normal' kind of person, the only kind about whom we may generalize in ways that affect us all.

Race ⊒

Race, too, has obviously been interlocked with the conceptual/
power hierarchy on a fundamental, and fundamentally skewed,
level. It can be said that race—which is a politically, economically,
and culturally constructed category—shapes if it does not deter-
mine class and status, just as, like sex/gender, it is in turn shaped by
them in some regards. That the majority of Black people in North
America have been poor and locked out of the higher levels of
power and status indicates that race is in some persistent and
critical way prior to, or in any case vastly influential over, class/
status allocation. (Class and status, while not the same, are closely
related.) At the same time, there are class/status distinctions *within*
the Black community as well. And gender pervades race and class/
status at all levels: Black women, whatever their class/status, are
considered and treated culturally, economically, and politically differently from Black men by both white and Black men and women.

Certain work categories have been and are (if unadmittedly, even
illegally) marked as 'proper' for people on the basis of race as others
are on the basis of sex/gender. These categories have been tangled
together in intricate ways, and they have been extraordinarily difficult to separate. For example, as Angela Davis observes, "Racism and sexism frequently converge—and the condition of white
women workers is often tied to the oppressive predicament of
women of color. Thus the wages received by white women domestics have always been fixed by the racist criteria used to calculate the
wages of Black women servants."[7] As these job categories begin,
however slightly, to be redefined and opened, the same kind of
cultural, economic, and sexual tremors created by opening all sex/
gender job categories can be felt throughout the system. Consider
the violence precipitated by the Civil Rights Movement, busing,
and fair housing efforts. Black people were to 'know their place,'
and that place was poor and powerless and separate in all respects.
But this hardly needs rehearsing here; we know well how dependent the economic and social and political systems have been on the
constructed category of race.

We also know that those systems have been intertwined with the
sex/gender system, have indeed been sexualized, as the horror of
lynching reminds us all too powerfully. Miscegenation laws were
once on the books in most if not all states, and 'mixed' couples are
still rare. Notions of love and laws of marriage, like economic and
political notions and laws and practices, have been both openly
exclusive and fundamentally unsound. And studies of "the Black

family" far too often reveal the power of the skew in our thinking and practices. I will not rehearse those painful debates again here; simply recall how often it has been noted that the "Black family" is 'dysfunctional,' that it is 'matriarchal' (and hence bad), that it is 'aberrant' insofar as it departs from the white middle-class, male-headed nuclear form of family. Prevailing notions of kinship, as of family, have been skewed by the basic error of faulty generalization. As Carol Stack notes in her classic study of Black families:

> Although anthropologists have long recognized the distinction between natural and social parenthood . . . until recently most ethnographic data has not clarified those social transactions involving parental rights. This omission has led to the persistent belief that each person is a kinsman of his natural mother and father, who are expected as parents to raise him. . . . Much of the controversial and misleading characterizations of kinship and domestic life can be attributed to this assumption and to the lack of ethnographic data that interprets the meaning people give to the chain of parent-child connections within a particular folk culture.[8]

Where one "folk culture" is generalized into the norm and the ideal for all, different cultures' systems appear as deviant or are not even seen as different (and hence are misinterpreted). Studies that should reveal that bias are instead skewed by the very error we need them to correct.

Since, in the dominant tradition, the white people who defined things took themselves to be the real kind of people, the norm, and the ideal, while defining Black people primarily as members of a race, the *concept* of race itself, like those of sex/gender and class, needs very careful reconsideration. One could make a case for the view that insofar as white people did not even admit that they belonged to a race (the prefix "white" is usually suppressed), race became an even more virulent if no more fundamental category or system than sex/gender and class. Men have taken themselves to be *both* male *and* all of 'mankind'; upper-class people have taken themselves to be *both* upper-class *and* the ideal for the 'lower' classes—in both cases, there was some recognition that the ruling few 'had' a sex/gender, a class status, so there was at least some sense of mutual implication. But white people may have gone further with the idea, involved also in constructions of sex/gender and class, that those who are not of their group are *utterly* different in kind from them. I have, to my horror, heard white people say that "Negroes" and white people should not "crossbreed" any more than "animals from different species" should. Here, too, sex is

revealed as a primary signifier and signification of power; interlocked with race, another falsely naturalized, essentializing construct, it serves to create a division that is supposed to be uncross-
able. That, precisely, is the role Nature has often played in the
dominant tradition's discourses of power.

‗ How race, sex/gender, and class intersect, interact, coalesce, *and*
differ remains to be studied very, very carefully. The major point
here is simply that all three systems consist of hierarchies that are
also, even in downright contradictory ways, monisms: the defining
few, generalizing from themselves to all, established their sex/gen-
der, their race, their class, as norms and ideals for all, while also
maintaining their exclusivity. Thus, they remain the ones who have
no prefixes, who are *not* defined primarily in terms of race, class, or
sex/gender, while for all others those systemically established categories become determinants not only of sets of prescribed qualities,
but of lives.

Further Complications

No discussion of the power hierarchies of sex/gender articulated
with race and class/status structures can conceivably be adequate to
all the shifting hierarchies Western culture has known. The lives,
functions, and meanings of the men in terms of whom hegemony is
constructed have themselves been stratified by religion, by degree
of education, by property ownership, by wealth, by physical capacity, by family name, by age, in criss-crossing, shifting ways within
and across historical eras, cultures, and subcultures. Still, I believe
it is correct to focus on the three fundamental variables of class,
sex/gender, and race, for when other hierarchical distinctions have
been most virulent, they have often partaken of the conceptual/
emotional 'language' of race, class, and gender, suggesting a basic
level of significance for those three.

In the anti-Semitism of Hitler's Germany and the Ku Klux Klan in
the United States, for example, we encounter raw racism, not religious prejudice reflecting differences in doctrine and religious
practices. Nazis, neo-Nazis, and Klan members do not think that
what Jews believe is wrong; they think *Jews* are wrong. In Hindu-
Muslim communal struggles in India, the opposing factions' charac-
terizations of each other have often gone beyond expression of
dislike of differing religious practices to what can only be called
racial readings of the character of "the Hindu" or "the Muslim." In
such situations, race is the most dangerous division of the articu-

lated hierarchy—but it is never without its sex/gender and class dimensions as well. In Hitler's Germany, a "Jewess" was distinguished not only from the "superior Aryan race," but also from "Aryan women," who were themselves relegated to inferior roles within their 'kind.' That does not change for a moment the fact that Jewish women and men were together subjected to genocide; it simply marks the persistence of sex/gender discrimination even when the hierarchy has been defined overwhelmingly in terms of race (which is also sexualized, and economically enforced).

Moreover, such is the complexity of humankind and our shifting realities that more than once people have strengthened themselves to stand against racial oppression by defiantly enacting gender prescriptions reserved for women and men of the oppressing race, or by embracing the style, or values, of a 'higher' class as a way to withstand race or gender prescriptions. Thus, some Black men in the United States have asserted their gender superiority over Black women in order to stand against the race and class oppression from which they suffer, and some Black women have refused to have anything to do with feminism because "the racial struggle comes first" (and also, I fear and must say here, because in a racist society feminism has itself too often been defined in ways that cannot speak to Black women, thereby painfully reminding us how deep and persistent the old errors really are).

Perhaps very, very few of us can find the strength to rethink, undo, and stand against *all* the most powerful systems at once. And perhaps, too, people within those systems have developed cultures and sources of strength that we really do not want to dismantle, to renounce.

But to keep trying to think ourselves free, we do need to return, again and again, to efforts to uncover and see the operations of the systems that have marked most of us as lesser human beings than the defining, hegemonic group of men. The point here is that race, class, and sex/gender (defined within a heterosexist system) are *the* persistent categories through which we find Otherness, and not just difference, expressed. It is in thinking through, and challenging, those terms/systems that we uncover the invidious hierarchical monism that expresses and shapes the hegemonic system of knowledge and of power within which we find ourselves.

"Reverse Discrimination"

Let me say it again: gender, race, and class do not persist in our thinking primarily as dualisms, as man/woman, white/Black, privileged/unprivileged—or even oppressors/oppressed. These are not categories that persist in equal but oppositional positions. On one level, that is precisely what the U.S. Supreme Court recognized when it finally found (in *Brown* v. *Board of Education of Topeka*, 1954) that "separate" in the American educational system is not and cannot be "equal" for whites and Blacks. For any and all groups within the dominant tradition we are trying to think through, to be "separate" from the defining kind of human is to be lowered on a scale of power and value as of attributed reality.

The problem is in the usurpation by the category *whites*, by the category *men*, of what it means to be human so that Black people and white women, men of unprivileged groups and all women, are seen as less human, less worthy, less real. That is the price of faulty generalization. Seeing that helps us see, too, one of the reasons why "reverse discrimination" is a useless-unto-vicious notion: in a hierarchical monism, as distinct from a dualism, there is no sense in holding to the reversibility of concepts and principles as if they were separate but equal. The root problem is precisely that they are not. They are related to each other as inclusive term to subkind, as norm to deviant, as ideal to inferior, as thing-itself to Other. Provisions for the continuing exclusion and devaluation of those defined and treated as inferiors are properly called "racist," "sexist." Provisions for the *disruption* of such systems are, on the contrary, antiracist, antisexist. There is no reversibility here. There is, instead, recognition that that which has oppressed people must be combatted in terms that openly and explicitly take that oppression into account. Since white people have oppressed and/or benefited from the oppression of Black people, Black people have grounds for categorically distrusting (at the least) white people that white people do not have for devaluing Black people. Suspicion of white people is justified by experience; it is descriptively based. Suspicion of Black people reveals the terrible tangle of errors that created that experience; it is prescriptively based. These are not interchangeable kinds of categories, and they will not be until there is genuine equality— at which time (and may it indeed come some day), we will still find that equality need not mean sameness, but, rather, that equality protects our right to be different. The idea of reverse discrimination is, in a hierarchical system, every bit as absurd as its suppressed premise—that we are all alike.

We also cannot speak of class as if it applied in the same way to men and women, to Black people and white people, to different ethnic groups, to different regions of the country, nor can we assume that racial hierarchies are experienced in the same way by men and by women, by poor and rich. We cannot accurately speak of "the oppression of women" and mean that all women are oppressed in the same way; oppression is experienced too differently at different levels of the hierarchy for similarity to override entirely or consistently our sensitivity to difference. We can speak of women as victims, but we cannot mean that women have been only victims, or that no women have victimized or benefited from the victimization of other women.[9] Not all women have been denied all privileges, nor has either privilege or victimization been the same for all women who experienced it. None of these categories are reversible; none are internally consistent. They have complex, shifting meanings and an extraordinarily varied range of uses.

It is, then, not enough to particularize the minority of men that has defined itself as all, has generalized from itself to all. We need to learn to particularize whatever and whomever we study, and then to contextualize, to historicize—to hold whatever abstractions we draw from the material of our study close to that material for as long as is necessary to keep us from thinking that apparently parallel but actually hierarchical categories are reversible. No one who has studied a transformed history that tells the stories of us all will fall into the error of thinking that the category white male functions the same way as that of Black female, that actions designed to control the power of the former are indistinguishable from actions designed to empower the latter. Again, supposedly parallel categories (men/women, Black/white) do not name parallel groups; the categories are indeed paired, but they are not expressions of a complementary dualism, nor even an oppositional one. In each case, one of the categories contains/refers to/constructs a group that has held the power to define what is, and has done so to the extent that all others are moved down the scales of worth and power. Faulty generalizations by those in power create and express not dualisms, but hierarchical monism.

Dualism would mean equal weight/power to each category. Not so. E.g. Black/white man/woman

Taking the Few to Represent All

The root problem is that the few took themselves to be the inclusive term, the norm, and the ideal. Through the ages, some have continued that set of mistakes through arrogance and a sense of entitlement: I have privilege, and that is all right because I and my kind should have it. They could, then, be kindly toward those who were 'less' than they, could even try to counteract the 'real' imbalance through efforts to 'protect' the "weaker sex," the "less developed" peoples (a kindness that turns quickly into outrage when the recipients of their condescension refuse to be grateful). As long as formal and informal education, wittingly and unwittingly, continues to perpetuate the idea that the few can indeed represent all, such paternalistic tolerance is likely to be the best those who are unrepresented in the generalizations and the systems built on them can expect. There is no ground laid for egalitarian respect in such a system.

The difficulty U.S. citizens have had envisioning women in Congress or the White House as their representatives directly reflects the problem and the complexity of the notion of *representation*, which is not quite covered by what I have said about generalizations thus far. Humankind in all its diversity is still for the most part simply not *seen* in 'high places,' and so continues to seem out of place there. Those who are used to encountering people who are similar to themselves in roles of power and authority cannot easily accept that they can be spoken to, of, or for by someone who seems not just different, but lesser. And, sadly, some of those who are defined by the dominant culture as different from and less than the defining few have also tended to choose against representation by others who share their marked category, against women and men from unprivileged groups. When people are well educated into the hierarchy, they can become uncomfortable with seeing those who are 'supposed' to be powerless in positions of power.

Clearly, representation has had different meanings for us. For privileged white males, it has meant having someone like them stand in their place to exercise their power on their behalf. For the rest of us, it has meant having someone unlike us stand in places not 'appropriate' for such as we. Our 'representatives' were to do for us what we could not do for ourselves; it was not our power they exercised but theirs. For us, being represented has been a lot closer to being *ruled*. I think perhaps it is that approach of representation to rule in our supposedly representative republic that, in part, makes many people deeply uncomfortable with the idea that a woman of any sort, or a Black man, might hold important elective office. To be represented by such a person can *feel* more risky because neither women nor Black men (nor men from other unprivileged groups) are easily recognized as powerful people. We are not used to seeing power in the hands of our *own* kind, and we have been led to believe that that is because we are not good enough, capable enough, to exercise it. Insofar as we have internalized that message, we become unable to trust people who might genuinely represent us because we cannot believe that they can do so well. And we are not entirely wrong, either; insofar as the system of representative government is defined, established, and practiced according to rules (overt and implicit) developed during the time of our exclusion, being a 'good' (that is, effective) representative has strongly tended to require being skilled in the practices that developed during that time. Just as, in scholarship, work on women is still often seen as less important, less significant, than work on men and can hurt a faculty member's chances for tenure, a representative who works for daycare, for comparable worth, or for any other provision necessary to the full inclusion of women risks being seen as an advocate of "special interests" and nonserious concerns. Generalizations about what are 'real' and important constituent concerns have not taken into full account what are still defined as "women's issues." As elsewhere, women are taken to be a mere subset of the citizenry, while men are the real thing. Those generalizations are in error, and it is our responsibility to correct them by making it evident to our representatives that they can no longer afford such errors—that we will no longer accept being ruled by those who are dependent on our votes.

Furthermore, what kind of person 'represents' us involves much more than the government. A woman who worked as secretary for a male colleague of mine marched into my office about a month after she had started work and said, "You know, you're making it hard on me." I asked what she meant. She said, "I've always worked for men. When I look at you, I think I should be doing something different myself. It makes me unhappy." An honest woman, that one; she recognized how much shakes when we disrupt the generalizations behind/within the hierarchy. Most of us have grown up in a world in which "growing up" means an increase in the power of males over females such that females remain in the private and/or unpowerful realms while males are supposed to separate from the home, go out into and rise 'up' in the world. We are then likely to have trouble with changes that violate what we learned was 'right' and 'natural.' Women who are uncomfortable working 'under' another woman are feeling what the hierarchy teaches—that our kind is not to be represented in powerful positions, that power in this world is properly exercised over us, not by us.

In our schools, "coming of age" literature has tended to be about

American white boys' struggles to grow up. Students read *Huckleberry Finn*, *The Catcher in the Rye*, *A Separate Peace*, and, sometimes, *A Walker in the City* and *You Can't Go Home Again*. It is considered a mark of worthy literature that it speak to all of us, that it speak universally, and certainly in at least some respects some of the 'great' literature we still study does so. But it remains true that we are not as likely to read about a Black girl's growing up and to be helped to see in it, too, what may be meaningful for many. Furthermore, it is difficult to understand how we can know what is generally significant about "coming of age," since we have, until very recently, had almost no studies of and very little easily available literature about what that complex process has in fact been like for white girls, for Black girls and boys, for those in other ethnic groups even within the dominant Euro-American culture—let alone outside it.

When the historian Gerda Lerner first tried to order some historical records of women's lives in America that she had retrieved from oblivion, she found that she could not use the available categories of analysis for her material. Her material taught her that the culturally shaped process of growing from girl to woman was not like that of growing from boy to man, even among privileged white people. She writes of those who had access to education:

> For a boy, education was directed toward a vocational or professional goal, and his life ideally moved upward and outward in a straight line until it reached a plateau of fulfillment; the girl's education was sporadic and often interrupted; it did not lead to the fulfillment of her role, but rather competed with it. Her development was dependent on her relationship to others and was often determined by them; it moved in wavelike, circuitous motion. In the boy's case, the life crises were connected to vocational goals: separation from the family for purposes of greater educational opportunity; success or failures in achievement and career; economic decisions or setbacks. For the girl such crises were more closely connected to distinct stages in her biological life: transition from childhood to adolescence and then to marriage which meant, in the past, confinement and loss of freedom, and greater restraint rather than the broadening out which it meant for the boy.[10]

The process differs for different ethnic groups and across classes and national cultures, too, of course, as it differs for some privileged young women today. There is no reason to assume that the story of a middle- or upper-class white North American boy's growth to manhood is the only kind that represents the rocky human process of maturation. In literature alone, Toni Morrison's *The Bluest Eye* and *Sula*, Maya Angelou's *I Know Why the Caged Bird Sings*, Gordon Parks's *The Learning Tree*, Maxine Hong Kingston's *The Woman Warrior*, and Paule Marshall's *Brown Girl, Brownstones*, among many others, are available to expand the imaginative horizons of all of us.[11]

A different way of taking the few to be proper grounds for generalization to all so that one group becomes representative of all (as others do not become representative for it) can be found in Lawrence Kohlberg's theory of moral development, which, although it is technically in the field of psychology, has had a profound impact on moral theorists, among others. As Carol Gilligan has pointed out, the people whose moral development Kohlberg studied were male, and the consequence of generalizing from them to all was, first, that females were not studied at all and hence the claim that "moral growth and development" itself, rather than (white, privileged, twentieth-century, North American) *male* growth and development, had been studied was false. This is the error of faulty generalization. Second, as girls came to be studied within the theoretical framework abstracted from the study of boys, those girls came out characteristically 'lower'—less developed morally—than males. This, as we shall see, is circular reasoning, the next category of errors to be considered here.

The same mistake (with the same kind of consequences) occurs whenever deviation from a partial, single model or norm is read as deficiency (the mark, as we have noted, of hierarchical monism). Those who have been generalized from emerge as representative of all, leaving all others unrepresented, with no recognized power or influence of their own. African art and Native American art are still too often studied not in their own right but only or primarily as they influenced modern artists of the European-American tradition such as Picasso—in which case they emerge as occasions for discovery by 'real' artists rather than as serious works in their own tradition. Here, as in politics, we can see a deep cultural inability to see the excluded in any role that might imply equality with, let alone superiority over, the category that has stood in for all. African art is not seen as representative of 'real' art.

The definition of whole peoples, as of whole fields, is based on faulty generalizations, from consideration of only some and by no means all materials, peoples, issues. Thus, for those influenced by the dominant tradition, it can be as difficult and disturbing to imagine a Yoruba philosopher as a woman boss, a Black president. And that means that it can be difficult, and disturbing, to *identify* with people unlike the defining few in such 'high' positions. It is difficult for those used to seeing people like themselves as philosophers, bosses, presidents, because, were they to identify with a woman, a Yoruba, they would be identifying with what they have learned is 'less' than and even threatening to them. It is difficult for those used to being represented in the mode of being ruled because we have little experience of true representation. We tend to feel 'put down' by seeing someone like us in a 'high' position because their exception-status implies that our 'lower' position is our fault and failure.

In work by the very influential philosopher Immanuel Kant, we can see just how hard it has been for representatives of the privileged few in the dominant culture to identify across the lines of the hierarchy. Kant felt perfectly free to characterize, and judge, other cultures on how they measured up against a standard of "man" that is evidently the product of faulty generalization. He simply could not see even how males from other cultures might represent humankind; they remained, for him, a particular and curious and lesser *kind*:

> If we cast a fleeting glance over the other parts of the world, we find the Arab the noblest man in the Orient, yet of a feeling that degenerates very much into the adventurous. He is hospitable, generous, and truthful; yet his narrative and history and on the whole his feeling are always interwoven with some wonderful thing. His inflamed imagination presents things to him in unnatural and distorted images.[12]

Of females in general, Kant wrote:

> The virtue of a woman is a **beautiful virtue.** That of the male sex should be a **noble virtue.** Women will avoid the wicked not because it is unright, but because it is ugly; and virtuous actions mean to them such as are morally beautiful. . . . Woman is intolerant of all commands and morose constraint. They do something only because it pleases them. . . . I hardly believe that the fair sex is capable of principles.[13]

The point is not just to collect absurdities uttered by European-American male philosophers, but to note that it is the mind that believed them that gave us the critiques of "Pure Reason" and of "Judgment" that are central in many ways to the field of philosophy as it is still taught. How can we assume that Kant's treatment of reason, as of judgment, was *not* skewed by his utter lack of respect for modes of thought and feeling he considered characteristic of the "fair sex" and the Arab man? At the least we know that he was exclusive, and so we must, surely, hesitate before we assume that his notions of pure reason can in any way *be* universal. He has taken the few to be the norm, and *from* as well as *for* them sought the ideal. He has generalized too far from too few.

In its false generalizations, what Kant says of the Arab man and of women is strikingly like what Thomas Jefferson says of the African writer Ignatius Sancho (who published his epistles in 1782 in London). Here we see how generalizations about *kinds* of humans different from the defining few both feed and result from notions of supposedly universal human qualities and abilities, such as reason, which have themselves come to be known through a process of faulty generalization. Jefferson, writing about a particular person and work, used a standard of 'real' and 'sound' reason to see in Sancho not difference but inferiority, deviance. Clearly, nothing in Jefferson's background and education, nothing in his culture, prepared him to read Sancho in terms that might have been appropriate to Sancho rather than to Jefferson's (limited, yet falsely universalized) notion of 'rational man.' Sancho's epistles may have been excellent or they may have been poor examples of their own kind; we cannot tell what they represent from Jefferson's comments, because Jefferson can see only how Sancho fails to be as Jefferson thinks he ought to be:

> His imagination is wild and extravagant, escapes incessantly from every restraint of reason and taste, and, in the course of its vagaries, leaves a track of thought as incoherent and eccentric, as is the course of a meteor through the sky. His subjects should have led him to a process of sober reasoning: yet we find him always substituting sentiment for demonstration.[14]

The idea of reason available to Kant and to Jefferson clearly precluded comprehension of modes of thought and expression different from those they wrongly took to be universal. 'Rational man' as we have been taught to think of him is a construct, a prescription, not an adequately rich and comprehensive description. He is neither normative for nor representative of all.

One way to see this error, generalizing—even universalizing—from too few instances, in *any* discourse is, as I have already suggested, to notice who is marked, who carries a prefix. Those who have no particularizing prefix are those who have been taken to be 'the thing-itself,' the few who stand in for the universal or general.

"Poet" means white male poet from the Western tradition. We have struggled to get rid of terms such as "poetess," but the prefixes persist. We do not teach "white male poets of America." We do (too rarely) teach "African-American women poets." A syllabus consisting solely of British, European, and American white men's novels may be called a course on "The Novel," and relatively few curriculum committees will ask, "Why so many white men?" Or, "Shouldn't this be an upper-level course because it is so specialized?" They will ask just that sort of question about a course covering only Black women's novels were it to be presented simply as a course on "The Novel." One group, one particular set of works, defines the field and has no prefixes; all others must be marked.

Our students, then, learn not about philosophy, or literature, or history, or psychology, or history of art, but about one exclusive tradition's versions of those subjects. And because they cannot tell from the unprefixed titles of courses and works that that is all they are learning, they internalize the notion that everything else, the lives and works and psyches and stories of all others, is at best a subset of the falsely universalized type they have learned. That is the result of generalizing too far from too few, a result that has very serious human consequences.

Invisibility

Although we here speak in conceptual terms, it must not be forgotten that concepts are by no means without emotional meaning and effect, just as they are not without political, economic, and social bases and effects. When generalizations to too many are made from too few, those who were not among the sample, or group, originally considered are not only left out; their reality is simultaneously eclipsed and falsified.

In being excluded, they are made invisible, and that invisibility itself teaches something. It is not just an absence. Students who never hear of a woman philosopher have trouble believing in such a creature. On a deep level, the level on which we learn cultural presuppositions of the most basic sort,[15] it comes to seem to them *wrong* for a woman to be a philosopher. The two categories, "philosopher" and "woman," exist for them as mutually exclusive. The same holds for all other disciplines and subject matters. For example, while History concentrates on the activities from which women were excluded and ignores—or depicts only from the male standpoint—women's lives and creations, students learn to think of all that is significant in the past as the domain of men.

Since the curriculum has indeed excluded works by and about women, it is not at all surprising that students taking a course in Philosophy that includes two or three works by women, and/or some works that include consideration of women, come to feel that the course is "ideological." They do not see the men represented and discussed in their courses *as men* but, rather, as philosophers, writers, painters, significant historical figures, important composers. But they do see the women *as women* because they have learned from the use of prefixes in course titles and the omissions in their courses that women are oddities in the dominant tradition, that women are always a kind of human, a kind of writer or whatever, and never the thing-itself. They do not notice it if a course concerns only men, yet they often feel at first that a course that mentions women more than a couple of times "overemphasizes" women (and sometimes complain that their instructor is "obsessed with women"). Their discomfort is but one more indication that such courses are very badly needed, not that "the students don't want them." What, after all, does it mean for us all that students find it odd, uncomfortable, uninteresting, even threatening, to begin seriously to study the majority of humankind—to learn about women, to learn about men other than privileged European-Americans? What does it mean for democracy that only some few kinds of humans can be imagined as our representatives? What does it mean for all of us on this shrinking globe?

Learning takes place on many levels. It not only affects what we hold consciously as knowledge but also establishes habits of association and expectation. It is part of the constant process of identity definition and development. While it can be very useful to make a distinction between psychological growth-and-development and intellectual training, it is disastrous to assume that psyche and mind are literally separate. Changes in what is taught and how it is taught produce such strong reactions that we should know better. The violation of what is expected, what is familiar, can startle or evoke anxiety and even anger, as any teacher knows who has tried to work in the classroom in ways that deviate from students' long-established and by-now preconscious—and so all the more influential—expectations. White male students, asked seriously to open themselves to an understanding of those with whom they have never been encouraged to identify (quite the contrary) can become troubled and angry. So can privileged white female students whose identification is strongly with those who have been in power. So can we all, as a matter of fact: it is not at all easy to shift or make less rigid one's sense of identification, to open to voices one has never been encouraged to hear—even when that voice is one's own.

To those who have taught Women's Studies and/or more inclusive courses in our disciplines, it is stunning how quickly white males begin to feel left out, threatened, upset, when the focus of a course is not almost exclusively on white Western males. Women of all groups, and men from those excluded from the curriculum, have spent all the years of their schooling in precisely that situation, but until very recently it has been rare indeed that any have expressed discomfort, let alone anger. In fact, as we have often noted, most of us *did not even notice that we were left out.* Women and unprivileged men fought long and hard to gain access to 'real' education, to 'the best' education—and that meant education into the dominant tradition. We wanted to learn the white male classics; they were, after all, taught simply as *the* classics. It is emblematic that the great fighter for Black and women's education at the turn of the century, Anna Julia Cooper, got her own Ph.D. (in her sixties) from the Sorbonne—in Latin.

We all notice when Western males are left out; many of us still do not notice when the majority of humankind is excluded. The omission of Western males provokes anxiety and anger; the omission of all the rest of humankind is not consciously noticed, is not felt in a way that easily comes to expression although it does indeed affect us. Our perceptions as well as our concepts and our emotions have been and are powerfully shaped by the dominant tradition.

Too true!

To change the curriculum is by no means to change only what we think about. It is to begin to change who and how we are in the world we share. Teachers joining in this effort become part of an educational project that recalls Plato's dramatic sketch of the cave in *The Republic*. There, Socrates makes it clear how well he knows that people do not find it easy to stop watching the same old images reflected on the cave wall, do not like to stand up, turn around, and begin the difficult journey toward a more complete and real knowledge. And he also notes that one who has made the journey and then returned to teach about a fuller reality will be in danger from all those who are used to the one-dimensional images on the cave wall from which all that passes for knowledge—and reality itself—has been derived.

But if we never startle our students, or any of those with whom we share our work, our life and world, if they never feel any anxiety, are never roused to anger or to sudden, intense, personal engagement by what we say, we ought to be concerned. Such comfort can indicate that the learning in which we are engaged is not touching the old errors built deep into the culture. It is, I believe, significant that although many teachers and scholars profess to admire and try to emulate the Socratic method of teaching, most conveniently forget that Socrates was put to death for "corrupting the youth of Athens." One who questions not as an intellectual game, not as a kind of conceptual muscle-building, but in order to make evident and open to serious reconsideration the deepest presuppositions and behaviors of the culture and state, *is* going to arouse discomfort and anger.

Alfred North Whitehead suggests:

> When you are criticizing the philosophy of an epoch, do not chiefly direct your attention to those intellectual positions which its exponents feel it necessary explicitly to defend. There will be some fundamental assumptions which adherents of all the various systems within the epoch unconsciously presuppose. Such assumptions appear so obvious that people do not know what they are assuming because no other way of putting things has ever occurred to them.[16]

Those are assumptions that can be made explicit and be questioned only at the cost of making the ground move under people's feet, an experience many respond to very emotionally. Faulty abstractions, generalizations, universals, are by no means 'merely' conceptual errors—not for creatures such as we for whom reality is rarely (if ever) unmediated by concepts. After all, for us reality is one of the most complex of all concepts, one with an ever-shifting, never finally knowable or even definitively specifiable set of referents. The point is not to attempt now to know reality correctly and finally; the point is to undo those errors in our thinking that quite clearly have consequences of which we no longer approve. It is not right conceptually, morally, or politically to construct, and mark, kinds of humans in a way that leaves only one such kind in the centrally defining, norm-setting, unprefixed position.

CIRCULAR REASONING

The profound connection between the ways we think and the ways we perceive, feel, and act emerges further as we consider the next conceptual error, circular reasoning. Our reasoning is circular when we end up where we began without recognizing, or admitting, that that is what we have done. Circling back to beginnings can be a part of profound learning, of course, as when we return and "know it for the first time" (T. S. Eliot). But circular reasoning is quite different. It is an error, for example, to start from an assertion and then 'prove' its truth by referring back to it, defining anything that might disprove it as irrelevant or out of order because, by the assertion that is supposed to be proven, that contrary evidence cannot be considered. "Girls are not good at arithmetic" and "Women are lousy drivers" are rather familiar examples of such assertions, revealed as circular when we point to examples of girls who are indeed good at arithmetic, women who are good drivers, and are met with, "But she thinks (or drives) like a boy (or man)." The assertion is not open to contradiction because it is not a descriptive statement, after all. It is prescriptive.

Another way of getting at this kind of mistake is to say that what appeared to be an empirical statement is actually a definition. That is, it *looks* as if "Girls are not good at arithmetic" is a summary statement made after observation, a statement of fact. But when contrary observations or facts are suggested, the speaker changes ground, saying, in effect, "It is a defining quality of girls not to be good at arithmetic. Anyone who appears to be a girl but is good at arithmetic is, then, not really, or entirely, or properly, a girl."

We are not after logical precision here; we are simply trying to undo quite obvious blocks to sensible thinking. However necessary it is to start somewhere, to have some principles or propositions or definitions or axioms that are themselves not open to proof or disproof because they themselves set the terms for proof, it is *not* right to elevate to that position statements or beliefs that have resulted from the fundamental error of taking the few to be the inclusive term, the norm, and the ideal. Faulty generalizations should not be used to justify their own continuing centrality so that we spin around and around in our cages, not only failing to further the on-going quest for knowledge, but locking ourselves into harmful, even dangerous, old ways of perceiving, feeling, acting.

Faulty Standards

In the dominant culture, much is made of the need to have young people study the 'best' of the tradition—as if learning about what has been established as 'the best' were a straightforward matter. But study of the 'best' is not a neutral, purely intellectual matter. Those who are educated formally and informally in this culture learn that they are to admire the best—to learn, even, to love it. And that means that it is to become a part of what motivates them, what draws and inspires them on a personal as well as intellectual level. Consider the study of Art History, for example. The "masterpieces" shown in slides in lecture halls are supposed to call forth the students' admiration in a way that responds to the respect their teacher shows these works. *These* paintings, their teacher says or implies, warrant your full attention. In them, genius is at work, greatness is made manifest. This mode of relating to art is by no means emotionally *or* morally neutral. A student who rarely responds on a personal level to the works discussed in an Introduction to Art History course, a new citizen who visits one of the established art galleries and does not respond to the "masterpieces" hung there, easily comes to feel that she or he is in some serious way inadequate. Good people—'finer' people—admire and enjoy 'great' art. Those who do not like what the tradition says is great art are seen as 'lower' than those who do. This scale of refined taste, from the 'cultivated' to the 'crass' and 'insensitive,' is compounded oddly of established definitions and moral and class-based judgments. 'Finer' people have 'finer' sensibilities—that is, they like what the dominant culture has selected as great. 'Lower' people have 'lower,' 'cruder' sensibilities—that is, they do not like the music, the drama, the literature, the paintings, that constitute "high culture."

This is a fascinating and complex subject in itself, revealing as it does the class-related nature of much of what is taught, particularly in arts and humanities courses, in our schools, and through the cultural establishments of states, cities, and communities. The point here is that whole traditions of creative works have been excluded from the collection of Great Works we are taught to admire, and that not only makes the excluded works and creators seem odd, startling, out of place, should they ever be mentioned, but marks them as less worthy of being loved, valued, admired, studied. A faultily generalized study of art leads one to *specific* accredited tastes, which

[handwritten margin note: E.g. Jazz & "lesser intelligence"]

are then used in circular fashion to 'prove' not just one's 'good' education but one's worthiness to be a member of a specific level of a specific culture, that which has had a corner on defining, cultivating, and protecting 'good' taste.

Circularity extends the error of generalizing too far from too few into the standards by which the hierarchy is maintained to such an extent that the few reappear, this time particularly tellingly as *the ideal*. Consider that the creation of Literature as a field was carried out by a particular sort of human, took place in a particular place at a particular time, and took as its focus particular kinds of works and some few kinds of writers. Then, the objects of this thought, the sources of notions of what is good (or great) writing, and finally early theories about literature lost their specificity as they were taken up into ever-grander theory. But those sources did not disappear, were not genuinely transcended. Had they been transcended, they would not reappear so predictably not as the *sources* for standards of judgment they actually are, but as *exemplars* of definitions, principles, standards of judgment.

That is, if the notions of what makes something literature, and the standards for 'great' or 'significant' literature that were derived from the original selection of works/writers/subject matters, had actually achieved a level of generality adequate to *all* literature, the application of principles of selection, judgment, and taste derived from them *would have resulted in far more inclusive literature texts and courses, in far more inclusive anthologies, play productions, novel lists, and so on than we presently see.*

Thus, faulty generalization leads to circular reasoning in which the *sources* of standards, justifications, interpretations, reappear as *examples* of that which is best, most easily justified, most richly interpreted by those standards. Many academic and culturally centered discourses are not so much coherent, effectively delimited conversations as they are hegemonic, closed, and circular constructs. They are not prepared to deal with works and theories and meanings and visions that spring from and require their own quite different discourses.

As Kohlberg's original *description* of levels of moral development turned around and became a *prescription* for 'higher' levels of moral development, Janson's and Norton's original criteria for inclusion in texts turned around and became prescriptions for any future inclusion. That is, of course, circularity, although it is often defended as "maintaining standards." It is as if redheads first defined red hair as an essential quality of humanity, and then—lo and behold—'proved' that red hair is necessary to anyone claiming inclusion in the category 'human' by appealing to their own definition.

We must beware of taking inherited standards of what is good, significant, meaningful, to be more than they are. They work quite well when applied to the works from which they were derived or to others that are akin to them. They do not work at all well when applied to that which was excluded in the first place, in part because they were formulated to explain and justify some of those very exclusions, and/or carry within them the results of exclusions. One cannot define art, or morality, or heroism, or reason, in a way that excludes the art, morality, heroism, reason, of particular groups of people and then turn around and use that definition as the basis for standards that justify the exclusion. As any child might say, that isn't fair. Circular reasoning is a prime example of unfairness: "You said you were going to pick the best hitters for the team after try-outs, and I hit the ball farther than anyone." "Yes, but you're a girl." Untangle that, and you find the threads that twist together to create the circular reasoning that concerns us.

False Claims to Neutrality

In philosophy, the claim is often made that we are more concerned with ways of thinking than with subject matter. Many teachers tell students that philosophy has no subject matter: it takes all subject matters, and the very idea of subject matter, as part of its purview. But the particular modes of thought considered to be properly philo-sophical were selected within a particular tradition, one that had long since relegated the intellectual activities assigned to women and 'lower' men and 'exotic' cultures to some different category, as we have seen in Kant and Jefferson, and in my students' reactions to Yoruba philosophy (which they assumed was too 'primitive' to belong in a Philosophy course). The criteria for a "sound argument," or "good reasoning," which are used to judge not just students' work but all works that might have some claim to be included in Philosophy courses, are turned around to justify not just their own soundness, not only past inclusions and exclusions, but the neu-trality of prevailing definitions.

Michael Patton, a scholar who specializes in evaluation meth-odology, notes, "In effect, identifying objectivity as the major virtue of the dominant paradigm is an ideological statement the function of which is to legitimize, preserve, and protect the dominance of a single . . . methodology."[1] Objectivity and neutrality are not quite the same, but both, attributed to a paradigm, method, theory, or attitude, give it a privileged, superior status in the dominant culture. And it is not insignificant that "objective" and "subjective" are often used in ways that indicate a lack of parallelism similar to that between Man and Woman in hierarchical monism. For example, the charge, not infrequently leveled at works refused entrance into the dominant tradition's favored curricula, that something is "merely subjective" is not reversible: one rarely if ever hears that some work or theory is "merely objective." And while we do hear that some instances of women's studies scholarship are "too political," we rarely if ever hear that mainstream scholarship is "too apolitical." The category of subjective scholarship, like that of woman, has had little positive content of its own, has been little studied as worthy in its own right, and is used most often as an indication of *lack*. That which is "subjective" is that which lacks a central source, or quality, of 'good' scholarship—that is, "objectivity," which is usually conflated with neutrality.

Objectivity, neutrality, disinterestedness, are qualities 'good' scholarship is for the most part *supposed* to have. I am not here taking on the question of whether or not these are indeed important to 'sound' scholarship; I simply observe that one function of *claiming* those qualities for scholars and works that speak from, of, and for a falsely generalized (even universalized) few is to hide yet again the hegemonic partiality that is enshrined at the base and still holds the center of the dominant tradition. And one effect of that hiding is to lock us into circular reasoning. Like the referee, the umpire, the judge, the "blind review," that which is 'neutral,' 'objective,' is placed both outside and at the center of the knowledge-making and evaluating enterprise. It is outside insofar as we are not to question the meaning or merit of that which makes it 'objective' or the appropriateness of objectivity itself. It is at the center because, as established knowledge and/or virtuous quality, it continues to justify itself in a way that marginalizes whatever differs from it.

In the early days of feminist scholarship, it became evident that "blinded reviews" or, simply, reviewing by established scholars judging by established criteria, worked to continue the exclusion of scholarship of, by, and about women. *For the process of judgment to have the old exclusionary effect, it was not necessary for the judges to be purposefully or consciously exclusive.* All they needed to do was to apply in a 'neutral' fashion notions of 'soundness' derived from exclusionary scholarship. The fault, the failure, was then neatly attributable to that which was judged. There was no way of judging swans in a world of ducks; the young swan was quite clearly, if regrettably, an ugly duckling.

Closet Platonism

To move still further into the question of how circularity works even when we do not intend it, we can turn to one of Ludwig Wittgenstein's famous de-essentializing examples. He observed that the only meter in the world that is not a meter is the standard meter. The standard meter is not a meter because it cannot be judged to be or not to be one, being itself the source and only warrant of what it means to be a meter. When feminist scholars suggest that Man is not defined with reference to an Idea that *is* essentially human but has simply been established in a way that is not necessary as "the measure of all things," it throws the dominant system into terrible confusion. By what, then, are we to justify our measurements? What, if that which is already established is now to be seen as 'merely' conventional, is to tell us what is significant, what is good, what matters, even what is real in ways that can continue to coerce our assent? It is such loss of necessity for fundamental cultural constructs that has led so many faculty members and scholars to claim that those who question the generality, even universality, of established concepts, notions, theories, methods, are threatening to reduce everything to relativism. If the meter itself, if Man himself, is agreed to be the result of unnecessary choice of what/whom to measure by, and then feminists refuse to abide by the now seen as merely conventional choices, what is to keep *everyone* from choosing to measure as s/he pleases? Chaos threatens. But, of course, an insistence on maintaining the meter, or man-the-measure, in an unquestioned essentialist position does not save us from choices. It simply locks us into perpetuating uncritically the choices made by others in earlier and different times. That is the real consequence of clinging to a kind of essentialism, of holding that the meter—or a particular group of males from a particular cultural tradition—that has been the measure is a true and necessary idea that is genuinely not subject to any human choice other than to acknowledge or not acknowledge it.

Few academics are actually closet essentialists, or Platonists, but

many sound as if they were when one questions the founding definitions and assumptions and standards that, as Whitehead noted,
they simply start from and do not even realize they hold *as* assumptions and standards. Thus, they stay within the circle, circle within
the set defined for them by the creators of their fields, even while
priding themselves on being critical thinkers. And in the culture at
large, the problem of being stuck with old definitions and assumptions can be at least as stubborn because there we do indeed encounter essentialists who simply do not know what is to hold
anything together if what they take to be real and absolute is ques-
tionable. More than one 'moral crisis' in the United States has been
credited to the undoing of essentialist notions of the Good, the
True, the Beautiful (usually as they are understood in religious
rather than philosophical discourse).

Feminist scholarship that is not just additive, that does not simply find what women have done that is as close as possible to what
men have done, necessarily breaks the closed circles of admitted
and unadmitted essentialism, or of conservative conventionalism.
It makes available to thought and to revision what was unquestioned. In the field of history, for example, as Joan Kelly noted,
women's history has made "problematical three of the basic concerns of historical thought: (1) periodization, (2) the categories of
social analysis, and (3) theories of social change."[2] It is not just the
stages of a woman's life in America that, once studied by a feminist
historian, reveal as male-centered supposedly neutral notions
about what "growing up" means. Women's history, studied with
women, not men, at the center and as the standard, reveals the
male-centeredness of supposedly neutral historical periodization,
analytical categories, explanatory theories—of the basic conceptual
tools of the field.

The problem of circularity is evident also in the abstraction, for
example, of the idea of a "Renaissance" from study of the lives of a
particular group of men. The "Renaissance" is not treated as a male-
centered term: it is presented as gender-neutral. But women, as
Joan Kelly suggested, may not have had a Renaissance in Europe
during the same time or in the same ways as (some) men did. And, I
would add, *whether they did or not* is a question that cannot be
answered in any case until/unless what is understood by "the
Renaissance" has been reworked through careful, extensive gender
analysis. That is, since "the Renaissance" as a complex notion was
developed from the perspective of and in central relation to men, it

is almost unnecessary to say "women did not have a Renaissance" for the same reasons we have not needed to say, for example, that women did not belong to fraternities. While "fraternity" *meant* "males only," the exclusion of women was by definition; it did not need to be noted. While "the Renaissance" was conceptualized and understood in terms derived from and suitable to the perspectives of males, the exclusion of women also took place and was continued by definition.

As long as regnant concepts are unquestioned because of their supposed generality and neutrality, research shaped by them tends very strongly to continue their reign. Such research can 'prove' the adequacy of its own assumptions much as some of the 'proofs' of God's existence work—starting with a definition of God as omniscient and omnipotent, then proceeding to base proof of His existence on the observation that imperfect humans could not have an idea of such perfection if there were no God to give it to them.

These are not just trivial or curious instances of circular reasoning. They matter, and deeply so: when tools of analysis, methods, concepts, based on unquestioned assumptions are claimed to be neutral, we yield power to those who developed them—and power that is by no means 'only' over scholarship. If we care about truth, meaning, and justice, we can no longer afford to yield such power to an exclusive past and its major beneficiaries.

Circular Definitions of Fields

Some years ago, when Peggy McIntosh and I were engaged in a study of curriculum-transformation projects, we stumbled on one of those naive questions that prove, in fascinating, suggestive ways, to be difficult for people to answer. I asked a very well known Art Historian, "What is the subject of your field?" There was a pause, and then she said, "I'm not sure. That's a hard question. I've never asked myself that." I asked, "Is it art?" "Yes," she said, "and no, of course. There is also history." "What is the subject of History, then?" The conversation sputtered into silence. A little later, we asked some Historians the same question: what is the subject of History? "The past," one of them said quickly. Then there was an awkward pause. "Well, not really," another said. "I mean, what is 'the past?' " "We study records of and artifacts from the past," said someone else.

In neither conversation were any of us comfortable implying that the subject of a field has some kind of separate, essential existence 'out there.' That is, while Historians may say that History has to do with the past and Classicists may say that Classics has to do with the study of ancient Greece and Rome, in fact most if not all are thoroughly aware that their subject matter has been, as it were, prepared for them by those who preceded them, and that the originators and subsequent practitioners of the field themselves worked with human artifacts that already reflected in their construction, use, and preservation, particular views, values, assumptions. One can ask, "Where is the art in works of art?" and initiate a complex discussion. Is it in the work? How? Is it in the artist? In the viewer? In some interaction between artist, work, and viewer? In cultural notions of and provisions for art? Likewise, one can ask, "What is the past?" Is it in artifacts, records, and the rest? In interpretations of such remnants? Is it what we in the present make it to be, or is it in some way there in the world and/or in us in ways we can find rather than create?

Such questions are (to some of us, at least) fascinating in any context, but the point in raising them here is to observe that, for the most part, they are rarely discussed in either graduate or undergraduate courses. When most faculty members actually decide what they will teach under the label of "History," "Literature," "Philosophy," they do not do so with reference to a clearly held notion of what the subject matter of their field is. We have found that what is selected as important to teach in undergraduate courses tends in fact to be shaped primarily by what has been taught before. When one compares syllabi from around the country and from all kinds of academic institutions, it becomes readily apparent that in a real sense History, Classics, History of Art, and the rest *are* what teachers of those fields teach—as "intelligence" is functionally defined as "what intelligence tests test."

While philosophy teachers claim to be teaching a subject that is primarily about reasoning itself, they in fact 'cover' certain texts, and the problems they treat, with stunning consistency. Then, not only do the problems treated in their classes become "philosophical problems" but problems defining of philosophy, while the texts become not just "philosophical texts" but texts defining of philosophy. Even a philosophy text organized around modes of reasoning, rather than texts or problems, will almost certainly introduce, or be correlated to, a reading list of the same familiar texts, now introduced as *examples* of the various sorts of reasoning—despite the fact that the texts (or passages from them) were the *sources* of the modes of reasoning studied and so are not simply examples of them. That, of course, is circular.

If academic fields were held responsible to the extraordinarily complex and fascinating, continuing, and evolving question of what their subject matter has been and could be taken to be, surely we would see far more variation in what is taught than any national study of syllabi reveals. In those fields that have proved most open to feminist and multicultural scholarship, questions about the fields themselves are far more common and more seriously discussed than they are in those fields that have resisted. In the 'hard' sciences, for example, alternative notions of what constitutes "science" are almost inadmissible. Students learn what science is by learning what professional scientists today have agreed is 'good' and 'real' science. Science—and not just 'good' science but *real* science—is what professionally recognized and validated scientists do. Thus, scientists say with confidence, "I can see how studying Women in Science might have something to do with the history of science, but real science has nothing to do with such issues." And when it is suggested to them that perhaps science has been defined in an extremely narrow way, one that excludes all historical, political, financial, professional, and moral considerations in ways that may indeed be dangerous, they are often either flummoxed or outraged. They repeat, "Those are interesting considerations and they should be taught as History of Science, or Ethics of Science, but they aren't *science*." That, again, is circular reasoning. Science has been defined so as to exclude its many contexts and consequences. Reiterating a definition does not justify it; it merely invokes its authority to stop questions.

At this point I confess to having a tremor of genuine fear, and sometimes anger. I think of scientists working in germ warfare laboratories, on nuclear weapons, on chemical defoliants for military use, all the while saying, "I just do science. It is no business of mine what others do with it." Narrow definitions of realms of knowledge that define as out of order all considerations of context and consequences serve our human capacity to compartmentalize, to avoid thinking about what we are doing, all too well. I have the same problem with business people, and politicians, who say, for example, that ethics should be considered, of course, but that "the bottom line is the bottom line" and other such silly, self-protective, circular clichés. It does no more good to tack a separate course in ethics onto a business school curriculum, or a political science program, or law school requirements than it does to tack on a single course that 'covers' women. The questions that need to be raised are intrinsic, not extrinsic, to what we are teaching, learning, practicing. Adducing circular arguments to justify the continuing marginality of all that has been for too long excluded does nothing more than protect the continuing hegemony of the inner circle.

In fields such as Literature, where almost every—if not, indeed, every—central notion has recently been put in question, feminist scholarship has much more readily been included. If what is meant by "text" is open for discussion, then works that not long ago would have been excluded not just as different but as non-texts, can indeed be considered. If what is meant by "author" is a serious question, then definitions of "author" derived from and circling back to justify a list of preestablished, accepted writers can no longer function in the old exclusive fashion.[3] Yet in undergraduate courses even in these areas, definitions of fields are for the most part (if in varying degrees) functionally collapsed into past practices that, for all the reasons we have been exploring, continue to justify themselves. This is an error akin to that in a famous philosophical example. "All swans are white," said European and British scientists who had only seen white swans, and philosophers took that to be an example of a definition not grounded in empirical findings but stating the essence of "swan-ness." Then black swans were 'discovered' in Australia. What to do? If white is a quality of swan-ness, then the black swans could not be seen as swans at all. If white is not a quality of swan-ness, then what had appeared to be a definitional (even a tautologous) statement, and not just a generalization from a particular sample, had to be recast.

As Women's Studies has challenged the definitional limits of all fields, we have produced the same problem for those who took limited generalizations to be essences—and many have found it hard to say, "Then what we have been teaching is not history-itself, but certain men's constructions of 'history.'" Like the European and British philosophers (and scientists) who were so troubled by black swans that they were sorely tempted to decide that such odd birds could not be swans at all, some faculty members have preferred to say, or (by not teaching it) to act as if, "Women's music is not really music"—and girls cannot do arithmetic, and women are lousy drivers, and a Black man cannot represent us all.

My students, as I noted above, had a terrible time recognizing Yoruba thought as anything other than "primitive" and aphilosoph-

Just as childrens' voices are "irrational", "not fully formed", "easily swayed" (by coercion) ical. Given their notions of philosophy, these different sorts of thinking (and ways of sharing thinking—for example, orally, rather than in a particular kind of written text, or ritually, rather than in a particular form designated "rational") had to be not-philosophy. They had, through their formal and informal schooling, come to mistake a limited empirically based, or instrumental, or conventional, definition (philosophy is what philosophers teach, and have taught) for an essence (designated philosophy books and courses are about philosophy-itself). They were more open to Zen Buddhism and to Jaina logic, but there, too, they had a hard time considering these highly sophisticated intellectual systems as anything more than exotic. The nontraditional (in the dominant culture of the United States) works I had the students read remained alien, of interest not on their merits but because of their exoticism. I fear it may also be the case that they found both Japanese and Indian philosophy easier to take seriously than African philosophy out of an ignorance, and fear, of African civilization and culture so profound that it left them convinced that all of "darkest" Africa is and has always been too "primitive" for something as sophisticated and "enlightening" as they assume philosophy to be. Black philosophy cannot be philosophy, just as black swans cannot be swans.

Prejudice

We cannot afford to forget that we deal here not only with thought and knowledge, with conceptual matters, but also with preconscious cultural assumptions and habits that are fraught with emotion and reflect not only the ignorance but the systemically created and reinforced prejudices of the dominant culture. Prejudice—prejudgment—may even be defined as circular reasoning, and vice versa: both rest on judgments made before the fact that are not open to reconsideration in the light of any new or particular experience or evidence.

In addition to having little to no cross-cultural knowledge, my students had no knowledge of the ways in which not only knowledge but the prevailing notion of reason itself has been linked with the power hierarchy intertwining sex/gender, class, and race in the dominant Western tradition. Sadly, such ignorance is not at all rare or surprising. I note it here simply because it is so rarely noted, or even noticed. Students in our colleges and universities know so little about other cultures that they assume, as Frank Newman has said, that "to be Bulgarian is to suffer from a moral flaw."[4] They are

& Age children

so trapped in circular justifications of hierarchical monism that they continue to believe, as the shapers of the dominant tradition did, that it is a moral flaw to be other-than the defining few—to be female, to be African, to be poor. That that belief can be and far too often has been internalized by those it robs of independent identity as of full human worth makes it all the more tragic. (Here, the works of those who have analyzed the effects of colonialism on the psyches, spirits, minds, and hearts as well as the political and economic systems of the colonized—for example, Fanon, Memmi, Cabral— are telling and helpful.)

Again, circular reasoning is another name for prejudice—for judgment-before-the-fact. Before they enter our classes, our students have strong inclinations to believe what far too many teachers then, however unintentionally, confirm for them: those who have been excluded from the curriculum ought to have been excluded.

We need, therefore, to move beyond operational definitions of fields that restrict them to what has been taught before in the construction in which it has been taught. And that applies to all fields. As the authors of *The Humanities and the American Promise* write, "When Congress established the National Endowment for the Humanities in 1965, it identified the humanities by a listing of scholarly disciplines." After quoting the list, they say, "We think it is misleading to regard the humanities basically as a set of academic disciplines or, even more restricting, as a set of 'great books.' We identify them, rather, with certain ways of thinking—of inquiring, evaluating, judging, finding and articulating meaning."[5] Having turned from humanities-are-what-humanists-have-taught descriptions that lock us into self-justifying circles to consideration of abilities available for cultivation by *all* humans, they are free to continue:

> A citizenry that is humanistically aware is a citizenry that is capable of confronting diversity, ambiguity, and conflict, overcoming prejudice and self-interest, enlarging its sympathies, tackling tough public issues, and envisioning possibilities beyond the limits of circumstance.[6]

From Classroom to Country

If the people of the United States had continued to abide by early ideas of who is and ought to be a citizen, all those who did not own property, Black women and men, Native Americans, Asian-

Americans, white women, and those who could not pass inappropriate "literacy" tests would still not be enfranchised. If citizens and those refused full citizenship had always accepted prevailing laws as fully expressive, even defining, of justice-itself, instead of calling on ideals of justice *not* derived from old exclusionary laws, women would not be allowed to vote (or even to wear trousers), "miscegenation" would be illegal, legally enforced segregation would still stigmatize our country.

In considerations of knowledge as in considerations of justice, there are ideas and principles that transcend, rather than simply repeat, any particular examples—ideas such as humanity, equality, inclusiveness, truth, and meaning. We need not, of course, locate such transcendent ideals and principles in some essential, unchanging realm in order to claim them. We can simply hold, once again, that humans are capable of thinking ideas that they cannot know. We know perfectly well that we have a dream of justice and of truth that is not limited to knowledge of particular sets of laws or systems of knowledge. It is the restlessness of mind and spirit kept alive and productive by the abilities we have to be imaginative, to think reflexively, to critique and re-form what we know, to learn to think in the place of others and to empathize with them, that makes democracy a real if not actualized possibility.

MYSTIFIED CONCEPTS

Learning to recognize faulty generalizations and circular reasoning can help to undo the old tangle of errors, but it is also important to locate and consider at least some of the more influential concepts that inform our thinking. This section involves, in one sense, an extension of the kind of critique we have been exploring; in another sense, it involves a different kind, one focused less on processes of thought and their effects and more on products, as it were. Here we take on more directly some specific conceptual tangles of inherited thought and meaning.

The meaning of *any* concept is, of course, extremely difficult to state unambiguously, let alone definitively, as is the meaning of "concept" itself—not to mention the meaning of "meaning." I have no intention of attempting here to develop (or even consistently to borrow) a single philosophic stance in regard to these old and haunting issues. What I do wish to do is to explore some of the particular concepts that have emerged as of particular significance during my years of work with faculty members on making the curriculum more inclusive, and with community groups trying to understand what Women's Studies offers them. It seems important to note that some concepts have, or reveal, particular power within the dominant tradition and hence need to be considered carefully. Somewhat hesitantly, because of their opacity, ambiguity, *and* power, I have called these concepts "mystified concepts." I am not using the term "mystified" in quite the same sense as Marcuse, for example, but I do wish to imply, with him, that that which is mystified is so not only out of some harmless conceptual confusion or sloppiness but, rather, persists *as* mystified because its opacity keeps us from seeing clearly how it reflects and serves powerful systemic interests. That is, mystified concepts are also mystifying— they *do* something to us.

It is not the effort to uncover or establish some 'truer' meaning for the concepts that interests me. It is the way they function within the Academy and dominant culture to lock us into old forms of thought, old hierarchies, old errors, while appearing neutral and, as it were, above the fray.

In this section, then, we will explore *excellence, judgment, equality, rationality/intelligence, liberal arts, woman, sex, man, war,* and *gender* (and with them, a number of related concepts). I hope to ameliorate somewhat the frustration of a necessarily at best tantalizing discussion by suggesting some of the richness of available thinking and resources. What is important to me is to make the very familiar begin to seem strange and worthy of a great deal more serious thought and conversation and reading, and to inspire searches for further source materials. The words, the concepts, we are about to consider tend to be mind-numbing either because they are worn smoothly into platitudes (as in pious invocations of "excellence") *or* because they are fraught with emotion and/or taboo and confusion (sex, war). I want us to *think* about them for precisely those reasons; platitudes and taboos are two sides of the same coin.

Excellence

A prime example of a misused, mystifying concept is that of *excellence.* It is, in particular, invoked with great frequency and solemnity in discussions of the mission of higher education, particularly as such discussions are provoked by consideration of possible changes in how that mission is to be understood and carried out. But it is very rare indeed that those who invoke excellence as a goal also say what they mean by it. Allan Bloom, an academic believer in the necessary conflation of excellence with élitism, has called efforts to make the curriculum more equitable and responsive to the needs and interests of more students "an unprecedented assault on reason."[1] For him and many others, the serious questions about and changes in the dominant form of education we have been considering constitute evidence of rampant irrationality, irresponsibility, and moral turpitude—expressions of a severe lack of respect for excellence in the Academy. But, of course, it is not the proponents of Women's Studies and/or multicultural education who have burned books and phonograph records in the contemporary and, historically considered, rather mild protests against established education we have seen in recent years. It is, rather, those who believe that public education in the United States, which is founded on the principle of separation of church and state, has been taken over by what they call "secular humanism." It is suggestive, at least, that these people, who want their children 'protected' from all but one set of religious beliefs and values, began their protests only when some few textbooks were somewhat transformed to include the lives, works, and perspectives of the majority of humankind. The old versions of 'good' education apparently posed no threat to their sectarian values, to their views that women should be subservient to men and the races should not mix.

Those in higher education who call on us to *return* to excellence are rarely so crude in revealing their prejudices, but then they need not be. The prejudices are so deeply interwoven within the dominant tradition that they need no longer be stated directly, as we have seen in exploring the root problem and its consequent errors.

☰ As it is called upon in the Academy, excellence can almost be said to take its meaning from the sentiment of loyalty: if someone feels it necessary to invoke excellence in a discussion, it is usually the case that the speaker intends to remind others of their commitment to the calling of higher education, to the reasons it not only exists but ought to exist. Excellence is a call to solidarity in loyalty to the best we all want for, in, and through higher education. But, of course, that solidarity in loyalty—which is strongly recommended if one wishes to retain credibility within the Academy—is entirely vague in its content. Or so it seems. In fact, it can be suggested that because there are so many possible meanings for excellence, a loyal adherence to it as a goal for higher education necessarily means, in practice, a loyal adherence to the measures as well as exemplars of excellence with which we were all trained to be most familiar. And that throws us right back to the root problem and its consequences, generalizing too far from too few and then abstracting apparently neutral standards for inclusion, significance, and quality from those few in circular fashion. That which has already been judged to be excellent within the dominant tradition is taken to express—to embody, as it were—the standards for anything else that might claim such high status.

The use of excellence as a term or concept around which we should all gather reverently maintains the conflation of its meaning with exclusivity. Calls for a new inclusiveness on any grounds, particularly when they are couched in terms of equity, are heard as threatening to excellence-itself, although, of course, such calls are in no way aimed at attacking excellence, any more than new laws, rules, and regulations necessarily threaten the overarching notion of justice that particular laws and codes are meant to serve. What is put in question by proposals to make the curriculum more inclusive is, quite simply, exclusivity. What is revealed by claims that these efforts are an attack on excellence is the lack of any idea of excellence that does *not* conflate it with exclusivity.

While it may well be the case that all judgments of excellence necessitate some exclusions—since if everything were excellent, nothing would be—the two terms ought no longer to be confused with each other. Exclusivity may be a necessary result where excellence has some real meaning, but the exclusivity of excellence is a by-product, not a goal. The best teachers try very hard to help all students do their best work and know perfectly well that the persistence of less-than-excellent work is a challenge to better teaching rather than something to be celebrated. Their goal is excellence, not exclusion.

Some country clubs and private men's clubs are exclusive, but that by no means makes them excellent. It simply means they refuse membership to some categories of people, and although doing so may make members feel special, it doesn't make them better. If we wish to make institutions as central to democracy as education, and government itself, less like the old white male clubs, we have to be very careful about the exclusions that take place as by-products of choices made, requirements established, practices followed. One sure test for the confusion of excellence with exclusivity is in consequences. A set of tests established to sort out who is and who is not prepared to work on the 'higher' levels at which excellence is approached that is consistently failed by more women than men, more Black people than white, reveals itself to be a protection of the old exclusivities, not a neutral, and certainly not a disinterested, test of abilities. A set of examples of excellent works that includes none from those long excluded (like most lists of the "Great Books") is, on the face of it, simply an exercise in the old circular reasoning that perpetuates the dominance of those who defined the terms of excellence to fit their own works in the first place.

It can, in fact, be held that equity, as a commitment to unbiased and appropriate consideration of significance and merit, is itself a prerequisite for adequate judgments of excellence. Without such a commitment, how are we to know enough, have considered enough, to trust that the standards by which we judge are adequate for any but a particular group or kind? Consider a dog show. The pinnacle of achievement for any entrant is to win the "best in show" ribbon. How would the dogs' owners feel if the judge for that final contest were an expert on terriers and spaniels only—and, regularly choosing a terrier or a spaniel as best in show, justified the choice as a neutral judgment of excellence of kind for all dogs? Could the owner of an Arabian horse expect an adequate judgment of her glorious animal in a show that had been running for fifty years but had never before included Arabians? Can a connoisseur of vintage French wines be expected to be able to judge beer (or, perhaps, even California wines—let alone retsina)?

But I have many times heard faculty members who are ignorant of African or African-American philosophy, of contemporary women's novels, of folk music—of *any* work other than that which is similar to that they themselves were taught in graduate school— say, "But surely we should not teach work that is less than the best? Surely we should not lower our standards just to be inclusive." We are not asking them to 'lower' their standards when we suggest that an exclusive tradition needs, at the very least, augmenting. We are asking them not to apply particular standards as if they were universal, and to take the time to learn something about new materials before they rush to judge them by old, inappropriate standards.

Defenses of past or present curricula that are characterized as struggles to "maintain excellence" can, I believe, be traced not to the need to judge what is important and outstanding, but to flight from the uncertainties that are necessarily present in any act of judgment, and particularly so when horizons are expanding, old forms are being refigured. To become able to make reasonable judgments of excellence, whether excellence of kind or excellence in a moral sense (two concepts that also, and dangerously, tend to be conflated), we require a broad and deep acquaintance with more than any single group, any one tradition, however abstracted and universalized, can offer. If we are to make any sense of excellence that is useful as more than a call for loyalty to the past, we need, then, to consider the nature of judgment.

Judgment

We may begin by considering something like the legal sense of *judgment*, in which to judge something is to bring it, in all its particularity, before a set of principles or standards or laws in such a way that both the particularity of that which is to be judged and the generality of the principle/law/standard are honored. That even that apparently straightforward and familiar act, the application of principle to particular, cannot be certain, cannot be the result of straightforward deductive reasoning of the sort so highly prized, and privileged, by the dominant culture is attested to by the institution of judges. If we believed that rules could be applied to individuals and individual cases *directly*, we would have no judges but simply law books. We have judges because we know that no law book imaginable could include before the fact everything that could possibly be done by anyone under any circumstances, and certainly could not tell us what we need to know to judge each individual's actions fairly in every possible case. Laws, like principles, are general; they not only do not, they cannot, contain within themselves the requisite specificity to allow a direct match between themselves and all possible particular, real, concrete people, acts, and situations. We have history to remind us that efforts to apply the law as if it were adequate unto itself for all instances of human action and behavior result in terrible cruelties—as well as absurdities. We recognize that it is not the same, and should not be treated as if it were, when a two-year-old takes a cookie from another child as when an adult steals a car.

In a different realm, we know perfectly well that we require something more than a trained mind in a judge of art. We speak of people with a "good eye," a fine "feeling" for art. We need someone who knows a great deal about art in general *and* has skill in seeing and understanding particular unique works of art. The pedant who knows only prevalent theories about art, who is familiar with all the established 'great' art of the Western tradition, is by no means necessarily a good judge of contemporary art, or of art inspired by a different tradition. Faced with genuinely original works, such people may well be rendered helpless simply because the works to be judged are, precisely, unfamiliar. Stories of such failures of judgment are familiar to art historians: Rembrandt is by no means alone in having had his art greeted initially with judgments that "*that* is not art," a classic expression of circular reasoning.

A story I heard once but have never tracked down makes this point in a different and intriguing way. As it was told to me, it featured Peggy Guggenheim. When the furor surrounding the Impressionists had finally died down and the works of some had come to be greatly admired, it turned out that Peggy Guggenheim had in her collection examples of precisely those artists who were now seen as 'the best.' Since the Impressionists had purposefully broken most of the standing 'rules' for 'good art,' even those who had liked their artworks had been unable to judge among them. Guggenheim was asked how on earth she had been able to exercise such good judgment when all prevailing norms and expectations had been violated. She replied, "I simply bought the works that most infuriated me."

The connoisseur has long been a fascinating figure in the world of art precisely because what s/he is able to do is so mysterious; it cannot be written down as so many laws, ready for application. To judge a work that not only does not fit within prevailing definitions but openly flouts them requires something special in the judge; so, too, does judging works that have never before been taken seriously, that have even sometimes been used as counter-examples to Art. Secure, accepted mastery of what experts in a field know can be a hindrance in such cases. This is not to say, of course, that ignorance is preferable to extensive knowledge of that which is to be judged. It is simply to recognize that judgment, particularly as it shades into something as elusive as taste (as Kant, in *The Critique of Judgment*, effectively claims that it does), is not the direct result of knowledge. A good judge, critic, connoisseur, is someone we cannot ever quite explain or characterize. We find ourselves saying things like, "She has exquisite taste," "He is a good judge because he has compassion," "She is remarkably perceptive about what the artist is trying to do." With such statements we recognize that the kind of mental and emotional engagement involved in judging what is good, important, significant, needs to be more like thinking than knowing, more like taste than like deductive reasoning.

Someone with good judgment is able to take into account *both* that which s/he has learned, that which is known, *and* that which appears before her/him, *both* what s/he thinks *and* what s/he feels. That same ability to cross realms, as it were, to move from the conceptual to that which appears, to connect the established with the innovative, to see in an individual case what is general and in what is general what illuminates the individual case, is required in good judges of any sort, from those in law courts to teachers grading classroom work. However, the dominance of the deductive model tends to push us away from a focus on the individual (person/work/situation) toward a focus on standards, standardized measures, rules, principles. In courts, however much we recognize that there is no certainty available for judges, however much we value compassion as a judicial virtue, the prevailing system works hard to keep judges, and even more so juries, from knowing anything more than what qualifies by highly rationalistic, predominantly white, non–working-class male standards as 'pertinent,' 'relevant.' And feelings are considered entirely out of order unless they can be established as belonging to some preexistent legal category such as motivation. It is therefore time to drop the legal model, as well as the deductive one. Both are, if pressed very far, ultimately subversive of our efforts to hear those whose voices continue to be excluded through the use of faultily abstracted, circular assumptions, definitions, standards, rules.[2]

We know there is no *necessary* connection between our standards for student work and the grade we choose to give in a particular case. If asked to do so, we can explain our judgment, but we cannot *prove* that it is correct any more than a connoisseur can *prove* the accuracy of her/his taste. As Kant observed in *The Critique of Judgment*, both taste and judgment can be developed but not taught, demonstrated but not proved (he makes the same point in the First Critique, A133B172). And, I would add, that does not make taste and judgment any less valuable than deductive reasoning. Uncertainty, which is the necessary result of openness to what is unique, individual, particular, new, and/or different, is, on the contrary, a virtue reflecting an open and enlarged mind and a capacity for empathy. The opposite of such uncertainty is not knowledge as we would have it be, but dogma and pedantry, which John Dewey describes in *Quest for Certainty* as all too characteristic of the dominant tradition specifically insofar as it carries antidemocratic tendencies from the past within it.

It is understandable that many flee the uncertainty of the act of judgment by trying to standardize that which is to be judged before it is necessary to judge it—for example, by giving tests requiring only information about which individuals are not supposed to differ at all. However much we say we value good judgment and good taste, their lack of certainty continues to make many people nervous. The discomfort of faculty members asked to take seriously works from cultures with which they are not familiar, or works by women that do not look or 'feel' the same as the male works that constitute the canon, similarly leads many to desire to go on teaching what they are more confident in judging, because they feel the support of tradition in taking established standards to be applicable to everything. Those who remain within the realm of the familiar, like those who lean strongly toward standardization, are, among other things, trying to avoid the risks of judgment. If we do not see new kinds of works, hear new voices, we can continue to appear to judge reasonably well simply by referring to "the judgment of the ages." However, by assimilating our tastes to those already enshrined as authoritative, in fact we avoid developing our own—and those of our students.

The arts of judgment and taste remain mystified in the dominant tradition as long as the principles by which we judge particulars carry in them recurrent conceptual errors, and we cannot get to work undoing those errors as long as we remain bemused by "the quest for certainty," a sense that knowledge is or should be a source of control. It is worth remembering that the idea that knowledge gives us not just familiarity with what is known but power over it is not a necessary idea at all. It was almost certainly alien to Socrates, for example, who was willing to accept the label of "wisest man in Athens" as long as everyone understood that his wisdom lay in knowing that he did not know. His struggle with the Sophists, at least as Plato depicts it for us, can be understood in part as a conflict between one who thought of teaching as an effort to remove hardened certainties from the minds of all who would converse with him, and those who sought to teach people how to win arguments and so gain power. The violent way that Thrasymachus enters the opening discussion in Plato's *Republic* is intended, I believe, to dramatize the differences between Socrates' efforts to find grounds for genuine harmony among different people, and a brash younger man's desire to establish his own dominance. With Socrates' death, Thrasymachus, we might say, triumphed.

It has been said before that the modern age of scientific knowledge was born with Bacon, who depicts Nature as a subject to be tortured until she reveals her secrets so that men may have, not merely certainty, but control. Today, "knowledge is power"—understood as most people understand it—surely indicates that the combative, power-hungry spirit of the Sophists and Bacon's dream of mastery of all Nature are still with us.

That many of us fear to be judged even more than we fear judging is, then, perfectly sensible: we fear being mis-taken, being marked as inferior rather than, simply, different, and we understand that someone is trying to control us by submitting us to such (faulty, but very powerful) judgments. It is a fear born of experience. As the authors of *The Humanities and the American Promise* suggest, too few have realized that "a large dose of humility is the first requisite for the humanist contemplating material for which old terms and standards do not necessarily suffice."[3] I am in complete agreement, and all the more so when I consider that the tradition has judged not just academic material but people, even whole peoples, by principles enshrining old errors and the old lust for dominance and so done terrible harm.

But when I have suggested, in workshops with faculty members, that it is absurd to judge works such as quilts made by women in the home by prevailing standards for 'art,' standards that were developed by those who considered creations such as quilts by definition non-art, I have been asked yet again, "But then how are we to judge at all? If we cannot apply the standards we have, must we throw out all standards?" The response seems to me to be twofold. First: if there really are no people who have the requisite level of general knowledge and particular experience to judge a newly considered category of works, then of course we cannot go ahead and judge anyway. That would be absurd: we ought not to judge on the basis of inadequate understanding. Instead, we should be willing to dwell with the new kind of works long enough, attentively enough, with enough commitment and care, to let those works develop in us the ability to respond to them well and truly. In doing so, we honor the advice of many writers and artists through the ages. T. S. Eliot wrote that his poems had to teach people how to read them, and

Susan Van Dyne, working with faculty members on how to teach women's poetry, has suggested that "the poem in refusing to answer old questions can teach us what new questions to ask!"[4]

Remembering such advice also helps us realize that we are rarely in such a state of complete ignorance even about what seem to denizens of the traditional Academy to be new categories of work. There may be no, or few, art critics trained and practicing in the Academy who know enough about quilts to be able to judge them, but many quilters can do so. Academic training is not the only kind of training, nor are academic standards the only standards in the world. The problem of including new kinds of works in the curriculum is not, then, that there is no way to judge their quality, their significance, their meaning. It is, at least in part, that those who are qualified to judge may not be academics at all. And that is hard for many academics to swallow. It needs to be recognized: efforts to make the curriculum more inclusive are indeed part of the effort to make our whole society more equitable and hence, among other things, better suited to helping us all become able to choose what to value, whom to admire, whom to elect, even what to enjoy. There are experts of all sorts 'out there' from whom those in the Academy can learn a great deal, some of which is even directly relevant to the specific tasks assigned to the Academy.

⎓ If we would honor excellence, and not merely exclusivity, if we would learn to make sensitive, appropriate judgments and not merely apply preexistent rules, we cannot remain within the closed circle. Judgments and the ways we make them need to be reflexively considered within a context of commitment to respectful openness and caring. The tradition offers some very helpful guidance in this quest; as is obvious, I have drawn heavily on Kant here, along with, in the background, John Dewey, Hannah Arendt, and Michael Polanyi (admired but still somewhat suspect figures who are only occasionally taught).[5] But the tradition needs correcting, sometimes, and tempering, with remembrance of the basic errors and the ways they are insinuated throughout the works even of such superb thinkers.

As Ruel Tyson has pointed out, even when we follow the contemporary move to consider the logic of narrative rather than deduction in order to move closer to genuine respect for individuals and particulars—to balance, as it were, the culture's traditional overweighting of the abstracted, generalized rule or principle—

some stories come to be paradigmatic, canonical, exemplary. Societies that did their teaching primarily through stories and examples were not in most cases less exclusive than our own supposedly
more rational and abstract system has been. *There is no preexisting,
consistent, and consistently helpful alternative to the dominant tradition
that we wish to open, enrich, and correct where necessary; we are going to
have to create it,* not, I believe, as a utopian vision, as a program, as
an ideology, as some final goal, but as an on-going process of active
engagement in thinking together. Fortunately, we can indeed do
that kind of thinking. Our relationship with the past is always ours
to negotiate. As Arendt wrote:

> This thinking, fed by the present, [may work] with the "thought
> fragments" it can wrest from the past and gather about itself. Like a
> pearl diver who descends to the bottom of the sea, not to excavate the
> bottom and bring it to light but to pry loose the rich and the strange,
> the pearls and the coral in the depths, and to carry them to the
> surface, this thinking delves into the depths of the past—but not to
> resuscitate it the way it was and to contribute to the renewal of extinct
> ages. What guides this thinking is the conviction that although the
> living is subject to the ruin of time, the process of decay is at the same
> time a process of crystallization, that in the depth of the sea, into
> which sinks and dissolves what once was alive, some things "suffer a
> sea change" . . . as though they waited only for the pearl diver.[6]

Equality

Here we need to consider the curiously distorted notion of *equality*
that prevails in the dominant culture and works its way through our
efforts to think well about "excellence and equity" in the curriculum, as about the achievement of equality in the political, social,
and economic realms. I have come to believe that without a transformed understanding of equality, and commitment to actualizing
it, neither excellence nor judgment can be well comprehended.

Equality, one of the basic political principles and promises of
the United States, has in fact long been confused with sameness.
Women of all sorts, Black men, and others excluded from the American promise have always had first to struggle to prove that we are
'as good as'—that is, the same as—those who excluded us in order
to gain any hearing or achieve any recognition from the dominant
few (and sometimes even from ourselves). That political as well as
intellectual fact is one of the most glaring instances we have of the

basic conceptual error of taking the few to be the inclusive term, the norm, and the ideal for all. It is that error that forces the absurd apparent ("apparent" because it is not really open to us anyhow) choice between being the same as those who have excluded us or being different from them—in a tradition in which difference is recognized primarily as deviance or deficiency.

We do not want to be the same *or* different: those are crude and confusing categories, but, more important in this context, they are not the same kind of thing as equality. The notion of equality exists precisely because humans are always *personally* both similar to and different from each other in infinitely complex ways and yet, at times, wish to speak and act together *politically*, intellectually, professionally, on protected common ground. Equality is established to give us such common ground, not to force us into sameness. As a matter of fact, if we never acted together as equals, we would know far less about our differences.

We establish provisions and protections for equality precisely so we do not have to be the same before we can act and speak together, precisely so that whatever differences we have do not always and necessarily divide us. Equality is specific: it is established externally and on purpose, so that we may say, for example, "Before the law, all citizens are equal." Obviously that does not mean that all citizens are the same. That is so clearly untrue as to be absurd. What it does mean is that all that marks us as the same or different can be held irrelevant for some purpose, with regard to some provision or standard or act or protection or intellectual inquiry. Very different works and voices can be given equal respect and attention in a class; they need not all be the same or even similar.

In a real sense, what equality is supposed to do is to challenge us to make distinctions that are relevant and appropriate to a particular situation or set of considerations or principles. What it means, what kind of distinctions it allows and disallows, differs according to the kind of situation in which we attempt to establish it. When we say, "We are all equal before death," we say that death is such an imposing human reality that it can force us to disregard all other distinctions among us. When we say, "We want equal rights in the marketplace," we mean that we wish only appropriate discriminations—such as, for example, those between people clearly possessing or not possessing essential skills for particular jobs—to be made. "Equal rights" does not, as a goal, ask us to disregard all distinctions—quite the contrary. To establish equality, and to protect it, we need to locate very carefully which distinctions must be recognized in order to be neutralized, which can be ruled entirely out of order, which may need (if only temporarily) to be privileged to allow all to start on an even footing. Equal rights is an enormously complex and changing goal; we simply frustrate and mislead ourselves when we assume that it has to do with absolutes, with absolute sameness, with blindness to all distinctions. Only in a world that had never known institutionalized discrimination, only in one utterly without the errors fundamental to ours, could blindness to all distinctions do anything other than preserve the centrality of those who have enshrined themselves as the only real and worthy kind of human.[7]

To say, "Women should receive an education equal to that received by men," is therefore not necessarily to say that women should receive either the same education as men or a different one. It is to raise the question that has vexed the history of education in this country from the beginning—the question of which distinctions are and which are not relevant to education. It is not an equal education for women when we study a curriculum that excludes or devalues us, although such a curriculum is the same as that studied by men. Black people, entering white institutions previously closed to them, may have achieved access to the same education as that given white people, but that did and does not make it an equal education. Nor were we receiving an equal education when our curricula were different from those of white male institutions. Then we were taught what some educators (men and women, Black and white) thought we should know in order to fulfill roles prescribed for us by a society premised on our continuing inequality, *or* what they thought we needed to know in order to become the same as those who were devaluing and excluding us. In neither case was the education designed for us.

As Jane Roland Martin has pointed out, the philosophy of education, like all fields, has excluded and devalued women's roles in education such that education-itself is defined solely in male terms. Either we see Rousseau's Sophie educated in coquetry and guile in order to please (and manipulate) men, or we do not see her at all. Should we then *add* what Rousseau and his peers prescribed for girls and women to what has existed for Emile? No. As we have seen, what is required is a profound rethinking. Martin writes:

> When the educational realm embodies only male norms, it is inevitable that any women participating in it will be forced into a masculine

mold. The question of whether such a mold is desirable for females needs to be asked, but it cannot be asked so long as philosophers of education assume that gender is a difference which makes no difference. The question of whether the mold is desirable for males also needs to be asked; yet when our educational concepts and ideals are defined in male terms, we do not think to inquire into their validity for males themselves.[8]

We are still working on the question of what equal education for all requires; clearing the ground for rethinking answers to that question is one of the primary purposes of this book. What we do know is that, whatever it means, an equal education for all women of all groups, as for the men of unprivileged groups, cannot be the same as the education that has been developed in a culture that is based on our exclusion. Only as we particularize what has been falsely universalized will we begin to be able to make adequate judgments about what is and what is not appropriate to all of us in any given situation. This basic conceptual work is essential to understanding what equality means, and accompanies efforts to figure out how to pursue it properly in all of the different realms of our life in which we take it to be a value.

Taking excellence to mean exclusivity and equality to mean sameness are related errors and both serve to fend off the need to exercise caring, appropriate judgment. Their persistence indicates that they work well within—and so help not just to hide but to mystify—a system of meaning that takes the few to be the whole, the norm, and the ideal so that the rest of humankind cannot be adequately comprehended in its own right. It is helpful to remember that, as Arendt liked to say, our commonality as natal creatures is that we are each unique, and capable of new beginnings.

Rationality, Intelligence—and Good Papers

In a philosophy class, I once suggested to my students that they find whatever way they wanted to show me they had understood the text on which we were working (Plato's *Republic*). I told them they could write a paper of the kind with which they were already familiar or, alternatively, draw a diagram showing how the central concepts in Plato's philosophy relate to each other; write a short story about someone coming to Plato's Republic and trying to fit in; give me a list of what seemed clear to them and what did not; come and talk with me about the text and tell me what they understood;

prepare a short play presenting the important ideas in *The Republic;* or discuss with me other ways they would like to work. I received diagrams, letters to friends about the book, 'regular' papers, journal-type entries, lists of thoughts and questions, and had several conversations with students who were more comfortable talking. When I had discussed each student's presentation with her, we talked in class about translating the different modes of expression into the conceptual form and language of the usual academic paper. I asked them all, then, to write such a paper, drawing on their own more comfortable ways of thinking about the subject to help them through it.

The papers were significantly better than any I had received before. I believe that, had I shown some of my colleagues a set of those same students' earlier papers and those written after the experiment, with names removed, they would have judged the second set of papers to be the product of "more intelligent" students. My experiment was designed to help me, and the students, see how they really tended to understand first, and then to help them work in the one way for which they were most likely to be rewarded in higher education. I believe one reason they did better on their second papers was that they felt more confident simply because I had recognized that the academic paper form is only one of many ways of achieving, expressing, and communicating fully 'rational' understanding.[9]

⎯ *Rationality* itself is a mystified concept in the dominant tradition (as was suggested earlier by Kant's and Jefferson's judgments of the 'irrationality' of those whose mode of understanding differed from the one these men recognized and valued). It has so many meanings that even, or perhaps particularly, among philosophers, it is difficult to pin down, yet it has an enormous prescriptive force in higher education and in the society formal education serves. Students are supposed to be learning to be "more rational" through education, and that is understood to mean that they are becoming better citizens, even better people. To be labeled "irrational" is to be discredited. But, of course, there are, as the experience I had in my course indicates, many modes of thought and expression that are not irrational but simply different from the primary modes of expression of rationality enshrined at the center of the dominant tradition. These modes tend to go unrecognized or be devalued in higher education because they do not match the presently privileged notion of rationality.

In the dominant culture of the West, a narrow view of what is rational has created educational systems that can make many of us feel inadequate and inept because our ways of thinking, of making sense, are not met, recognized, given external form, clarified, and returned to us refined and strengthened. Instead, too many people are made to feel 'stupid.' Their minds or their own most comfortable mode of expression tend to work differently from those particular constructs, academic 'intelligence' and 'good' papers. I have worked a great deal with older students returning to higher education, and time and again I have heard painful stories of early experiences of that sort from people who, when they got up the courage to return, have gone on to prove to themselves and their teachers that they are capable of good to excellent work. And many times, after I have given a philosophical paper, women (students, faculty members, members of the community) have come up to me to say, "I always *thought* I would like philosophy, but when I tried to study it as an undergraduate, I felt like a real failure." When we discuss what happened in those unfortunate classes, what I hear is that the professor intimidated students, argued with them, seemed to delight in "putting us down," and that the students who did well were those who flourished in what these women felt to be a very unpleasant, combative arena in which only one mode of discourse was acceptable. I always think of these people when I notice yet again how often academics (I include myself) speak of good papers as "presenting a good argument" (which is often characterized as an "impregnable" position, a revealing phrase if ever I heard one).

I have worked with many undergraduate and graduate students, and I have consistently found that they do better with 'straight' academic writing when they are encouraged to prepare for it by locating and building on the ways of understanding and communicating which are most comfortably their own. We do them a serious disservice when we refuse to recognize as rational their own approaches to understanding work, and when we label "irrational" all that has to do, in particular, with the emotions and/or with experience reported as such.

Especially in the so-called hard sciences, which are at the pinnacle of respect in the Academy, the more distanced the knower is— claims to be—from the known, the more 'pure' the knowledge produced is supposed to be. This is not the place for another critique of the currently dominant mode of science, but it is important to recognize that the rest of the liberal arts, and the culture in general, are by no means free of the tradition that led not only to the development of modern science but to its near apotheosis as the exemplar of human rationality. In every field there are strains of thought that indicate a craving for the apparent certainty, the 'toughmindedness,' of the sciences (which is contrasted with the 'soft' humanities, attributions on which I am sure I do not need to comment).

Perhaps eventually the work of people such as Michael Polanyi, Michel Foucault, Jacques Derrida, and Jacques Lacan, and all the developing schools of thought loosely gathered under the headings "Critical Theory," "Poststructuralism," "Deconstructionism," "Discourse Analysis," and/or "Postmodernism," that are reshaping our notions of reason as of reality (of reason in relation to reality) will have the effect of changing the forms of expression of reason that are privileged in the Academy today. But they are not adequate challenges to the dominant tradition in and of themselves except, perhaps, as they emerge through the works of feminists such as Gayatri Spivak, Toril Moi, Monique Wittig, Nancy Miller, Alice Jardine, Chandra Mohanty, and others who, joining the critique of a masculinized, colonial Logos, have enriched the critique of "phallocentric reason" by exploring what it might mean for women to speak *as women* (an effort in which they are by no means alone, of course—I mention them here not only because they are admirable but because they are trying to work with the new schools of thought that are having a remarkable effect on academic thought).

The feminist critique has other sources of support and inspiration as well. For example, in his introduction to *Philosophy Born of Struggle: Anthology of Afro-American Philosophy from 1917*, Leonard Harris reminds us that "philosophic texts, if products of social groups doggedly fighting to survive, are texts born of struggle. They must cut through the jungle of oppressive deeds to the accompanying labyrinth of words masking the nature of the deeds. Fraught with controversial intuitions that reflect the coming accepted beliefs of the new world, such texts challenge prevailing ways of viewing the world."[10] Those "controversial intuitions" are the product of active intelligence honed through 'book learning,' community conversations, and conflict, and they are invaluable in helping to demystify prevailing notions of rationality as well as other hegemonic definitions. The "intuitive," like the "irrational," has been defined in contradistinction to narrowly constructed notions of "the rational," but it need not be. Once freed from that particular old discourse, intuitive reason may be open to less simplistic consideration. The ways we have of comprehending are many; we need not assume that all that are different from those specialized in by a particular group in a particular tradition in a particular time are threatening, strange, 'primitive'—Other.

At present, however, not only are students taught "phallocentric" and "colonial" notions of reason as *the* forms of rational expression, but the full possible range of expression of human intelligence also tends to be forced into a severely shrunken notion of intelligence. Intelligence is far too often understood to be that which the IQ test tests, and the results of that test have been used to mark whole groups not different, but inferior. That not only hurts those so marked; it impoverishes our understanding of intelligence. Children grow up knowing about IQ tests (and ACT tests, and SAT's etc.), and it is almost impossible to convince them that these products simply assess their ability to take a particular kind of test, cover only particular skills that have been isolated as those that have to do with a particular kind of success in particular kinds of institutions. People of all ages believe that their intelligence is being tested when they take IQ tests—as if we knew all that intelligence might be. Intelligence, like one of the qualities it is supposed to express, rationality, is a mystified concept. It is by no means a neutral, universal concept. Our belief in it, as it has been defined and given power through the use of devices such as IQ tests, works to maintain the dominant system.

Kathryn Pyne Parsons notes that "some philosophers have insisted that criteria for judging whether something has a certain characteristic may be entirely factual, and yet the characteristic be evaluative."[11] We overlook the evaluative meaning and function of our most central concepts at our peril; as Phillipa Foot continues, "We might give such an argument for the evaluative term IQ," because "there are evaluative consequences of networks of factual concepts, and some of the evaluative consequences may be moral."[12]

Such mystification of the moral implications and consequences of apparently neutral systems of definition and explanation is evident when great civilizations such as those of the Yoruba and the Jaina seem, to our students, 'primitive,' meaning 'illogical,' less than fully rational. That view reveals a narrow, and circular, notion of logic—once again, the error of generalizing too far from too few. Not only are there other systems of logic in the world—in the sense of systematized descriptive and prescriptive sets of statements about how reason works—but they deserve our serious attention. Consider an example in which I have found students to be profoundly interested once they get past their initial scepticism. Jaina thinkers—who have a seven-pointed logic, not the two-pointed logic with its law of excluded middle that characterizes the Western tradition—had their greatest influence in Gujarat, the area in India from which Gandhi came. It is perhaps not surprising that Gandhi was able to develop his philosophy and practice of non-violence by bringing together many different Indian traditions with what he learned of the West, particularly Christianity. He was nurtured in a culture that prepared him to think syncretistically, not exclusively.

In the Jaina system, as A. L. Basham describes it, "there were not merely the two possibilities of existence and non-existence, but seven." The seven are derived by bringing into the place of the Western excluded middle (in this context, "something either is or is not"), a third possibility: that in one aspect something is, but in another it is not. That possibility recognizes existence as relative rather than absolute. Another possibility is that something exists, "but its nature is otherwise indescribable."[13] There is, then, also a recognition of limitations on knowledge; it cannot encompass all. We need not go into the technicalities of various logics to see why this one appeals to students. As I understand it, the familiar story of the blind people and the elephant is of Jaina origin. The lesson of the story is that the one who, feeling the tail, thinks an elephant is like a rope is not wrong unless s/he thinks s/he is right, that that is all the elephant is; the one who, feeling the leg, thinks the elephant is like a tree is not wrong unless s/he thinks that is all the elephant is; and so on. This is not a story that promotes relativism; the point is not that each of the blind people is right and so there is no knowledge of the elephant on which they can or must agree. The point is (I believe) that knowledge requires many of us, and that even apparently incompatible models or metaphors can provide part of the picture—if we can give up the notion that there is one right way of knowing it, that only one paradigm can or must rule.

Along these lines, it may and may not be true that women learn and come to understanding differently from men, as works such as those by Carol Gilligan, Mary Field Belenky and her colleagues, and Nell Noddings suggest (although these authors are very careful not to claim that modes of knowing and responding are either sex-determined or absolutely consistent within the genders). But it seems very likely indeed that many humans think well and effectively in ways that do not fit within the narrow confines of the dominant culture's notions of rationality, of intelligence, of logic. There is little doubt in my mind that that is one of the reasons for the stunning popularity of Gilligan's work. Across the country, I have found women and a remarkable number of men for whom arguments for the existence *and worth* of "a different voice" strike a powerfully resonant chord. Some of the wide popularity and frequent citation of these women's work is no doubt due, then, to their courageous effort to ask the very difficult question, What would it look like if we were, today, to put women in the center, as feminists have long said we should? What would we learn about alternative ways of being rational, of learning, of being moral?

The responses to such questions that are suggested by these books may and may not be adequate, of course. It has frequently been suggested that the effort to say what women are like risks perpetuating the old errors resulting from faulty universalization (or essentialism). All women are by no means alike, after all, not only across but within cultures, and subcultures. That is one problem. Another is that the ways of reasoning, of knowing, of judging, depicted in these books, precisely insofar as they may be general (if not universal), may derive from the general oppression of women. That is, what we find by studying "the woman's voice" *now* may not only not be *the* woman's voice, but may specifically not be the, or a, voice that we would hear had women not been oppressed so systematically for so long. The debate around these works is complex and important, but I wish here only to note that their popularity tells us that many of us are deeply hungry for public recognition of ways of thought different from the few that have been in the ascendancy for so long. I would also note that, as Sara Ruddick demonstrates in *Maternal Thinking: Toward a Politics of Peace*,[14] we may indeed need to find the suppressed voices not just to make ourselves feel better, or to change education, or even to enrich our understanding of 'rationality,' but to make the peace we must have if we are to survive on this earth. For that essential effort, *nonexclusive* universals may indeed be helpful—again, not as things we can *know*, but as ideas we can think, as we can think but never know the idea of justice, as justice is approached but never realized in any particular set of laws, institutions, or practices.[15]

⎯It is the circular, self-referential, and self-justifying meaning of reason that needs to be particularized if we are to think more freely about thinking, about knowing. But many respond to the effort to particularize as if reason-itself were under attack. It is only under attack as long as one persists in claiming for a particular version of it the totality of human reason rather than a particular share or mode of expression of that infinitely rich gift, which can always overleap itself and so cannot catch itself in any of its particular constructions. By including reason in this discussion of mystified concepts, I am suggesting that the narrow view of reason we can find functioning in (rather than consciously held by) many academics (among others) has served some purposes. Among other things, it has worked quite effectively to allow the dominant few in the Western tradition to brand others "irrational." And that, in a tradition that has taken rationality to be *the* characteristic of the truly and fully human, has had very serious consequences. As Aristotle said, slaves and in different ways 'free' women, being less rational than free men, *need* to be ruled—and, the tradition added, "the Dark Continent" *needs* to have enlightenment brought to it. Conquest, rule, mastery, are all served well by a notion of reason that is both narrow and absolutized. When one has said, "That's an irrational idea," one has not only exempted oneself from asking whether it is true, but also from considering whether or not it is expressive of some real experience or is indicative of someone's good-faith effort to remedy a situation—from asking whether that which presently seems "irrational" is, perhaps, born of an "intuition" of a "new world."[16] The irrational, judged as such against a narrow (or even an adequate) definition of "rational," is not the same as the *anti*-rational.

Liberal Arts

In practice, as we have seen, the liberal arts tend to be defined by a list of standing disciplines. In both the particular fields and in the liberal arts generally, that kind of operational definition serves to encapsulate, to protect what is against serious change even if such change can be justified by appeal to more thoughtful definitions. Here we go even further: conceptions of the liberal arts themselves tend to hide the old errors that mystify and perpetuate the articulated hierarchy from which they sprang.

In liberal arts institutions, studio courses—*doing* courses of any kind—are barely recognized or, if recognized, are often not given full liberal arts standing. Technical schools are considered intellectually inferior, and illiberal. Those divisions reflect the privileged, male, Greek (largely Athenian) division between those who use reason and lead a life devoted to it and to politics, and those who should be ruled by those reasoning few. The standards of what is and what is not liberal arts are used to justify themselves, and with them the class as well as gender hierarchy of old. As Martin puts it, even the division between liberal arts and technical schools is only between kinds of "productive" knowledge; neither takes into account the "reproductive" knowledge that has long been considered appropriate only to women.[17] It is as if we still believed that "those who do, do not think, and those who think, do not do," which can be found in an updated version of the old saying, "those who can, do; those who can't, teach" (with a still more recent addition, "and those who can do neither, consult"). And then many profess to worry about the ethics of professionals, and of citizens, and claim to be—and often are—bewildered that teaching people something does not seem to make them good at it, in either the technical *or* the ethical sense of "good."

Openly professional graduate schools, such as business, law, and medical schools, tend to try to combine practice with theory in ways that the less openly professional Ph.D.-granting schools that prepare researchers and professors in the liberal arts rarely do. Thus, the former schools make it evident that they recognize the 'doing' dimension of what they teach. Recently graduated M.D.'s have characteristically had more experience practicing as physicians than newly minted Ph.D.'s have as teachers. But it is in nursing school that one finds serious attention paid to the care of human beings, as it is in the training of elementary school teachers that one is likely to find open admission of the fact that teachers need to be able to practice their art with and for the benefit of students (rather than doing their most important work primarily for 'the community of scholars'). The 'higher' the profession in the articulated hierarchy, the less emphasis there is on practice *or* on care—and the smaller the proportion of people who have traditionally been 'lower' in the hierarchy.

In the United States a long subtradition of educational thought has struggled to undo those curious separations that derive directly, I am suggesting, from old class, race, and gender hierarchies. Oberlin's motto, "to learn and to work," stands as a striking reminder of that subtradition, as does the continuing if no longer very influential progressive education tradition. John Dewey, Alexander Meiklejohn, Maria Montessori, Sylvia Ashton-Warner, Paulo Freire, Ivan Illich, and others still inspire some to try to bridge the gap in education between knowing and doing, and between the liberal and the civic arts, and feminist educators are attempting to undo the mystifications built even into some progressive views.

But the notion most educators involved with higher education have of the liberal arts remains a peculiar one. It is assumed that the liberal arts liberate, that they counter human limitations, enrich human abilities. But can they do so while we retain the old monistic hierarchy, which, despite the pairing of terms, does not create mind and body, knowledge and action, theory and practice even as separate but equal? Certainly not so long as those paired terms continue to reflect the same errors we have been exploring, errors in which all that has to do with the 'lower' human activities is defined as appropriate to women and lower-caste men, and so as 'improper' for the educated 'free man.' To help liberate humankind from past prejudices and beliefs that derived from and justified the assignment of physical and daily maintenance work to lower-caste people, we need to know much more about all that truly makes life possible and humane, from mothering,[18] to community-building, to surviving with imagination and dignity intact in deprivation and poverty, to working with our hands with art and integrity.

The "liberal" in liberal arts was never intended to mean "liberating" except insofar as the arts that were taught 'liberated' some men from concern for mundane, useful, care-taking concerns, ostensibly so they could give their full attention to 'higher' things. The history of the liberal arts curriculum in America is one of struggle between such 'higher,' classical and theologically oriented learning, designed to preserve the past and prepare minister–teacher–scholars for the future, and pressures exerted on it to educate men for the professions and according to the "new learning" emerging from the 'Enlightenment.' Thus, even as education in this country began to take account of the world around it, it continued its role of selecting and training those who were to hold positions of power. As Frederick Rudolph writes:

> By the time this course of study had moved out of the medieval university, passed through the universities of Renaissance and Reformation England, and landed in the American forest, much had happened. . . . A broadened view of letters and language, knowledge appropriate to the responsible use of leisure, and an interest in

Greece and the Greeks before they fell into Latin translation en-
tered. . . . *What had been a curriculum for theologians now carried the*
burden of training a governing class of gentlemen and men of action.[19]

Over and over again through this history, we see the proponents
of the liberal arts trying to ward off subjects and concerns that
would, they thought, lower that 'high' calling by making the course
of study suspiciously useful for any other kind of life or inclusive of
troubling new views (let alone 'new' people). Mathematics, for
example, was long considered "a slight remnant of the ancient
quadrivium," and therefore teachable, but nevertheless "of use to
mechanics but of no value to gentlemen, scholars, and men of
affairs."[20] Yet these were the schools and programs in which attention was to be paid to questions of meaning, of worth and character,
in ways neither required nor expected of those designed specifically
to teach skills to men who could expect to have no leisure for the
scholarly life, the life of the gentleman, or civic leadership. The
liberal arts that descended from the education of gentlemen still
carry within them all the errors that exclusiveness, that snobbish-
ness, built into them—and yet it is to the liberal arts that we turn
today to show and promote concern for the enduring questions of
human life and meaning.

The problem is not that no one in the liberal arts cares about
either the enduring questions or those that press so hard on us
today. The problem is that those who teach 'useful' skills are neither
prepared for nor expected to be concerned with anything other than
the technical training they offer, while those whom we expect to do
more are not prepared to do so either. Professionalization has en-
tered the liberal arts too, so that undergraduates are basically of-
fered entrance-level training to the academic disciplines it is de-
voutly hoped they will pursue through graduate school (thereby
becoming qualified to become professional professors), while far
too little has been done to bring into the curriculum the new learning of *this* age, which raises fundamental questions about what it
means and ought to mean to be human.

So long as the liberal arts continue to be directed primarily toward the preparation of the few 'best' students for the kind of life
this age's professors consider worthy (remarkably often one that
emulates and thereby validates the professor's own choice), and do
so by perpetuating definitions of subjects that enshrine the old
exclusivities and hierarchies, we cannot expect the liberal arts to
liberate. The widespread belief, and faith, that they do reveals the

mystification of their real history as of their present condition and role in our culture.

Woman

As long as liberal arts institutions continue to reflect the idea that the body is 'lower' than the mind, women are likely to continue to seem out of place there because we have long been held to be defined by our bodies as men are not by theirs. *Woman* is a concept mystified in much the same way as the others we have explored; this concept, too, has been defined through the same skewed and error-twisted tradition. In many ways, in fact, the understanding of woman we need to untangle is vastly more complicated because it is deeply related in unadmitted ways to almost all, if not all, central expressions of the dominant culture.

The constituted meaning of woman, thought through, reveals the articulated power hierarchy not only in its broad outlines but in its most intimate expressions because women, and/or imagery of the female, are to be found in almost all groups and activities of the culture and polity. And where women are not to be found, prohibitions against women *are*, revealing that the exclusive group, the "masculine" activity, depends on the *absence* of women for its own meaning—while often making use of appropriated imagery of the female. Think of pin-ups in male-only armies, dormitories, work places, of the female muse inspiring male artists who did not believe women could themselves be artists, and of the irony of "lady liberty" and the female figure that holds the scales of justice by which men have consistently found real women unequal.

Although women were not the subject matter or central issue of any professional academic field before Women's Studies, women have, indeed, been thought about. All that I have said about the exclusion of *women* both physically and conceptually as valued contributors to the human story does not mean that nothing has been thought or written about *Woman* by the men who defined and maintained the dominant culture and its institutions. Quite the contrary: Woman has been used as the delimiting boundary for the meaning of Man and so has been present even when apparently absent. As Spinoza noted, in the dominant system of thought everything is what it is by not being something else (commonly phrased as "all determination is negation").[21] Stunningly often, Woman has been that "something else," that which almost everything (and everyone) that made it into the dominant culture and polity *was not*, albeit in importantly varying degrees of immediacy.[22]

The problem is that that which pertained to Woman was thought through systems and in terms that made it impossible to think well, let alone accurately, adequately, and in ways appropriate to women rather than to a few men's conception of us. Woman has been Man's Other, an absence required by the ways he was defined: Woman was that from which Man issued, that from which he had to distinguish himself, that in himself he denied, that through which he symbolized his own meanings. That Woman had no meaning of her own, no real and positive content in the dominant system, was thus both perpetuated and mystified.

To keep women lumped together in the concept Woman was to keep us, in all our extraordinary diversity, available to be the Other for the faultily abstracted, singular universal Man. Thus, the singularity and universality implied by "Woman" as by "Man" did not mean that the concept penning us in was replete with all relevant meaning; it meant that it was empty of meaning, was only negative. But at the same time, Woman was defined as for-Man as well as not-Man, and that complicated matters. The men creating and working within the hegemonic meaning system held that Woman referred directly back to biology, to Nature; she was not-Man and yet was available for his use, to take care of his 'natural' needs. As *A Feminist Dictionary* notes, "The word *woman*, and its etymological companion, *wife*, have together received from the English etymologists an astonishing number of interpretations, most of them based on the presumed sexual or domestic function of women."[23] Thus, women are turned into the empty singular universal Woman, who is not-Man, and then are reattached to men through sexual/reproductive and related domestic functions. As I have said, Woman has been thought of primarily as a condition for the life, and the good life, of Man. It is worth remembering that "husband" is a verb as well as a noun, and that it means to cultivate, to manage, to administer. Men can husband their resources; women cannot wife theirs, because, of course, as women/wives who are 'properly' domesticated by husbandry, we are that which is cultivated, managed, administered (along with men's animals and fields, the other primary objects of "husbandry"). Sherri Ortner's groundbreaking article, "Is Woman to Nature As Man Is to Culture?" brought out some of the meaning of this lack of parallelism between Man and Woman, husband and wife—Culture and Nature.[24]

In the dominant tradition, since Man was pronounced the generic and normative term for human and that term's dependence on
the Otherness of women was rarely acknowledged, any more than
it occupants' dependence on real live women was, there had to be
some *reason* for speaking of women directly. Thought about her
began and usually ended with what supposedly made her most—
and most safely—*distinct from* men, the centrally defining kind of
human, on the one hand, and with what held her *in relation to* men,
the only significant kind of human, on the other.

Thus, Woman was primarily constructed with regard to her 'natural' (that is, 'proper') reproductive and sexual being, as Man was
not. It is worth remembering, when the 'obviousness' of sex differences is adduced to explain hierarchical gender constructs, that
humans differ physically in a great many ways. Some are tall, some
short; some are young, some old; some are blond, some dark-
haired; some are strong, some are weak—and women and men are
to be found in all those categories. Furthermore, not all women can
or do conceive and bear children; and even those who do, actually
exercise those capacities for only part of their lives. It is not physical
differences that account for cultural and political inequalities, nor is
it being an egg-bearer or a sperm-bearer that 'explains' the division
of humans into two kinds that are considered fundamental from
birth to death (and beyond—even the deceased are either man or
woman). A prior move ('prior' conceptually and historically) selected from among human characteristics those that are to be focused on to establish and/or justify inequality.[25]

For whatever reasons, Woman came to mean the human creature
who is different from Man with regard to reproductive function
while men were *not* defined exclusively with regard to their reproductive role—here, too, we are not dealing with parallels, with
dualisms. And women were defined as related to, not only different
from, men in the complex area of sexuality, which is by no means
only 'about' reproduction. Woman was mother, daughter, sister,
wife, breeder, lover, object of pleasure—for men. She was not-Man,
yet she was intrinsic to men's lives. Hence, it had to be specified
in what regard she was most indubitably extrinsic to his self-
definition. For men, self and life, personhood and physical being,
were split apart with the division of Woman from Man. That left
men with the infamous mind/body problem to think about in the
study, while women suffered a fraught definition of relationship if
ever there was one—Woman is alien to Man, Other than Man, and

yet essential to men on all levels, from the definitional to the domestic, from the erotic to the procreative. Man needs her, yet cannot admit mutual implication with her. Is there any wonder that misogyny is every bit as much an expression of the dominant culture as romanticized heterosexual love—is, indeed, its unavoidable obverse?

Thus, we have a mystified conception of Woman; and still today, while it is held that she is indeed human, and apparently well-intentioned efforts are made to treat her/us as equals in Academia as elsewhere, it is nevertheless also held that we are fundamentally and significantly different from men. But neither position is tenable while Man remains on any level the inclusive term, the norm, and the ideal for humankind. If we are to achieve genuine equality, to approach real comprehension of women, Man must be deuniversalized so that our own meanings can emerge in plural and differentiated terms. We cannot be equal until we can be different in our own ways, not those imposed on us. As Chandra Mohanty notes, "The experience of being woman can create an illusory unity, for it is not the experience of being woman but the meanings attached to gender, race, class, and age at various historical moments" in various cultures "that [are] of strategic significance."[26]

If education is to become truly concerned with what it means to be human, it is essential that we dedicate ourselves to fundamental rethinking and new learning about what *human* might mean were it not conflated with a particular view of Man that both depends on and denies its intrinsic uses of Woman, and of women. At present, the category *human* is filled with notions derived from the privileged few males. When those notions have been honestly particularized, the category may reveal itself as empty. It will then become the exciting work of new generations to begin to rethink it. We cannot, I believe, *know* what it is to be human; that would require that we know ourselves as objects, a knowledge contradicted from the very beginning by the fact that it is we who are subjects of our own 'objective' knowledge, as well as by the surely obvious observation that in knowing ourselves we change the knower–known. What we know when we know ourselves is always, at best, what has been, not what is at the moment and what is, always, coming to be. But that does not mean that we cannot *think* about the meanings of Woman/women, Man/men, and human in inclusive *and* very carefully differentiated senses, clearing the ground of all that has blocked our thinking as we do so.

Sex

Sex, far from being a safely settled ground, a biologically given license, as it were, for conceptions of significant differences between humans, must also be considered a mystified concept/construct. To begin with, we need very careful feminist analysis to uncover and remedy the prevalent blurring of the meanings of sex, sexuality, reproduction, and gender, beyond the early feminist distinction between sex (as biological given) and gender (as sociopolitical, or cultural, construct). Any comprehension of humankind that continues the old mystifying bifurcation and simultaneous blurring of these very powerful constructs is necessarily crude. Let us, then, consider sex, sexuality, and reproduction. They are by no means or in any way 'simply natural': they are, in different if intricately related ways, central to the sex/gender *system*, as to the whole articulated hierarchy of power, and should no longer be relegated to dark corners of the dominant culture, there to be enjoyed (or inexcusably used) by those who benefit from that hiding.

One of the first premises of feminism is and should be that what has been declared 'private' in the male-dominant system is in fact deeply implicated in all that is public, in constructions of power, just as power is expressed and enacted in the "private realm." It is not a private matter that whole cultures have consistently relegated over half of humankind to a devalued, even feared, 'natural' realm, which is then seen as something to master, to control, to repress, to dominate, to transcend. The concept of sex, like those of reproduction on the one hand and sexuality on the other, is an expression of established, and enforced, political/cultural relations and meanings that are not only not private, but are implicated throughout the culture and its power structures.

Sex, Women's Studies scholars used to say, has to do with biology, while gender has to do not only with the social but also with the political realms. But even that helpful distinction is, I have suggested, too simple and hides within it a continuing identification of the biological with that which is simply and necessarily given, as if in this realm human knowing can and should simply reflect the given 'real'—as if, in speaking of the biological, we speak a language not of human construct at all. But what is known about human physiology is, like all knowledge, the result of intention, of dominant forms of meaning, expression, explanation, discourse. One need only explore some slightly older texts on the biology of human reproduction to discover striking examples of cultural constructions.[27]

Furthermore, sex is not the same as, is not fully contained within or expressed by, sexuality, and vice versa, and neither is fully understood as or expressed through reproductive capacity or experience. All three have had different meanings in relation to each other, to conceptions of what Woman means, to the articulated power hierarchy. All three are differently experienced not only through history and between cultures but between classes and racial cultures and communities, and in religious and ethnic groups as well. And some of those differences are both curious and dangerous, for class and race have been sexualized in ways that reflect and reinforce old patterns of dominance. Dominance itself has been sexualized.

We cannot untangle the meanings of sex, sexuality, reproduction, and gender yet; that is the continuing task of theory as it becomes finer and more sensitive in all these dimensions of meaning, power, and experience. What we can say with ease is that these are no longer topics only for certain areas of science, of psychology and sociology, for "sexologists" or anthropologists. They are subjects we must study as fundamental to our meaning and power systems, *and* they are revelatory concepts needed for the undoing of old mystified, essentialized, naturalized, meanings the dominant culture has preserved even in eras of supposed 'enlightenment.'

Among the developments promising to hone our ability to use these concepts are those emerging from the work of international feminists concerned with the new reproductive technologies. For these scholar/activists, it has become evident that *all* our thinking about sex, gender, and reproduction is being forced to the surface by what is now possible through the intervention of technologized science in ways that both demand and make possible profound reconsideration. The problem of "surrogacy"—in which the woman whose egg and/or womb is involved is called a "surrogate" mother, while the man who donated but did not implant sperm is called a "father," a peculiarly revealing set of constructs to say the least—is only one of the most publicized of such issues.[28]

All our modes of transforming knowledge are going to be required to undo the knots in our comprehension left by the mystifications of sex. The peculiar construction of the meanings of woman-as-natural-creature whose essence is somehow expressed as it is locked into sex, sexuality, and reproduction within a hierarchical gender/class/race system has perpetuated the root error of taking

the few to be the norm, the inclusive term, and the ideal. Woman
was seen only insofar as she was part of the condition of men's
lives, locked on the biological or 'natural' level, denied the central
defining quality of humanness. As it becomes increasingly possible
for women to be used as sources of eggs to be externally fertilized
and implanted in another woman, or as incubator-wombs for eggs
fertilized by men with whom they have no personal relationship at
all, we begin to see the dominant definitions and their power relations still more clearly, even when those possibilities are greeted by
some women as liberating means to increase choice. It is, I believe,
no accident that the antiabortion movement came back to virulent
life in the mid-1980s. The power struggle over women's bodies is
out in the open once again, and now it is fueled by years of fear,
anger, and resentment raised by the Women's Movement as well as
by economic, technological, and political developments that have
made significant portions of the population feel more helpless and
less able to understand what is going on. At such times many turn
back, with a particular vehemence, to the most basic of the old
systems of meaning and behavior, such as those espoused by fun-
damentalist religious sects. Since the control of women's bodies,
and through it the control of sex and sexuality, has always been
deeply important to patriarchal religions, a turn to fundamental-
ism, whatever its motivation, entails also a turn against anything
that might even appear to empower women to make our own
decisions about our bodies.

It is worth considering seriously and stubbornly that *all* talk of
sex concerns the issue of power over women's bodies, and perhaps
this is particularly true of that which takes place on the more abstract and/or transcendent levels of the dominant culture—for example, in the discourses of science, religion, history of ideas, "Western Civ." It is remarkable how often, in the implicit as well as explicit
stories in such fields, Man is depicted as 'ascending' *both* biologically *and* culturally from Nature to Civilization, while Woman remains closer to the level of Nature, necessary to Man, yet to be
transcended by him. As de Beauvoir put it, Woman was locked into
immanence and hence was seen as unable to achieve transcendence; as she seems not to have observed, it is a radically impoverished concept of transcendence that depends for its meaning
on a dichotomous contrast with (nonparallel, 'lower') immanence.
If there are qualities of Woman-as-the-immanent that *cannot* be
taken up into transcendence, then transcendence, like the defini-

tion of Man, is only partially conceived. To put it simply, it will no longer do to conceive of humankind in any terms that do not recognize the dangerous artificiality of nonparallel (or, indeed, any kind of) dichotomies between the natural and the cultural, the immanent and the transcendent, body and mind/spirit.[29]

We need to remember that with the definition of women in terms of sex in ways that included and justified control of our sexuality and of our reproductive capacities by 'ascending' and/or 'transcending' men came the exclusion of what we can call dailiness and nurturance from recognized, valued human qualities. The matrix of life was placed in that strange non-category of Otherness, of intimate, threatening strangeness—threatening, to the men who exercised the power of creating their culture's knowledge, precisely because intimate yet supposed to be strange to them, to be not-their-place. The realm of women was that from which they had to distinguish themselves in order to be men, and so they shut off involvement with intimacy, with dailiness, with physicality as relational (rather than a negotiation of dominance), with 'feminine' emotions, making these crucial aspects of human life strange, feeling their attraction as threatening.[30]

I know I appear to be doing something odd here: I am suggesting, among other things, that the supposedly *least* physical/physiological aspects of human be-ing, the most spiritual and 'uplifting,' have been understood in ways that are skewed by the non-inclusion of the supposedly *most* physical, least spiritual, most elemental aspects. How odd to discuss transcendence and immanence in a section on sex—to put it bluntly. But to those who have read a lot of mythology, and/or some of the autobiographies and biographies of the saints, not to mention Freud, Jung, et al., the conjunction will not seem so strange. I neither quarrel nor entirely agree with those other systems. What I wish to do is to suggest that insofar as Man has been constructed in ways that differentiate him sharply from Woman and justify the ascendancy-as-dominance required by patriarchy, human being itself has necessarily been misunderstood. Since, to be universal, Man cannot be admitted to be male (that is, sexed in a particular way), yet at the same time must be male in some (incomprehensibly) nonsexual way in order *not* to be akin to woman, who is primarily defined in biological/sexual terms, notions of and so quests for transcendence have had to deny sexuality so vehemently that they have by that very effort been deeply tied to it. It is no wonder at all that men seeking transcendence have feared, above all, the 'power' of women. The 'power' of the temptress is the obverse, the Other, of men's power in the mystified sex/gender system. As the master is utterly dependent on the slave to be a master, and so hates and fears the slave, man in patriarchal systems is utterly dependent on woman to be man, and so hates and fears her. Sex and sexuality, as the primary determinants of woman in the sex/gender hierarchy, then become the locus of that distorted relation and so take on an enormous power.

Hence some serious problems in considering what human life is and means: having defined all that is essential to the creation and maintenance of life, of intimacy, of community, as "women's work," the men in position to shape the dominant culture publicly could not then *think* about these rich and critically important functions and qualities, precisely as they could not think about sex, sexuality, and reproduction, or study these essential concepts/constructs/ experiences as aspects of being human. The dominant tradition was created such that knowledge supposedly of humankind, but actually about a few functions of some men's lives, grew airily unconnected with reality, as any study must that proceeds without consideration of the essential activities of life that have been defined as "women's work," of the reality of dailiness, of the groundedness of immanence.

Where a 'high' position is defined by not being the 'low' position, where the transcendent is defined by not being immanent, where Man is defined by not being Woman, where the spiritual is defined by not being sexual, where productive labor is defined by not being reproductive, we find a tangle of mutual implication denied and feared on such a deep, somatized, emotional, level that it is no wonder violence is so endemic—and so often sexualized. White men have violated Black women and lynched innocent Black men for supposedly violating white women. Immigrant women have been seen by those who exploited them as more sexual than privileged women, who were themselves then blamed for being asexual and 'driving' privileged men to turn to those 'lower' women. It is stunning how consistently those who have been most exploited have also been seen as most sexual. The conflation of nature, biology, sexuality, and physical and emotional expressiveness, and the projection of that tangle upon 'lower' beings, has been deadly.

Jessica Benjamin writes about "the violence of erotic domination . . . the strange union of rationality and violence that is made in the secret heart of our culture and sometimes enacted in the body." "This union," she continues, "has inspired some of the holiest imagery of religious transcendence and now comes to light at the porno newsstands," where "the slave of love is not always a woman, nor always a heterosexual; the fantasy of erotic domination permeates all sexual imagery in our culture. This rational violence mingles love with issues of control and submission."[31] There are terrible difficulties of all sorts in undertaking such discussions; what is promising is that they are, indeed, being undertaken nevertheless. We do not know where they will go, of course; what we do know is that the most taboo acts and subjects of all have been and are revelatory of a critical locus of power that calls on us to attempt, with humility and with courage, together and individually, to try to comprehend it.

Eve Sedgwick, responding to the need to think better, writes, "Before we can fully achieve and use our intuitive grasp of the leverage that sexual relations seem to offer on the relations of oppression we need more . . . daring and prehensile applications of our present understanding of what it may mean for one thing to signify another."[32] She is clear that sexuality is broadly revelatory of relations between humans, by no means a new realization, but does not at all consider that that settles, let alone explains, anything. For her and those working along similar lines, sexuality *is* signification, on the one hand, and must be comprehended as such in ways for which we are not yet fully prepared, on the other. Approaching sex and sexuality, reproduction, nurturance, and daily life with a commitment to demystify them as concepts, as experiences, as expressions and significations of meaning and of power, requires us to be willing to rethink not just what we have thought but how we have thought it.

What it means to be human is profoundly implicated in and implicates these concepts, which may be among the most mystified of all—and therefore require the finest and the most subtle, differentiated, and far-ranging work to disentangle from all that overlays, hides, and/or distorts them.

Man

Implied in all that I have been saying is, of course, that *man*, the apparent subject as well as object of the whole story, necessarily became a mystified concept as well, and in a way that led to all kinds of strange contradictions and confusions. The root error feeds a vast and luxuriantly leaved tree. We need not only to plant new trees, but to prune the old to keep it from blocking the light, to cut back its roots to keep it from growing back again and again. *All* knowledge, all meaning, is skewed when the concept that has been central to the pursuit of knowledge—Man, Mankind—is partial yet taken to be inclusive; claimed to be neutral, yet used normatively; a particular subject matter universalized and then taken to provide ideals of and for all. Man is mystified in ways that keep us from comprehending, taking in and grasping, not just what he means but how his meaning is dependent on all that is present only as absence, as contrast, as lack.[33]

How odd it is, when we think about it, that even though male is the privileged category of human, in the dominant tradition it is often very difficult to think about men *qua* males, as in interesting ways those involved in the new "Men's Studies" movement are doing. That oddity is, in part at least, the result of the basic error: if Man is the inclusive term for humankind, then Man cannot be admitted to be *male* in any real (that is, particular, contextualized) sense—biologized or not.

We are faced with the intriguing, to some people troubling, need *always* to take into account gender, sex, sexuality, reproduction. All of these powerful constructs and experiences have been mystified as a consequence not only of forces of repression (which I obviously do not think of as only or even primarily psychological) but of the related need to hide Man's limiting particularity as male. If Man's particularity as male were once fully recognized and thought through, not as some kind of 'natural' given but as a very elaborate construct, much that is present only as anomalous, secret, trivial, 'only' private, and threatening in the dominant tradition would be illuminated. We would not like all that we brought into the light that way; the universal ideal Man has achieved his luminosity by creating a dangerous shadow world. The 'privacy' of the home, which for Man has been "his castle," has been a nightmare for far too many women and children, whose story is rarely told in the tales of Great Men. And the degree to which it is particular, and changing, constructions and *not* just 'expressions' of 'normal' male sexuality that have created pornography, prostitution, and homophobia as defining limits that are made to be transgressed is terribly difficult to admit. But where too much is denied, too much is also permitted; darkness breeds an addicting intensity that the dominant culture has protected with ferocity.[34]

Even on a far less fraught level, we note that while Man and mankind are not just falsely universalized but *singular* terms, problems that have serious consequences persist. It is very difficult to think well about plurality, diversity, difference, while the very form of the words pushes toward abstract singularity. People speak easily of "the student," "the author," and, even more problematically, of "the enemy," "the criminal," "the whore," creating and expressing a singularity of image, of meaning, that usually remains both highly abstract (to get beyond multiple images, meanings) and dangerously particularized (because, to have any meaning, the singularity must have some content, as it were, and that content comes, as all content does, in a particular form). Thus, we continue the press toward abstractions that claim generality but are actually particular in ways that tend very strongly to be congruent with the dominant meaning system. "The student" still tends to be thought of as a young white male; 'older' women returning to college have long encountered the more or less open prejudgment that they are not 'real' students, that having too many of them marks a school as inferior (as night classes designed for working adults are always considered a sideline to the 'real,' prestige-conferring work of schools).

In a very telling analysis of one such term, "the enemy," J. Glenn Gray writes:

> Always, the definite article is used with the noun, not *an* enemy or *our* enemy. The implication easily drawn is that the opponent is mankind's enemy as well as ours, and also that this enemy is a specific, though undifferentiated group, an implication that is only pseudo-concrete. That is, by reference to *the* enemy we seem to mean a unified, concrete universal. . . . By designating him with the definite article, it is made to appear that he is single and his reality consists in hostility to us.[35]

Not all singular universals are so dangerous, of course, but we should nevertheless be careful of them in a tradition so attached to that form. Thus, when students and colleagues of mine have stumbled over the "she or he" of properly inclusive language, I have often suggested that it is actually not only easier but helpful to try switching to plural subjects. To say "the students" where we might have said "the student" makes it much more likely that we will remember their plurality and differences in the sentence/proposition that follows. And that is no small thing; as our student bodies become as diverse as our ever more diverse population, we are going to have to do a much better job of *recognizing* them.

Yet as the deeply inscribed meanings of the defining few that are behind and reinforced by singular terms are challenged, commonality and community themselves may seem to some to be disappearing. Of course, what we are really doing is clearing the ground so that it may indeed accommodate us all, be common equally to all. What cries out to be created is an understanding that would allow "all members to rejoice" in their common human differences, in the uniqueness that characterizes all human be-ing.

As Hannah Arendt put it, "Human plurality is the paradoxical plurality of unique beings."[36] Recognizing that generative paradox as those who are bemused by the singular universality of Man and Mankind cannot, Arendt also won for herself the ability to think well about change, about action—about precisely those realms that usually seem to threaten knowledge (because singular universals must remain constant if they would remain unitary). Arendt, looking for the human condition of action because she did *not* see it as a problem, a falling away from the eternal, the certain, the 'highest,' found natality, one of the aspects of human being that men have long tried to ignore, to shroud in secrecy and shame, to control. Natality, the fact that humans are born, guarantees plurality ever enriched by newcomers, thereby creating the condition for action, the human capacity that disrupts what already exists through its characteristic unpredictability and boundlessness.[37]

If we remember that we are natal and not only mortal, that we are many and diverse, and that we can therefore act and not merely behave, we also remember that dominance, control, mastery, cannot succeed except by such extreme means as those we see in the violence-enforced 'order' of tyranny and the obliteration of visible plurality of totalitarianism. Man's efforts to master Nature (referred to as "she," as "Mother Nature") can be seen as dangerously perverse efforts to *become* the part that is the whole, to turn mystification into reality: "*L'état, c'est moi.*" The nuclear threat under which we now live is one awful indication of how far that strange mixture of domination and consuming identity, cast in terms haunted by all that has been Man's not-self, has gone.

War

The deep importance of learning how to think about humankind as diverse and equal, a way of thinking toward which we are working when we demystify these central concepts, emerges vividly when we look with new eyes at the central concepts and experiences of the dominant human story. Consider, for example, what the tradition does with *war*. It *appears* to be something men do, while women—depicted as absent from the scene of war, from the real thing—do no more than suffer at home while at the same time serving men as symbols for all that is worth fighting for, and as the trophies seized by the 'winners.' In the way war has been presented to us by the dominant tradition, we may see almost all, if not indeed all, of the uses that tradition has imposed on women.

First, as we have seen, women have been forced into the dangerous singular abstraction Woman, whose meaning is held in necessary relation to men, creating Woman as feared, desired, and needed use-object. In the story of the warrior, she is symbol of the home he fights for, excuse for fighting, comfort-giver and healer when he is in pain, goad to stay and fight so he can be a 'real' man ("come home with your shield or on it"), opiate when he needs to forget, diversion when he needs to relax, help in bonding with other men that masks the eroticism of such intense relations. Woman is used to raise the spirits of the warrior and to relieve his body; between spirit and body, there is for her no room for particular personhood. She is virgin/wife/mother, country/cause, and she is whore, temptress, and, far too often, nothing but body to be 'taken' and once used, thrown away, even killed.

If we are to approach comprehension of war, as of all that pertains to humankind, we are going to have to undo such mystifications. In all these constructions of Woman for and by soldiers, there is no real, and certainly no safe, place for individual women. And while real, diverse, individual women are not seen as they are in the story of war, there can be no honest picture of war either, or of warriors.

While *Woman* has been created by and for warriors, *women* have been part of and actively opposed to war throughout the ages and across cultures. Women have fought; women have tried to stop the fighting; women have been on the front lines as suppliers, as nurses, as spies, and have worked behind the lines as cooks, secretaries, seamstresses, drivers, experts in language; to keep the country going, women have moved into positions vacated by men going to war, and women have been forced out of their jobs when the men returned. Without women, as the historian Gerda Lerner has said, no war could ever have been fought. The meaning of wars as constituted within male-dominated cultures cannot be understood adequately without analysis of how we have been used, and abused, in

the service of man-made wars. Of course, unprivileged men who
had no part in making wars have also been used, and that use has
been 'justified' in terms that reveal how they, too, have been defined primarily as physical beings who are expendable as sub-
stitutes for privileged men and as "cannon fodder." But, as always,
we see here not only parallelisms between sex/gender, class, and
race but also their interpenetration: the exploitation of some groups
of men by others does not keep either exploited or exploiters from
participating in male uses of females.[38]

On a different level, consider the centrality the dominant culture
has given to mortality as a defining characteristic of Man, and the
deep silence surrounding the paired characteristic of natality mentioned earlier. Without natality, there would be no mortality—since
there would soon be no one left—but the dominant tradition focuses on the nobility and tragedy and spiritual transcendence of
Man facing death with barely a mention of birth. Birth, because it is
dependent upon women and so recalls all that men have projected
onto them, has been ignored, trivialized, and, at the same time,
feared. "All men are mortal" resounds with high sentiments; "man
is of woman born" reminds men of what they have felt to be their
humiliating, even sin-perpetuating, origins. One universal human
given—mortality—is called on to ennoble; the other, its essential
complement and balance—natality—to humble.

But what sense does it make and what does it cost to focus so on
death, to forget the miracle of birth? To focus on endings, forgetting
beginnings? To emphasize the aloneness of dying as if it were not
balanced by the relatedness of birth? A self defined under the
shadow of "all men are mortal" feels itself threatened and alone. But
we do not begin our lives alone or threatened; we begin protected
by the womb, connected to another. Being defined as those who are
mortal—but not natal—cannot help but make those so defined feel
the need to identify with death and so, too often, also with killing,
an act that seems to return to men their agency in the face of what
we must all suffer.

Natality, it seems, has been treated as Other for mortality, as
woman has for man, as peace has for war. The mystifications we are
exploring are deeply intertwined, and they are dangerous. Thus,
analysis of the mystification of war, which is increasingly becoming
a focus for some important feminist scholarship, leads us to the very
deepest constructions of meaning in the dominant tradition. If we
wish to think about peace as well as war, we need to recognize that

peace, like natality, like women, is strikingly absent from the dominant meaning system and so from our curricula and courses. We don't even have a plural for peace parallel to "wars"; we don't speak of "peaces." Peace appears in most courses as an absence of war, unnamed in its own right (except, perhaps, when secured through a treaty so that it can be marked—by reference, of course, to a war). Courses are not infrequently organized around wars ("America from 1776 to 1865," "Europe Between the Wars"), but never around 'peaces.' Thus, we see peace as an absence, a supposedly highly valued state that is rarely in fact studied at all; as the 'natural' state of affairs that can simply be assumed and so is not 'interesting' or 'significant' as are the great disruptions, wars.[39]

Mutatis mutandis, that is stunningly similar to the ways women are, or rather are not, treated by the curriculum. And that similarity is no accident: consider also that Peace is often symbolized as a woman, and is considered to be feminine in direct relation to the rampant machismo of war. Male pacifists have always been taunted by being called effeminate. The remarkably intense opposition initially expressed to women in the military reflected these constructs, as, particularly, does continuing opposition to women in combat. It *frightens* men to think of women being "in the trenches" with them. They assume women are always and everywhere 'soft' in ways that admit of no contrary evidence; they think that, to be men, they will have to take more risks to 'protect' female soldiers; they cannot imagine taking an order from a woman; they worry about having to watch their language—and avoid the use of women as occasion and excuse for eroticized male friendship. Think about that fear, listen to those who express it, and much if not all of what we have been discussing becomes almost glaringly evident. The most dangerous, deep, and pervasive mystifications are by no means subtle, and they tend to be very emotionally defended even as the defenses are publicly put forward as dispassionately 'rational.'

In the dominant European-American male tradition, war, a particular notion of rationality within systems of thought that are obsessed with mortality while virtually ignoring natality, and the male use of women for inspiration and physical release intertwine to vicious effect. It is absurd to study war as if it could be comprehended, let alone ended, within the exclusive, hierarchical, dominance-oriented systems that have prevailed. The male attachment to war is an old and deep one, as psychological and mythic, as well as economic and political, as any Oedipus Complex. And it is profoundly related to men's need for and willful incomprehension of women. As the poet Muriel Rukeyser wrote:

> Long afterward, Oedipus, old and blinded, walked the roads. He smelled a familiar smell. It was the sphinx. Oedipus said, "I want to ask one question. Why didn't I recognize my mother?" "You gave the wrong answer," said the Sphinx. "But that was what made everything possible," said Oedipus. "No," she said. "When I asked, What walks on four legs in the morning, two at noon, and three in the evening, you answered Man. You didn't say anything about woman." "When you say Man," said Oedipus, "you include women too. Everyone knows that." She said, "That's what you think."[40]

Oedipus, we might say, did *not* think when he answered the Sphinx's riddle. He gave an answer from the conventional, dominant system, and thereby earned a kingdom. But the plague came to his kingdom, forcing the king back into conversation, into the asking of questions, questions that revealed to him who his mother was. He ceased being a king and took up wandering with his sister/daughter Antigone until he died in a grove sacred to the "daughters of darkness and mysterious earth." There, no longer a king or a warrior, he became a blessing.

Gender

Man suffers, perhaps, not from the Oedipus Complex, from desire for his mother, but from the Oedipus Error, the blinding insistence that Man includes women. To undo the Oedipus Error, we now have the emergent, complex, powerfully useful concept of *gender*. Discussion of gender as it is coming to be theorized by feminist scholars belongs under the heading "mystified concepts" only— and this is, of course, my reason for including it—because its meaning emerges in what we find as we work on other concepts and as we think about that work. The concept of gender is a basic tool for the process of demystification; it is also an emergent concept of that which has been mystified.

Gender, in its broadest sense, is the term feminists use to evoke the conceptual and experiential, individual and systemic, historical and contemporary, cross-cultural and culture-specific, physical and spiritual and political construction of what it means to live in a world that has created them not human, but always woman or man (a division that is not a dualism but a hierarchical monism). Humans are, then, either men or the lesser beings created for them (by Nature? by God? by History?—various languages are used) called "women." For those of us who live enmeshed in that system, which is, of course, shaped by the root problem and its related conceptual errors, to be human, sexed, and uniquely individual at once is virtually impossible. Both the generic and the particular are formed/informed/deformed by the hierarchy that made some males into Man and the rest of us into failed men, deviants, primitives, saints, or whores.

In terms of our analysis, we can say that gender is the primary and fundamental result, as, in an equal sense, it is a primary and fundamental cause, of the root problem of taking a few males to be the singular universal Man, the inclusive term, the norm, and the ideal for all. In the language of Aristotle, gender—and genderized sex—could be seen as the first, final, formal, *and* material cause of one of the most basic ways human being is constructed. That is, gender is so fundamental to the dominant systems that it is said to be the result of natural cause (we must be women and men because we are naturally female and male), while at the same time women and men are what we are supposed to become, are ends we are to achieve by enacting, in highly prescriptive, formalized ways, what our bodies supposedly just are. Or, again in our terms, when we trace the conceptual errors through the dominant tradition, we are uncovering critical aspects of what gender has meant, which is also what gender has been.

Gender, then, is a *subject matter* that is approached through exploration of the dominant meaning system, including its political, economic, historical, and social expressions, and it is a *revelatory concept* that starts us on that exploration, emerges through it, and is refined as we continue our work (much as history is both the subject matter of History and the concept that allows us to construct that subject matter). And since we can and do make subject matter of our concepts (as we can study the concept of history/History), the concept of gender is itself also a subject to be studied, a *meta-concept.*

I know this is complicated and perhaps frustrating to those who are not intrigued by distinctions. But it is important to recognize the different meanings and uses of "gender" to avoid confusion of the sort that is bound to arise when one word is used so many ways. Furthermore, it is important to realize that we think, as I have noted earlier, reflexively: we can and do think about our thinking, and that is a basic ground for our freedom. Gender reveals the importance of reflexive thought because to think about gender is to think about what it has meant to be human in a way that helps us break out of old traps. This is not just one more new concept, one more specialization, one more technical term. To think about gender in its various forms and functions is to bring to center stage something that has influenced all thinking from behind the scenes, thereby allowing us first to see and then to question its directorial power. That is why we need to make distinctions, to pull out threads, to vary our focus, to circle around. We want to retain the complexity and multidimensionality of our understanding of gender and avoid premature and unduly narrow definitions without losing all specificity.

The concept of gender is at least as complex, after all, as that of race or class, neither of which has ever been resolved into a neat category, an undebatable definition. That these terms are not finally defined is not a failing, a problem, but an indication of something very important. We deal here with the transactional relation of thought and action, with terms that are not and cannot be finally defined because defining them is itself an act with particularly serious consequences. Gender, like race and class, is a *strategic concept* as well as a subject matter, a revelatory and a meta-concept. It reflects, shapes, suggests, demands action; its definition *matters*.[41] When we have realized that, we can begin thinking about what gender might mean in a nonhierarchical world, whether it could be constructed differently so as to become empowering rather than constraining, whether it might be much more a matter of choice, whether it is something that ought to be perpetuated in any form at all—about the visions that might inform our strategies.

But we must also not forget that gender is strategic even when it is not consciously so. It is not something we just think about; it is something we *do*, preconsciously much more than consciously. Gender prescriptions that tell us how we ought to be women and men, girls and boys, reflect, in a sense, the 'strategy' of the sex/gender system. Although our conception of gender becomes strategic in the more usual sense (entailing a conscious plan for specific action) as understanding increases, while we are doing that work it is far too easy to be influenced unknowingly by the old tangle of errors. If we are not very careful to remember the political and personal commitments that led to the work from which gender as concept and subject matter emerged—if we leap too fast to a focus on the meta-level, to using and refining the concept of gender as if it were our starting point and end—we are, I fear, likely to create just one more rather interesting academic subject.

That is one reason why I am both interested in and wary of the emerging field of Gender Studies, which is in some places replacing efforts to develop Women's Studies. Just as many people early on encouraged us to stop focusing on women, to move quickly to the goal of studying humankind, others today are urging an immediate move to a study of gender. We need to notice that the pressure is to ensure that what we study includes men (as subject matter, as teachers, as students). Some give that advice in good faith, trying to get to what seems a deeper level of analysis, to look at what makes us women and men in a way that recognizes their profound mutual implication. For others, I fear, the motivation is akin to that of people who get nervous when we talk 'too much' about women. There are threads here from the old tangle: study that does not involve men cannot really be significant, cannot become general enough, cannot raise 'the basic and most important' questions or introduce works that are 'good' enough to merit all that attention. Studying women feels like studying a *kind* of human, and a highly particular one at that . . . so let's hurry on to the 'real stuff,' which means that men *must* be more than present and in all roles.

But if we do not study women, we will not become able to think about humans well, nor will our work on gender be equally informed by knowledge of and about women. It has taken millennia for the knowledge we have from and about men to develop; we can hardly critique it adequately in twenty or even a hundred years, nor can we discover or create knowledge of and about the equally diverse creatures who inhabit the category of women. I know very well how uncomfortable it makes men and some women to remain in the company of women for long, but that discomfort is precisely why we need to do so. Gender Studies requires Women's Studies, just as Women's Studies requires the study of gender. One does not substitute for the other; they are mutually enriching.

Gender is *out there* to be studied in the sense that our identities, our relations with others, our systems and institutions, our stories and histories, are cast in its terms. What has been done has been done by women and men who appear vividly as such as soon as we give up the mystifying Man. Gender is also *within* our ways of studying (even our ways of studying gender, which is why we require Women's Studies), unconsciously before we think reflexively about the dominant tradition, consciously as we become aware of and more informed about it. Once we have started that thinking, gender becomes a specific revelatory and strategic concept that we work with and on, and it becomes a subject matter, even a field (as economics became a field when certain complexly interlocked modes of behavior, relationships, power, thought, and formal and informal institutions were called to our attention).

Turning it another way, we can say that as subject matter, gender is one of the primary expressions of human being as it has been mystified, *and*, as concept, is one of the tools we use in demystifying. It is what we suffered when we had not thought through the constructions within which we live; it is what we comprehend when we do think about them. In the movement from unnamed to named, unthought to thought, we discover what we are, and in discovering it, we become able to question it, to consider change. At the pivot point between what has been and what could be is the long moment in which we realize that the past is not our entrapping fate but our inheritance. The power available to us through that inheritance lies not only in understanding the terms of the will by which it was left to us, but also in how we become able to think about it, and what we do with it in the present.

In this present, we have progressed from the relatively simple early feminist notion of gender as the socially constructed and highly varied cultural expression of biological sex (gender as a slightly more politicized understanding of the old "sex role") to a point at which sex itself seems to be constructed by gender rather than the other way around. That is, the concept of gender expresses and then furthers our growing awareness that there is no starting point for thought about what it means to be human outside the distinctly human. Nature and history do not cause us to be human; they are expressions of our human abilities, symbols and systems of explanation created by humans. They do not cause gender; they are themselves gendered.

The horizons of meaning of gender in all its various related uses are so all-encompassing as to be simultaneously inspiring and intimidating. But the idea that gender refers to one of *the* fundamental human systems and its conceptualizations helps; of course thinking about it is complex. As the feminist philosopher Sandra Harding wrote in 1983: "Like racism and sexism, the sex/gender system appears to limit and create opportunities within which are constructed the social practices of daily life, the characteristics of social institutions, and *all of our patterns of thought*" (emphasis added):

Not only are the "macro" social institutions the way they are in the vast majority of societies because the sex/gender system is interacting with other organic [i.e., primary] social variables to structure them that way, but also the very existence and design of characteristics of daily life to which sex and/or gender seemed irrelevant now appear suffused with sex/gender. Now we can detect sex/gender in the details of domestic and public architecture, in what THE problems of philosophy are supposed to be, in the forms of technology a culture chooses, in the intensity and forms of the very distinction between nature and culture, and even in the forms of the state. The genes of the sex/gender system now can be detected in most of the social interactions which have ever occurred between humans of any sex, age, class, race, culture.[42]

Gender as subject matter, that which we study when we use the concept of gender as a primary lens, is, in our shorthand, the powerful fundamental system of patriarchal hierarchical monism and all that has been 'Othered' by that system understood *as* Othered. When we look for gender, we bring to the surface the immensely complex construction of power, knowledge, identity, and culture of the articulated hierarchy—which, you will recall, is informed by and informs also race and class, as well as other human systems of differentiation.

In other terms, we could say that everything of and by humans expresses gender precisely because it does *not* express comprehension or enactment of what "human" means—that is, what "human" might mean if it had been thought or lived free of the fundamental errors we have been exploring. In many ways, as we have seen, gender is a concept that reveals absence, lack, alienation, negation, in ways that force us to understand that these, too, can be constructs and not mere spaces of omission, or deferral of attention, or recognition of simple limit. To not-be a man of a particular sort in a system that takes Man to be inclusive, normal, ideal, is much worse than simply to be different from men.

Another turn: as a concept, gender reveals dominant systemic constructions to be patriarchal, where "patriarchal" does not refer to an external quality (as we say, "That flower is red") but to an internal characteristic (as we say, "Water is wet"). Gender analysis allows us to see male power expressed in forms and arenas of human practice and theory that have been mystified in the sense that, without gender analysis, they have appeared to be neutral, and/or necessary, and/or natural rather than profoundly related to power. As Heidi Hartmann puts it, bringing class and gender analysis together, *patriarchy* is "relations between men, which have a material base, and which, though hierarchical, establish or create interdependence and solidarity among men that enable them to dominate women."[43]

The emerging association of gender with power takes different forms in feminist works. For Joan Scott, "Gender [is] a primary way of signifying relationships of power,"[44] a way *so* primary, indeed, that I find myself thinking that perhaps we can go on to explore the obverse—how power is a primary way of signifying gender. Neither way of putting this complex relation means that gender *is* power, or vice versa; we are not dealing with essential definitions, on the one hand, and, on the other, we continue to benefit from the use of both terms, gender and power, and their rich associated languages.

Using the concept of gender allows us to see articulations of power in revealing new ways. Scott, for example, undertakes specific, contextualized analyses that are very interesting indeed:

> When middle-class reformers in France . . . depicted workers in terms coded as feminine (subordinate, weak, sexually exploited like prostitutes), labor and socialist leaders replied by insisting on the masculine position of the working class (producers, strong, protectors of their women and children). The terms of this discourse were not explicitly about gender, but they relied on references to it, the gendered "coding" of certain terms, to establish their meanings.

Generalizing from several such examples, Scott calls gender "one of the recurrent references by which political power has been conceived, legitimated, and criticized. It refers to but also establishes the meaning of the male/female opposition."[45] Consider, then, the *effects* of the gendered power conceptions of the labor and socialist leaders studied by Scott. Is it any surprise that more than one movement for major social and economic change whose male leaders promised also a change in the unequal relations of women and men has not delivered on that promise? Having understood and fought for power gendered in the old ways, they could not later undo the sex/gender system.

Gayle Rubin's classic paper "The Traffic in Women" is cast in quite different terms, although the profound relationship of gender and power is nevertheless explored. Here it appears in terms of "the exchange of women," which is "an acute, but condensed, apprehension of certain aspects of sex and gender" central to kinship systems, while kinship systems are "imposition[s] of social ends upon a part of the natural world" within which "men have certain rights in their female kin . . . that women do not have . . . either to themselves or to their male kin."[46]

Rubin's analysis includes the far too often overlooked, or suppressed, observation that

> gender is not only an identification with one sex; it also entails that sexual desire be directed toward the other sex. The sexual division of labor is implicated in both aspects of gender—male and female it creates them, and it creates them heterosexual. The suppression of the homosexual component of human sexuality, and by corollary, the oppression of homosexuals, is therefore a product of the same system of rules whose rules and relations oppress women.[47]

What these and other theorizations of gender give us is a way to demystify concepts, relations, and systems within which women and men are both differentiated from each other and directed to desire only each other, and men are given powers over women that women do not have over ourselves or men. Obviously, the scope of any man's power over any particular woman or group of women varies enormously according to his own placement in the articulated hierarchy. But the point holds insofar as we find some kinds of power belonging to or claimed, even fought over, by males *qua* men even as that gender power is mediated through constructions of class and race. Many a man has rebelled against class and/or racial oppression because that oppression, even when it was understood as the result of systematized racism or a particular economic system, denied him his 'rights *as a man.*' And remember that in the articulated hierarchy, gender is encoded sexually, thus linking *sex/* gender and power, and so also sexualizing racial and class power. For example, some white male southerners expressed their gut-level fear of the Abolition movement—which threatened their economic interests as those depended on enforced racial hierarchy—in starkly sexualized and gendered terms: "If you are tame enough to submit, Abolition preachers will be at hand to consummate the marriage of your daughters to black husbands."[48]

Sex/gender, race, and class can be and have been expressed in terrifyingly explicit relation as males struggle to maintain their entitlement to women as sexual possessions to be 'taken,' used, 'given away' to other men. That entitlement has often seemed to them to be *the* indication of their place, their status, their power. Not to be able to "protect your woman" was to be unmanned, and that did not mean simply that it is terrible to be unable to protect those you love. Women are not 'unwomanned' by being unable to protect men they love, or even their own children. Friends are not 'unfriended' by being unable to protect those they care about. Being in the position of protector is specific to the definition of man as it is not for those to whom it has been 'proper' to be powerless, to those whose definition does not require entitlement to power over others (as with friends). Power is not gender, and is not *only* genderized, but it is *also* profoundly genderized, and sex/gender is in multiple yet very basic senses an articulation of power.[49]

The obvious implication of all this analysis is that the gender system is unjust and dangerous. But the point of using the concept of gender to demystify, to develop new subject matters, to allow us to create rather than participate without choice in systemic 'strategies,' is not utterly to discredit all that is and has been created and expressed in gendered terms. That is not necessarily the goal, any more than the goal of comprehending race is to eliminate all that we find expressed and enacted within systems where race is an organic variable of power, culture, identity. There are qualities, experiences, values, works, systems of thought and culture that express gender, and race, and class, that we may wish to affirm, to revalue, not to dismantle.

That is, it is fully possible that within the articulated hierarchy, qualities, experiences, and strengths have been developed that are valuable to humankind. If we did not hold that to be possible, we would fall into the fallacy of holding that all that makes and has made females into women—and women into females—is bad in a way that makes all women 'bad,' and/or that all that constitutes Black culture and working-class culture is bad. And that, of course, is to view the majority of humankind only as victims in an extreme way: it is to turn us into nothing but the objects of victimization, and so to see our lives, actions, and creations as nothing but expressions of that victimization. It leaves us still with no subject status, with no identity or past or culture that we might have forged in the interstices of the dominant system and/or in defiance of it—with no sources of meaning to be re-membered and built upon in new ways. As mere objects of the patriarchy, we have nothing to offer that could counter its hegemonic meanings except mute suffering or, in Derridian terms, our utterly disruptive because unspeakable, unthinkable, non-phallic non-selves.

But while it may well be the case that it is important now to decenter by deuniversalizing man-as-subject, and/or author, and self, it is just as important to *center* as subject those who have survived subjection for so long. We have not only been acted upon; we have acted; and it is time that we claimed the authorship and authority, the selfhood and subjectivity, that we have created and can create. We need not, indeed cannot, do so in the same terms as the hegemonic culture. Those terms have been defined in contradistinction to us; we cannot just add ourselves to them, or adopt them for ourselves. But we can find our own stories and wisdom, our actions and creations, our struggles, the ways we have indeed genuinely and fully lived within and without the dominant system. We have not waited millennia for scholars to use us to disrupt systems; we have been disrupting them for ourselves all along. As we retrieve that knowledge of ourselves, we can demystify, pluralize, particularize, contextualize, historicize old faulty abstractions and generalizations in the light of, as well as in preparation for, immersion in study of our own multiple stories.

When we shift toward the quest to find ourselves in our own terms, it is helpful to view gender, race, and class as demystifying revelatory lenses focused so that we can study women, African-Americans, social and economic history—so we can study those who were excluded in an effort to let them/us tell their own story at last. Women's Studies makes use of the revelatory concept of gender in ways that allow the concept to be further critiqued and honed, and that keep us from seeing women only as victims. Women's Studies allows us, asks us, to approach the study of women in whatever ways we may need—mythically, historically, poetically, philosophically, theologically, politically, economically, culturally— so that we can contextualize our subject matter and so reveal its diversity. At the same time Women's Studies, by using concepts such as gender, race, and class, asks us to move toward an understanding of these powerful constructs that becomes ever more consciously strategic. We hold together a commitment to honor our subjects in their particularity and diversity *and* a commitment to try to act together for the sake of all. As I have suggested, it may not be universals *per se* that are to be undone but faulty universals. Universals properly understood and responsibly thought through can be inspirational, suggestive—ideas we cannot know but can think. In this and only in this sense, Woman can perhaps be reclaimed as a strategic concept, an inspirational idea even as, and because, it is renounced in its old form as Man's Other *and* its newer one as a faultily generalized abstraction derived from too few (the infamous Euro-American heterosexual, privileged woman generalized to be the inclusive term, the norm, and the ideal for all women). An idea that suggests coalition is quite different from one that enforces sameness.

⸻ In the classroom, when we work with sex/gender, race, and class as subject matters, as revelatory, meta-, and strategic concepts, we move to the foreground what has always been present but has not been admitted. We begin to see with both eyes, to see the whole where we saw only a part, to see with new eyes, to see more clearly—the phrases we use to express the change shift, but they all suggest the healing, empowering, demystifying effects we seek. Even if/as we first see ourselves as Other, Otherness is thereby transformed for and in us. The act of seeing, of comprehending, unleashes the power of being the knower in/for the known. For an object to know itself even as an object is, precisely, for 'it' to begin to experience itself also as a subject.[50]

In the act of coming to know himself as invisible, Ralph Ellison's "invisible man" ceased to live only as others defined him. He took on the freedom, and burden, of consciousness. De Lauretis writes, "Representing the conditions of existence of those subjects who are muted, elided, or unrepresentable in dominant discourse, this new understanding of the nature of identity actually opens up the possibility to 'set about creating something else to be,' as Toni Morrison writes of her two heroines in *Sula*."[51] The invocation of Morrison here reminds us, as do Ralph Ellison's earlier work and Richard Wright's *Native Son*, that becoming conscious of what has been mystified, hidden, denied, can indeed be agonizing and dangerous even as it is liberating. Few capture the pain lived by those caught in the 'triple oppression' of gender, race, and class as brilliantly as Morrison. And even fewer catch also the strength, the love, the subversive and creative wisdom, that call also to be recognized and affirmed.

It is not easy to teach with such consciousness, nor to respond to changed consciousness in students. Some traps into which it is easy to fall are those of romanticizing oppression and/or leaping from teaching in ways that hide the very existence of oppression to a kind of patronizing suppression of any serious thought about it—as some white professors say, "I would teach Black women's writings, but I'm white, so how can I?" But leaping to new extremes (very like the old in their effects) is not necessary. While it is important to take serious notice of oppression and victimization as of power and privilege, the horizon of possibilities for and the real, multivoiced story of humans precludes collapsing people into their condition. We seek finer, subtler, more complex and more inclusive ways of knowing, not crude reversals. Many have been victimized in the articulated hierarchy, but we/they are not and never have been definable only by victimization.

⸺I must confess that discussion of these points always evokes a line from *West Side Story*, delivered by a teenaged gang member who has learned very well how to deal with his social worker. As I recall, he sings defiantly but cheerfully, in a spirit that recognizes as it mocks the ways he has been explained in systems not of his own making, "I'm depraved on account of I'm deprived." Something of that spirit has been experienced by feminist scholar/teachers and our students. It will be experienced, I believe, by others who re-nounce the deadening effort of refusing to see all that has been hidden in a mystified meaning system, even when at first it seems that all we find is absence, devaluation, distortion. As the other eye opens and we begin to experience clearer vision, "every member rejoices." It has taken far too much energy to keep our eyes and minds closed; the release of that energy is enlivening, empowering in and of itself. And need I add that some of the very best humor has always emerged from those who see with both eyes wide open? It is repressed anger that is always serious. The Sphinx herself/himself always wears a slight smile.[52]

PARTIAL KNOWLEDGE

Before we move into an exploration of some occasionally rather complicated thoughts, let me say that my major point throughout is really a very simple one. The touchstone is in the observation that a part defined as the whole leaves no place for anything that differs from it. All else must, then, be squeezed into similarity with the defining part, or remain Other to it, outside it, in no-place, no-time. I remember being about ten years old and trying desperately to understand how the universe could be all there is *and* be expanding. Into what can it expand, if it is everything? I have often sensed that people coming to understand why it is that we cannot just add the majority of humankind to established knowledge are undergoing a similarly shaking realization that what has seemed like common sense is being undermined: how, after all, can the universal Man/ Mankind be expanded? Into what unthought, unimaginable space/ time can it grow?

What we must do, of course, is to rethink what we thought we knew, recognizing now that the knowledge established by the dominant tradition is indeed *partial* in both senses of the term. It makes the part the whole, and that whole is partial to the interests of those thus enshrined at the defining, controlling center. Thus, we realize also that supposedly objective, disinterested, nonpolitical knowledge not only is constructed rather than 'found,' but has often been faultily constructed.

Undoing Traditional Authority

Today, as a result of work in many fields and from several schools of thought—for example, poststructuralism, postmodernism, critical theory, deconstructionism, a reconsidered pragmatism—the male European 'Enlightenment' vision of certain knowledge that is available to and achieves its authority from reason exercised by and on behalf of Man has been put into question. There is a profound shift taking place throughout the Academy. Male thinkers as diverse as Nietzsche, Foucault, Polanyi, Kuhn, James, Pierce, Geertz, Lacan, Derrida, Rorty, Lyotard, Jameson—to mention only a few of the presently more influential nonfeminists—are called on to remind us that knowledge is not only a human construct but suggests an always deferred meaning within, and between, its own texts/discourses, its own cross-references, and that those presences are themselves playing against what is absent, denied, suppressed. In a helpful comment, Barbara Johnson, translator of Derrida's *Dissemination*, observes, "The deconstruction of a text does not proceed by random doubt or generalized scepticism, but by the careful teasing out of warring forces of signification *within the text itself*. If anything is destroyed in a deconstructive reading, it is not meaning but the claim to unequivocal domination of one mode of signifying over another."[1] 'Authoritative' readings of texts as of whole traditions are thereby not demolished but disestablished.

Through such work as well as that of feminist scholars, even the most basic assumptions about sources of authority for knowledge and modes of knowing, those long assumed rather than considered, have been (as the emergent language has it) *problematized*. And that problematizing, that undoing of traditional authority that could be called on to settle problems of meaning as of interpretation, is not, as Alice Jardine reminds us, gender-neutral. Whether we are considering constructions of knowledge in the company of nonfeminists (male or female) or feminists, gender is now an essential prism, however variously it is understood and used. Jardine writes:

> Over the past century, those master (European) narratives—history, philosophy, religion—which have determined our sense of legitimacy in the West have undergone a series of crises in legitimation. It is widely recognized that legitimacy is part of that judicial domain which, historically, has determined the right to govern, the succession of kings, the link between father and son, the necessary paternal fiction, the ability to decide who is the father—in patriarchal culture. The crises experienced by the major Western narratives have not, therefore, been gender-neutral. They are crises in the narratives invented by men.[2]

One such 'crisis' is well described by Foucault, who, questioning the notion of *author*, also puts in question root notions of *authority:*

> The coming into being of the notion of "author" constitutes the privileged moment of *individuation* in the history of ideas, knowledge, literature, philosophy, and the sciences. Even today, when we reconstruct the history of a concept, literary genre, or school of philosophy, such categories seem relatively weak, secondary, and superimposed scansions in comparison with the solid and fundamental unit of the author and the work.[3]

A great deal could be unfolded from that statement, including the reminder that even proper participants in the singular universal category, Man, were not always conceived of in the highly individuated terms so familiar to us today—*and* that those terms are so powerful now that it is exceedingly difficult to undo them. The (male) author and his work are, in fact, together seen as an expression of one of the most individualistic (and therefore also masculine) acts of all, that of making one's name through making a work that bears it (which cries out for the observation that this is male birthing, a process from which women were long excluded except as inspiration —inseminator?—in the form of the female muse). Foucault then proceeds to undo precisely that apparent solidity, that seemingly unshakable fundamentality. In place of questions about who the author is and what the author meant, Foucault moves us to ask, "What are the modes of existence of this discourse? Where has it been used, how can it circulate, and who can appropriate it for himself? What are the places in it where there is room for possible subjects? Who can assume these various subject functions? And behind all these questions, we would hear hardly anything but the stirring of an indifference: What difference does it make who is speaking?"[4]

Joining this undermining of partial traditional notions of (generic male: "his") author-ity, feminist theory can add—or, perhaps, object—that to those who have been excluded from authorship, from authority, even from being the subject-who-speaks, it does, in fact, make a great deal of difference "who is speaking." And it makes a great deal of difference that only some kinds of "works" can, within the dominant tradition, be said not just to have been written, but to have authors. As Foucault notes, "In a civilization like our own there are a certain number of discourses that are endowed with the 'author function,' while others are deprived of it. A private letter may well have a signer—it does not have an author. . . . The author function is therefore characteristic of the mode of existence, circulation, and functioning of certain discourses within a society."[5]

Precisely: who we are to 'know' as an author and what functions as a 'work' both reflect a culture's constructs *and* what are taken in a particular time and place to be meaningful and fruitful questions to ask. And these things make a difference; they express and perpetuate the exclusions we have been exploring. For example, so long as "a private letter . . . does not have an author," one of the main forms of literary expression and creation of women denied the freedom to publish remains in the category of non-"work." As Edmund Husserl and the phenomenologists have held, we know what we *intend* to know—and, I would add, what we intend to know is by no means always or primarily an individual expression or matter.

Behind such complex undoings of that which had for long seemed most obvious within the dominant culture, and perhaps especially so in the humanities (for example, that we can start from an unambiguous idea of *the author*), is a reminder that we know what *we* know, that what is known is always known by us (wherever it comes from—or, whatever its ontological status), an epistemological truism that requires no resolution of the status of that which is known. That which we know may be absolute and depend in no way whatsoever on us for its existence, or it may be nothing but a figment of the imagination. Still, for it to be "knowledge" it must be comprehended—taken in and understood—by a human mind, and human minds are formed (not determined) within a reality-framing language that is not itself private (cf. Wittgenstein).

That which is known has been that which is comprehended and accepted *as* knowledge by specific people who have achieved credibility, and so power, in particular groups. In this view, knowing is a social act deriving its legitimacy from specific historical professions (from priests to academic experts). Knowledge is a public construct in many ways: it is established as legitimate through social forms such as professions; is created and expressed in and through shared languages; reflects and perpetuates accepted modes of thought and views of reality (and challenges them in terms that must also be recognizable); forms the common stock of the culture that is carefully transmitted to rising generations; appears in forms, in kinds of works, that are already acceptable as 'authored' and as authoritative; and reflects, throughout, the basic constructs of the dominant culture, including gender.

Consider it this way: if someone 'knows' something but cannot gain the agreement of anyone else at all, the product of that 'knowing' has not been called "knowledge," and may well be suspected to be the product of madness (even if perhaps inspired madness). Similarly, if a nonlegitimatized group 'knows' something and makes claims for its general validity, what is 'known' is easily written off as prejudice, sectarianism, 'merely' experiential, biased, or 'ignorant' by the legitimate authorities (Women's Studies initially encountered just such reactions). In the dominant tradition today, insofar as something is thought in the mode of knowledge, it partakes of the human mind, is communicable (language is of it as well as expressing it in a way that is available to others), *and* is cast in a form accepted as 'proper' by relevant others who have met recognizable tests of legitimacy (such as earning a Ph.D., holding a high office, publishing a well-reviewed book).

Behind any particular body of accepted knowledge are the definitions, the boundaries, established by those who have held power. To disagree with those boundaries and definitions, it has been necessary to recognize them; to refuse them is to be shut out even from debate; to transgress them is to mark oneself as mad, heretical, dangerous. The assumptions and the form of a position mark it as admissible or inadmissible to the discourses of knowledge. So, too, does the kind of person (a person whose 'kind' has been pre-established by the culture) affect whether what is said or written is listened to as knowledge or not. The insights of a mad person, the utterances of a god-possessed saint, the "intuitions" of a woman,[6] the "hunches" of "the common man," the "myths" of non-Western cultures, the "folklore" of lower-caste people, the expressions of women that were written but not "authored"—none of these have been acceptable as expressions or examples of knowledge. Nor have they been considered as proper subjects/objects for knowledge unless they have had recorded impact on the dominant culture in ways defined within that culture as significant. The 'voices' of Joan of Arc have been studied; the voices of most women of her times have not.

There is in these exclusions not only the necessary delimitation of definition, the necessary marking of boundaries and noting of patterns of relation that allow us to recognize things, categories, kinds, but also evidence of the familiar error of circularity. It is circular reasoning when what has been accepted as knowledge is considered as definitional of or essential to knowledge-itself, a move that disguises partiality as impartiality. For example, "women's work" has been excluded along with works by women, along with women. And, having been stopped at the gates of the dominant tradition and the curricula that preserve and continue it, these subjects have continued to be excluded because, as we noted much earlier, they have not seemed to *fit* when judged by partial standards not admitted to be such. The construction of knowledge has thereby lost not only whole realms of subject matter but modes of thought and populations of people whose knowledge was not 'the same' as the defining, ordering kind.

As Foucault puts it, writing about his study of the human sciences and particularly of 'madness':

> I am concerned . . . with a history of resemblance: on what conditions was Classical thought able to reflect relations of similarity or equivalence between things, relations that would provide a foundation and a justification for their words, their classifications, their systems of exchange? . . . The history of madness would be the history of the Other—of that which, for a given culture, is at once interior and foreign, therefore to be excluded (so as to exorcize the interior danger) but by being shut away (in order to reduce its otherness); whereas the history of the order imposed on things would be the history of the Same.[7]

What Foucault says of madness applies, with frighteningly little alteration, to the study of women, and/or of male lower-caste and/ or 'primitive' people; to find us in the dominant constructions of knowledge is to find the Other, excluded, exorcized, shut away from the "history of the Same" that was written out of the root problem of taking the few to be the inclusive term, the norm, the ideal. To focus on us in our diversity is, precisely, to undo traditional authority. That is why so many contemporary nonfeminists like to invoke the feminine, or Woman: we are useful to them precisely because we have been included only as excluded, as Other.

Writing about literary traditions, Henry Louis Gates, Jr., gives a description of what a tradition is that suggests at the same time how these culturally prolonged conversations not only rest on what has already been included but also and by the same means exclude:

> Literary works configure into a tradition not because of some mystical collective unconscious determined by the biology of race or gender [or necessarily *purposeful* perpetuation of race and gender-exclusive definitions] but because [published] writers read other writers and ground their representations of experience in models of language provided largely by other writers *to whom they feel akin*. It is through this mode of literary revision, amply evident in the texts themselves—in formal echoes, recast metaphors, even in parody—that a "tradition" emerges and defines itself. This is formal bonding, *and it is only through formal bonding that we can know a literary tradition*. (Emphasis added.)[8]

Using the notion of informed traditions as continuingly self-referential conversations operating within texts, Frederic Jameson describes his method so that we can see literary criticism constituting a similarly configured tradition. Jameson tells us that his approach

> turns on the dynamics of the act of interpretation and presupposes, as its organizational fiction, that we never really confront a text immediately, in all its freshness as a thing-in-itself. Rather, texts come before us as the always-already-read; we apprehend them through the sedimented layers of previous interpretations, or—if the text is brand-new—through the sedimented reading habits and categories developed by those inherited interpretive traditions. This presupposition then dictates the use of a method . . . according to which our object of study is less the text itself than the interpretations through which we attempt to appropriate it.[9]

Such a method, extended to suggest an approach to what has been presented as knowledge through being taught in our curricula, can indeed keep us from falsely universalizing, or essentializing. It reminds us that what we know, what we have learned and what we teach, does not appear before us uninformed by human intentions, interpretations, meanings. We are then in a position to approach the "always-already-read" as it reveals *who* did the reading in conversation with whom—and whom those conversations first excluded and then could not include except as exclusions, negativities—Others. The work of the nonfeminist scholars I have cited is in part an effort to help us learn to excavate the strata of traditions of many sorts that have constituted, among other cultural artifacts, knowledge, revealing complex discourses that include by excluding, exclude by the ways they include. These are efforts that join feminist efforts in helping us see how meanings have been established and maintained. From these perspectives, we can see power at work without having to look for any singular, purposeful intent either to include or to exclude. Such an intent may be present or absent: the point is not that it does not matter, but that it is not necessary.

But all this intriguing and effective work is not adequate without full consideration of feminist critiques as well. Gayatri Spivak, agreeing with the need to give up forms of knowing that claim suprahuman, falsely universalized, 'neutral,' scientific status, suggests a feminist disruption of "public rigor" through the telling of ("private") stories.

> The fiction of mainstream literary criticism—so generally "masculist" that the adjective begins to lose all meaning . . .—is that rigorous readings come into being in a scientific field, or in the field of legalistic demonstration of validity. The other view, coming from a mind-set that has been systematically marginalized, may just as well be called "feminist": that the production of public rigor bears the strategically repressed marks of the so-called "private" at all levels. . . . This is especially the case with feminist alternative readings of the canon that will not find their comfort in citing the demonstrable precedents of scientific specialism. Women must tell each other's stories, not because they are simpleminded creatures, but because they must call into question the model of criticism as a neutral theorem or science.[10]

In different language and with a slightly different emphasis: to end our exclusion, women must undo not only self-justifyingly exclusive traditions of knowledge and modes of knowing that masquerade as neutral and "scientific," but also the newer discourses that are internally configured and "always-already-read"—*but not by us.* We must undo the false universalization that has excluded us, and refuse even its critics and our allies when they leave us out even as they make use of us. That is, *feminist criticism and scholarship, women's voices and traditions, do not constitute just another perspective, one among many that are now more readily recognized because hegemonic meaning and authority systems are being disestablished.* There are many of us and we differ in important ways, on the one hand, and, on the other, we cannot be adequately fitted into any categories, perspectives, modes of knowing, or discourses that are uncovered or created without our full participation. To use us as the Others of the dominant tradition that is to be undone is, once again, to use us.

And that realization takes us back to the necessity of critiquing *all* claims of authority *and* all attacks on it, including those that have so quickly (and so perhaps suspiciously) become very powerful indeed inside the Academy. A palace coup is not the same as a revolution, and we know very well from history that women have been very useful to the men engaged in both, only to wake up the morning after to find ourselves once again excluded.[11]

Objective Knowledge

"Feminist theories," Jane Flax has written,

> should encourage us to tolerate and interpret ambivalence, ambiguity, and multiplicity as well as to expose the roots of our needs for imposing order and structure no matter how arbitrary and oppressive these needs may be. If we do our work well, "reality" will appear even more unstable, complex, and disorderly than it does now. In this sense, perhaps Freud was right when he declared that women are the enemies of civilization.[12]

When the Others—and by no means only women, among whom there have always been some who participated in the work of maintaining patriarchal structures—break into the dominant tradition *and* into the camps of its critics, controlling limits necessarily fall, and insofar as those limits have defined the dominant discourses constitutive of 'civilization,' of 'rationality,' of 'knowledge,' it will—and does—feel like what best-selling author Allan Bloom has called "an unprecedented assault on reason." Revealed in such strong language is a level of identification with, and need for, the old limits that has suggested to many feminist scholars the need for a psychological interpretation of the structuring and functioning of that which is established as knowledge in a patriarchal society. In particular, many feminists have taken on the question of what 'objective' knowledge not only is but reveals or expresses. Miller, Chodorow, Harding, Rubin, Belenky and her colleagues, the Hintikkas, Dinnerstein, and others develop a connection between the notion of objectivity and a male epistemology and logic that reflect the formation of male psyches in a boy's 'need' to differentiate himself from his care-taking mother, to individuate by becoming vehemently not-female. Flax also observes that "because historically women have been the caretakers as well as the bearers of children, they represent both the body and our first encounter with the sometimes terrifying, sometimes gratifying vicissitudes of social relations. They become the embodiments of the unconscious, just as men become the embodiment of reason and law (the ego and the superego)."[13]

A passionate—and by no means calmly objective—defense of the privileged position of 'objective' knowledge can express, then, the workings of the articulated hierarchy in the production, character, and validation of knowledge on a deep non- or pre-rational level of consciousness. A self individuated through a process of radical separation from origins, care-takers, and contexts is very likely to need (rather than choose) to project such separation into and onto constructs such as knowledge so that it can feel safe. The objective then appears as that with which the masculine subject needs to identify to maintain a hard-won individuation. Again, Woman appears as essential to Man in her absence, her difference, her Otherness. She is what he is not; he is capable of objectivity, she is 'mere' subjectivity. He is separated, differentiated, individuated; she is in-relation-to him, an Othered shadow dimension of his achieved masculine separateness.

The root error of partiality claiming wholeness is here seen as originating on a deep psychodynamic level; according to this analysis, that is what gives particular force and passion to familiar defenses of the dominant definitions of knowledge as objective and reason as dispassionate, disengaged, disinterested. Remember Kant's and Jefferson's as well as Bloom's reactions to expressions of reason that seemed to them alien to this notion of reasoned knowledge. Their reactions were hardly disengaged, dispassionate, disinterested. Order, personal and social and political and epistemological and moral, seemed to them to be threatened by a thinking African or Arab man, as it has seemed threatened by Woman. Those onto whom is projected all that is denied and repressed threaten order-as-control, or mastery, or rule, as soon as they appear in the foreground and speak in their own rather than their masters' voices. Robert Coles and others have suggested similar dynamics with regard to some white southerners' projections of taboos, fears, desires onto Black people.[14]

In philosophical rather than psychological language, Hegel has interesting things to say about the dialectical relation of 'subject' and 'object.' In his work we see a powerfully telling analysis of the problem of an as-yet-unhealed partial self that craves that from which it has nevertheless separated itself. As Hegel scholar Elliot Jurist writes: "Insofar as one removes oneself from the realm of interpersonal and social interaction, one's life is impoverished. Not only does one suffer from such isolation, but self-knowledge becomes impossible to achieve.[15]

Claims that knowledge, which not only includes but entails self-knowledge, ought to be solely or 'purely' objective betray what Hegel calls an "unhappy consciousness" in which the self is divided, alienated from itself in a radical fashion. That alienation is found in, created by, expressed through modes of knowing *and* of relating to other people. We need to bring together "being for itself" and "being for another" through *recognition*, a moment of healing mutual interdependence that transcends the splitting of known from knower. Such recognition, the goal of the dialectical process of development of the self as of human history, is possible only between people who are equals. In the development of knowledge, it is possible only when that which has been held to be utterly separate from the knower is re-cognized as an expression of the same reason that is doing the knowing. Difference is maintained, but oppositional, hierarchical division is undone.

It is worth noting that Hegel's work, "stood on its head" so that not Reason (or Spirit—*Geist*) but material conditions move development toward equality, informs not only Marx's thinking but that of Sartre, Fanon, and de Beauvoir. When we move to the level of epistemology to carry out our critique of exclusive traditions of knowing, we continue to find ways in which we can use those traditions on themselves. Neither Hegel, nor Marx, nor Sartre developed epistemologies or political philosophies that allow us to think fully and adequately about women. They either took no account of gender in any of its meanings or reflect the gender hierarchy of their times. But de Beauvoir thought with them and went on to write *The Second Sex*, to give us, in particular, the invaluable notion of the Other thought through as it implicates and is implicated by gender.

Similarly, Freud can easily be seen as downright dangerous to women, yet there is the work of Juliette Mitchell, Nancy Chodorow, and some of the French feminists working along Lacanian lines to suggest that this system of thought and practice can yield to feminist critique and gender analysis and then, re-formed, be suggestive and illuminating.

In a different way the philosopher Susanne Langer, in her monumental *Mind: An Essay on Human Feeling*, puts feeling at the center of her consideration of mind and from that perspective has some startlingly subversive things to say about objectivity (having started with feeling, she could hardly have been other than subversive, of course). She does not draw on psychoanalytic or Hegelian or existentialist positions, or on gender analysis. But what she says joins this conversation. Her thinking is so rich that a rather long quotation is necessary:

> Logical conviction is such a pin-pointed feeling that it has, in itself, none of the widespread and involved character of emotion; it seems the very opposite of emotion, although all sorts of highly cathected ideas may gather around it, and make it a tiny firm center in a maelstrom of fantasies. . . . And, furthermore, it leads to the peculiar social circumstance that it is relatively easy to confront different individuals with the same challenge to feeling [of logical conviction arising from following the operations of that particular set of rules], unimpaired by the usual modifications due to personal context. This makes for a unanimity in logical convictions that has few if any parallels in the realm of human feeling, and gives to logical perception an air of "objectivity." . . . But there is much more to rational thinking than the highly general form which may be projected in written symbols or in the functional design of a machine. Thinking employs almost every intuitive process, semantic and formal (logical), and passes from insight to insight not only by the recognized processes, but as often as not by short cuts and personal, incommunicable means.[16]

Knowledge has been established as objective when it comes closest to *forcing* unanimity. Because we differ so much, because reality is always more than we, and changes, those who would *know* something have, it seems, retreated ever further from us and from reality. By establishing highly specified abstract definitions and tightly systematized relations and functions and rules, those who created some areas of knowledge provided for themselves and those who followed them the opportunity of achieving Langer's *feeling* of certainty in the midst of the usual "maelstrom" of emotion—and, we can add, of differing social realities and political views. Yet these modes of knowing have come to stand at the pinnacle of what is considered 'real,' 'sound,' 'hard' knowledge— and those who work within them are widely considered to be the most brilliant as well as the most disinterested of all. Sadly, and wrongly, very few today would consider a superb teacher of preschool children to be on the intellectual level of a logician or mathematician. Knowledge that arises from the ability to work with individuals, with change, with emotion, with the full range of modes of thinking, is devalued as 'subjective.' Knowledge that arises from the ability to move skillfully within tightly defined, timeless, spaceless, entirely abstract systems that are self-enclosed is highly valued as 'objective.'

Need we note that such a view of what is the 'highest' knowledge, which the most brilliant intellect, is fundamentally gendered and—not surprisingly, since gender is perhaps *the* signifier of power—is also dangerously akin to a craving for absolute domination, beneath which all is forced either into the unanimity of agreement or into the silent defeat of being wrong? The dominant tradition has many other modes of knowing, of course, including the poetic. But the hierarchy of modes of knowing, and of knowers and subject matters, reflects the errors of the invidious monism we discussed earlier. Masculine 'hard' science reigns supreme over a hierarchy that slides downward to the 'soft' knowing of nonquantifiable fields, approaching near bottom with the 'intuition' of women and the 'instincts' of "primitive" people.

The error of circular reasoning is then unavoidable. As Sandra Harding puts it:

> To repeat the metaphor I borrowed earlier from behaviorism, science functions primarily as a "black box": whatever the moral and political values and interests responsible for selecting problems, theories, methods, and interpretations of research, they reappear at the other end of inquiry as the moral and political universe that science projects as natural and thereby helps to legitimate. In this respect, science is no different from the proverbial description of computers: "junk in, junk out."[17]

As we noted in the beginning, the old errors do indeed create tangles, traps, closed and exclusive traditions. But that does not mean that we must either remain within those entrapping circles or create different epistemologies *de novo*. It is not an either–or situation. We are in many different ways, through many different conversations, struggling toward finer, more subtle, and more complex ways of thinking. Some of those ways are emerging from critical, reflexive conversation with established systems of thought. Others are developing from immersion in traditions, modes of thinking and knowing and acting, that were not seriously or respectfully thought about before by those in power. There is no need to force any kind of choice between these approaches; we are precisely *not* in pursuit of a single epistemology, a single philosophy, a single ideology. We are trying simultaneously to open space for new thinking and modes of knowing; for heretofore suppressed voices to speak and be well heard in ways that may express and/or call for the creation of different epistemologies; for critique and reformulation of thought that has been entangled in unnecessary yet profound errors.

Epistemology and Power

The old errors and exclusions and hierarchies are by no means 'only' conceptual; they reveal and perpetuate the articulated hierarchy in intrapsychic, educational, social, historical, and political relations that have very serious consequences indeed. Power is involved in many ways in the construction of knowledge, which is a specific practice that differs among, as it is controlled by, professions. Such differences, however, tend to follow lines with which we are now familiar. Hannah Arendt observed about scientists:

> It certainly is not without irony that those whom public opinion has persistently held to be the least practical and the least political members of society should have turned out to be the only ones left who still know how to act and how to act in concert. For their early organizations, which they founded in the seventeenth century for the *conquest of nature* and in which they developed their own moral standards and their own code of honor, have not only survived all vicissitudes of the modern age, but they have become one of the most potent power-generating groups in all history. (Emphasis added—note the ease with which bellicose notions of scientific reason emerge.)[18]

Why do we keep rediscovering that it is very often precisely that which is "held to be the . . . least political" that functions as the most political? There is no more powerful position than that which dominates while appearing not to, no more influential position than that which sets the standards for and informs cultural meanings and their expression as knowledge. Even Plato, who certainly believed that what we come to know is absolute and unchanging *and* that it is in our souls to be found (rather than being of our own creation), also knew that the state, as he put it in *The Republic,* is the greatest sophist—the most influential teacher—of all. He knew very well that it is what is accepted by the denizens of the cave that functions as knowledge. He did not like that, but he knew that it would be changed only by a complete change of the state to one that gave power to those who had the kind of knowledge in which he believed. That is, he knew that knowledge claimed as such by those who have only the warrant of their own thoughtful experience is not received as knowledge in the world, even if it is 'real' knowledge (of the sort he thought a true philosopher has).

"Knowledge is power" is perhaps a truer statement than we often realize; like many clichés, this one may have persisted because it expresses something common sense stubbornly grasps despite mystifications. In any case, like power, knowledge depends on the agreement of a significant group of people and establishes itself more firmly as their organization grows. And when that organization is of professionals whose knowledge is itself high in the hierarchy, power takes on the further mantle of authority. In such organizations, it is not at all surprising that the articulated hierarchy of 'kinds' of people is also replicated. All you need do here is picture a room full of elementary school teachers, and another full of professors of physics. Which group is composed of representatives of the top of the gender/race hierarchy? And yet we are supposed to believe that science is of all fields the most disinterested, neutral, nonpolitical. Of course it seems that way; it so fits the dominant system that it isn't even seen as systemic. Those who are taken to be the inclusive term, the norm, and the ideal for all come also, and devastatingly, to seem the most *real*.

Feminist scholarship, in pointing out the social, historical, and political construction of what is taught as knowledge, is doing nothing new or exceedingly peculiar at the same time it is indeed doing something radical and necessary. Feminist scholarship emerges time and again in opposition not to the quest for knowledge, but to its persistent inability to achieve what it claims for itself because of persistent errors that cannot be overcome without feminist critique. In a sense, feminist scholars are like Civil Rights activists who call

the dominant tradition on its own best principles *as if* those principles were not tangled and self-contradictory: if "all men are created
equal," and "men" is inclusive, then *we* are created equal, and you
are, of course, in favor of our full inclusion. If the pursuit of knowledge is to be disinterested, nonpolitical, then it cannot mean to
exclude us, so you will, of course, welcome Women's Studies,
Multicultural Studies, and the other marginalized 'special' studies
into the center of learning.

But we need also to remember something that is both obvious
and stubbornly elusive. We cannot *simply* be included, because the
part has defined itself as the whole, because the hierarchy is so
firmly entrenched, because power is indeed at stake. It has been
and remains the task of *feminist* scholars and activists to transform
knowledge and that which it reflects and perpetuates, not because
the task could not be taken on by non-feminists, but because it has
not been. Persistently we rediscover differences in our thought-
projects that correspond to our different 'places' in the world in
relation to power. In the Academy as elsewhere, feminists can
indeed find allies, but allies cannot be counted on to maintain the
constant effort of critique, of reformulation, of creation, necessary
to the radical undoing of the old power-conferring and -protecting
errors. At the same time, feminists require allies from among those
whose work may not focus on gender but does center on class, race,
ethnicity, relation to colonialism. Such alliances do not remove the
need for an adequate feminist analysis, one that does not fall back
into the old errors by taking Euro-American heterosexual middle-
class women to be the inclusive kind, the norm, and the ideal for all
women. Quite the contrary: such work must be done to make it
possible for alliances to be formed. Women excluded from a mystified, faultily generalized Woman cannot be added on after the fact,
any more than women can be added to Man. But it is important also
to attempt coalition among all those excluded. We need to know
each other as best we can, to live with and learn from our tensions
as well as our commonalities. The critiques we make of the dominant tradition are stunningly similar, and where they differ, they
extend, correct, and enrich each other.

At the center of work to transform knowledge ought to be all of
those who have been on the margins; we have been excluded by the
same error-ridden systems in ways that have made us appear to be
'minorities' while the defining group at the center, which *is* a minority, has appeared to be all there is, all that is real, all that matters.

Look around the margins of the contemporary university and you will find courageous, creative scholar/teachers and students who are taking on the central questions of our age—in Women's Studies, African-American Studies, Multicultural Studies, Peace Studies, Nuclear Studies, Environmental/Ecological Studies. The critiques that these fields have had to make to think themselves into being are remarkably similar, and the work they have developed differs and overlaps in fascinating ways.

Scientists are not the only people whose power has been and can be increased through organization. The test for us is whether we can come together without the old objectivist insistence on the suppression of subjectivity, difference, the "maelstrom" of feelings, in favor of an unreal unanimity. What matters now is that we prove ourselves able to enjoy and learn from our differences as well as from our agreement in critique and in the moral/political concerns that made these new fields necessary in the first place.

The Personal

The political and the conceptual are profoundly related to the personal. Passionate scholarship that is inspired neither by a desire to dominate, to control, to possess certainty, nor by external rewards emerges from people who are pursuing their own questions. We know that on the level of myth—there are many works on "the journey"—although it has been denied on the level of knowledge.[19] But it is there to be relearned in the unavoidable observation that feminist scholarship is the creation of women (some of whom prefer not to use the term "feminist" in favor of Women's Studies, Black Women's Studies, Alice Walker's suggested term, "Womanist" Studies, or some other indicator), as African-American scholarship is the creation of African-Americans, as Deaf Studies is the creation of deaf people and those whose lives have been profoundly touched by someone who is deaf. Perhaps no one can take our journey for us; that is certainly the message of myth.

Furthermore, the prize of knowing brought back by people who have been passionately engaged in their own quest is first and most eagerly recognized by others whose experiences have been similar to those of the seeker. But such knowledge is not thereby proven inaccessible to others. Paradigm shifts (to use the Kuhnian notion) may be repudiated by the established order at first, but when they make it possible to account for more phenomena better, they are indeed comprehensible, at least to those who are not locked into a posture of defense of knowledge-as-established, knowledge-as-taught. If the journey has to be taken by those who feel the call as a deeply personal one, and if at first only those who are akin to the journey-makers welcome what they bring back, still the rest can *if they will* participate in wisdom so hardly achieved. Teaching rests on that faith, that commitment; we differ profoundly, we have profoundly different stakes in learning and in what is available to be learned, but we can approach, at least, comprehension even of that which appears to be utterly outside our own private experience. Translation is never perfect, but it is possible, and the effort to achieve it rewards us not by giving us an exact copy (which would be of little real interest, after all), but by expanding our boundaries. Good teachers of any kind are not restricted to teaching themselves or their own culture; they are, preeminently, creative translators.

Maurice Merleau-Ponty, considering the possibility of cross-cultural understanding, wrote:

> It is a way of thinking, the way *which imposes itself* when the object is 'different,' and requires us to transform ourselves. [When we] let ourselves be taught by another culture . . . a new organ of understanding is at our disposal—we have regained possession of that untamed region of ourselves, unincorporated in our culture, through which we communicate with other cultures.[20]

Starting instead from 'home,' proponents of "standpoint epistemology" and "identity politics" belong here, too, as extensions of "the personal is political" to the conceptual. Such personal/political epistemologies, and epistemological politics, raise questions about and suggest alternatives to the dominant mystified, partial systems of knowledge by claiming fully what was once labeled 'merely' subjective. The 'private,' the 'subjective,' the 'biased' stance of the knower who not only rejects the quest for some universal standpoint but positively affirms a particular one, is a real challenge to hegemonic systems. By insisting on a political, historically located positional self, we reground knowing in the real world, where we are indeed different and things can and do change.

When one is committed to knowing as a particular person, one can, of course, slide into a kind of radical privatism, but that is by no means necessary. We can speak honestly of and from ourselves in ways that challenge *and* permit others to understand us. And although there is always a risk that one who seeks some kind of privileged 'free zone' from the dominant culture in personal/political experience may unknowingly perpetuate that culture, so deeply is it in us, that, too, is not necessary. As I said earlier, we are neither trapped nor free; we are always in interaction with our culture, our times, our realities, and we are always able to think about as well as within them.

It occurs to me here that Alcoholics Anonymous suggests something of the power of speech from and about who and what we are, even when that speech is utterly uninformed by political or historical or any other kind of analysis. In AA, as I understand it, people tell their own stories. Simply by doing so, they begin the process of change. Feminist work that seeks to ground knowledge in particular experience, claimed as such, has become much more sophisticated than the earlier discovery of consciousness-raising groups that the personal is political, and that speaking it helps free us. But it is worth remembering, when we become embroiled in complex epistemological and political analysis, that there is something very powerful in the direct, nontheoretical turn to speaking oneself with others who really listen.

We do not reduce, or elevate, ourselves to being representatives of our 'kind' when we speak of, from, and for that kind, if only because by speaking we shatter the silence that has been prescribed. To seek knowledge as who and what we are, even when the 'what' has been imposed on us by an oppressive system, can enliven our ability to think reflexively, to free even as we express ourselves. It is empowering to claim the self that one was taught to hate, to explore its strengths, its resistances, its originality, its suffering, its personal and collective history as that story looks from the standpoint of those who lived it. "Black is beautiful" is not just a statement of defiant opposition to white racism; it is a statement of genuine discovery, of a moment of transforming knowledge. It reflects a move outside the standpoint of the dominant few, a step out from behind the veil, as W. E. B. DuBois put it.

We are each, after all, not only a mysterious and elusive and unique 'who' that cannot be known as an object at all (although we are also that); we are people who live in the real world, where what we are matters. We have been labeled, categorized, branded, but we have always also been much more than our labels. Chandra Mohanty, who is suspicious of women speaking *as* women (of assuming that the female is a direct line to the feminist), writes nevertheless of the power of claiming our *multiple* identities:

In this country, I am, for instance, subject to a number of legal/ political definitions: "third-world," "immigrant," "post-colonial." These definitions, while in no way comprehensive, do trace an analytic and political space from which I can insist on a temporality of struggle. Movement *between* cultures, languages, and complex configurations of meaning and power has always been the territory of the colonized. . . . The struggles I choose to engage in are then an intensification of these modes of knowing. . . . There is, quite simply, no transcendental location possible in the U.S.A. of the 1980's.[21]

The Threat of Relativism?

Obviously, I do not share the fear that recognizing the profoundly personal in the quest for knowledge leads us ineluctably to the slippery slope of relativism. To put it most simply, the questioning and particularizing of previously mystified absolutes need not catapult us into a radical relativism. What it does do is open up space for the renewal, discovery, creation of ways of thinking that are compatible with diversity, plurality, particularity, change—and relationality. People and things need not be viewed as encapsulated monads suddenly released by destruction of the dominant, ordering Absolute to whirl madly in a void. Instead, we can shift our attention from static vertical ordering of independent entities beneath an *arché* of universals to *relations* we are then free to see between interdependent, changing entity-moments, between things and people and events and systems that are more organically than mechanistically related.[22]

We then see 'order' as patterns within rather than rules imposed from without; matrices rather than rigidly demarcated typologies. As in ecology, we can see what we focus on as "nested" within a more or less supportive system on which it depends, and which depends on it, an intriguing alternative to rigidly schematic knowledge in which *transactional* relations cannot be thought. We become open to serious consideration of narratives as well as, and sometimes perhaps instead of, deductive arguments, to exploration of an ethics of care as well as an ethics of rights.[23] In political terms, we can admire and/or create epistemologies, logics, ethics, and whole philosophies that do not undermine democracy, however inadvertently, but support and strengthen it by their recognition of plurality and necessary relationality.[24] In all such moves, such changes in the ways we construe and construct knowledge, we are recognizing that knowledge matters, that it has effects, and that it does so not only insofar as it may be applied to the world but also in how it teaches us that the world is put together. Epistemology, in other words, is profoundly personal and political. Those who believe that the only alternative to the Old Order is radical, chaotic, and hence finally paralyzing relativism reveal thereby the degree to which they are still seeing from the perspective of the few who have been taken to be the whole. The rest of us know very well that there are many ways of making distinctions, of understanding differences, that are neither locked into the old scale of descending worth nor reduced to the entirely individualistic, the private, the relative.

I am reminded here of students with whom I have worked in courses on political philosophy and ethics. Over and over I have found them retreating to a position of relativism when they fear that there is about to be conflict over moral positions. They say, "Well, that's your opinion," and "It's just a matter of semantics," or "I guess it's just how I was socialized." I have come to believe that such retreats from discussion of moral differences are 'caused' not by the relativism with which students are so often charged, but by moral absolutism. The dominant tradition has not helped young people learn how to converse together about the most important values they hold; it has taught them that those values must be absolutely right or they are not values at all. So, when students encounter serious differences, they are startled, troubled, frightened. And rather than fight with their friends over who is absolutely right, they prefer to say, in effect, I hold my absolute values, you hold yours. *Both* absolutism *and* radical relativism make it possible, even necessary, to avoid serious engagement with differences. Thus, if we want people to cease being absolutists *or* relativists, we need to open to them the challenge of exploring a rich complexity of differences understood from the beginning as being in transactional relation to each other. We will not get past the problem of relativism by retreating to the good old established certainties; when we do that, we simply ensure that those who want to get along with people who are not already just like them will have nowhere to go but relativism.

Continuing Resistance to Transformation

Since these are clearly values and goals shared by many non-feminists as well as feminists, why the persistent, widespread discomfort-unto-anger we find when questions are raised about the curriculum? What is so disturbing about the claims of feminist scholars that the knowledge passed on should be examined with a radical doubt before it is accepted as genuinely inclusive of, and having the same significance for, all? The Cartesian move to adopt a radical doubt is familiar, after all, and more than one faculty member prides him/herself on helping students achieve a more critical stance toward inherited meanings and established knowledge. Why the profound discomfort when it is suggested that the curriculum perpetuates basic conceptual errors resulting from a partial tradition that claims to be universal? Does anyone really believe that the purposeful exclusion of women, as of nonprivileged men, as of whole cultures labeled "primitive," left no significant traces? Could such exclusionary thinking, which until recently was not in the least abashed, have proceeded *without* creating tangles that perpetuate the original exclusions even when the will to do so is less widespread? That would be rather like concluding that a structural error in the foundation of a building has disappeared because we have learned how to build the top floor differently.

Yet resistance persists, and not only among those whose prejudices block their thinking, who feel their power and privilege threatened, or who fear the implications of the new scholarship for their 'private' life. (More than one man in faculty development groups I have run has sat silent through discussion of the intellectual and ethical reasons for making changes in courses only to burst out suddenly with some only apparently irrelevant cry such as— and I quote one of them—"But my wife *likes* doing the dishes!") Resistance occurs also among those who are or have been a great deal more open, and one reason is, I believe, that the more critical we are of the dominant tradition, the more sophisticated we become in critiquing and redoing it, the more it seems we are undertaking a Sisyphean task.

Some early feminist thinkers carried on a heroic struggle personally, politically, intellectually to become able to think about women by insisting on thinking for themselves *as* women, only to be accused of having carried their white, middle-class, heterosexual privilege into the defining center of a new scholarship and politics that was itself exclusive.[25] Some Black feminists courageously turned to thinking about their experiences as Black women, only to find themselves accused of betraying racial politics that seemed to require them to stand in unbreached solidarity with Black men.[26] The rock rolls up the hill, and then it rolls back down, by no means without damage to those who were brave enough to try to move it at all.

And then, compounding the problem, feminist critique and scholarship persist in reminding even their apparent allies that feminism is not just one of the new 'isms,' a helpful partner that can be brought in to help them roll *their* rock up the hill. No: it criticizes even those who think they share a similar, if separately conceived, task. Thus, feminist scholarship seems more demanding, more troubling, more risky, more irritating, than many other schools of thought that have not only found homes in the Academy but even seem to be on the verge of taking it over.

We continue to hear what we have been hearing since the new scholarship on women began to emerge and claim its place in the Academy. It may be worth returning for a moment to that time when the reasons given, and revealed, for resisting feminist scholarship were more direct than they sometimes are now. I do not believe the reasons have changed; they are just masked in more sophisticated language and theory.

When we started trying to add the missing majority of humankind to the curriculum, we encountered the curious notion that knowledge is somehow utterly separate from human life and history and purposes, a notion relatively few would have affirmed even then if questioned about it directly. A Platonic view of knowledge, which I have found behind remarkably diverse positions, is rarely intended, let alone claimed. Yet I have found over the years that faculty members, wanting to continue teaching what they were themselves taught or believe they know, slide into the belief that what they teach *is* the subject matter of their field. That is, they did not then (when I first started this work), nor do they often now, want to think that they teach a particular construction of history; they want to be teaching history-itself, philosophy-itself, literature-itself. Again, few would claim that position. They know perfectly well that there are many views on and versions of history (or whatever). But another, more stubborn belief reveals itself when their courses are challenged. Then, works and authors and modes of thought and creativity, and forms of life and of meaning, that are not already recognized by their professional colleagues are dismissed as not belonging in their courses—because that "isn't history."

"That's not literature," I have been told. "You're raising sociological questions"—that is, a question about why and how literature-as-taught excludes or distorts a view of women is *not* taken to be a question about literature, but about societally defined behavior having to do with women. "That's not philosophy; that's anthropology"—that is, exploration of the search for meaning among people other than the particular male philosophers who are taught is exploration not of wisdom but of 'culture,' and 'exotic' culture at that.

Regularly, when I and others raise the question of including women, we are charged with wanting to turn an extant field into something else. To teach about the history, politics, economics, and profound effects of science is, science teachers have told me, fine—but, "It isn't real science." The prevailing definition of the field is used in circular fashion to justify its own perpetuation. The particular view of what science (or literature, or psychology) *is* is taken to encompass the whole of the subject matter. There is, then, no place for subject matter or approaches that are not very much the same as the already-included material to go, except, teachers tell me helpfully, into someone else's field. The newcomers, like Alice at the tea party, are shuffled cheerfully around the table to someone else's seat. And the unacknowledged but shaping assumption that knowledge about a professionalized academic field is knowledge about its *subject matter* is perpetuated. A partial, particular view retains its seat in the chair of the field-itself.

But the field of history is actually about interpretations of a particular past based on particular preserved evidence that itself reflects the choices of those in a position to make them as to what deserves recording and preserving and in what form it should be recorded. Religious Studies is about what has been taken to be 'real,' 'significant' religion, and then about how its theorists and practitioners have themselves construed what is important, the records they have kept, the practices they have chosen to continue. Disciplinary knowledge concerns subjects as they have been historically expressed and then as they have been shaped through the theories and methods—and professional development—of the fields. Again, in a very complex sense, "knowledge is power." A scholar in Religious Studies, wishing to know how some actual people express and experience what they themselves consider religious, teams up with an ethnographer and goes into the field to find out. S/he then runs the risk of confounding colleagues: is that what a scholar of religion does, or is it what an anthropologist does? In which department should a course based on that approach be placed? One who steps across the boundaries of professional fields becomes an anomaly and is likely to be viewed as a poacher and perhaps even a traitor. Discipline-based fields, like all professions, patrol their boundaries fiercely.

Again we encounter the errors of faulty generalization and circularity: religion is what Religious Studies teachers teach, and Religious Studies is defined in terms of a list of texts, of issues, of thinkers, not in terms of direct approach to a phenomenon of human life and activity. Bounded disciplines, established for various reasons, take on the status of real, essential, categories. And circular arguments are adduced to protect the centrality of the partial knowledge that defines the field.

But the knowledge that is taught in our curricula can be and often has been changed, as have the disciplines themselves. At any point in its history in any field (more in some, less in others, but always to some extent), any accepted field is ambivalent, ambiguous, and often downright contradictory when all that it includes is considered. One cannot simultaneously be an existentialist, and a logical positivist, and a Marxist, and a Platonist, and an ordinary language philosopher. It is even exceedingly difficult to try to draw on and use aspects of several such schools; they arise from, draw on, and to varying degrees are designed to universalize such fundamentally different premises that they are simply not additive. One can *teach* these different philosophical approaches sequentially, or even in dialogue with each other, but one cannot *espouse* all of them at once, any more than one can *be* a Protestant, a Muslim, and a pantheist all at once. One cannot easily hold onto the notions of literature enshrined in the New Criticism and be a Marxist critic and follow the postmodernist and critical theorists' lines, nor easily use methods drawn from several of these schools of thought at once. One would think, then, that teachers and scholars used to such diversity would have little trouble dealing with materials deriving from different premises, developing new methods, focusing on different questions.

In fact, some principles, some methods, some modes of thinking, some specific insights, can be picked up and used without pulling their whole system-of-origin with them. Feminist and other innovative scholars perform such delicate operations all the time, as we have seen. But practitioners of the systems-of-origin themselves often remain prickly toward each other, sometimes jostling for priority, sometimes co-existing in mutual benign neglect, sometimes fruitfully recognizing, even teaching, the unresolved tensions.[27] Univocal, conceptually coherent, essential definitions of the fields covered in the curriculum are simply not available—but one would think they were when the pipe-smoking professor of philosophy leans back in his chair and says calmly, "The course proposed on feminist social and political thought may be very interesting, but it doesn't belong in our department."[28]

We all speak about Kuhn, and about paradigm shifts, but many somehow do not use that understanding when they feel challenged about their own discipline as an organizing framework that allows them to feel clear about what is and what is not their subject matter. They forget, once they become authorities in their own field, what they knew as graduate students. Generations of graduate students have wended their way through the minefields of interprofessional competition, carefully figuring out which approaches they must use with which professors on which exams lest they get caught in the cross-fire. And yet, once certified, many then proceed to defend their own views of what 'properly' constitutes their discipline with the same totalizing vehemence from which they once suffered.

Let me say explicitly what is again implied here: *it is precisely that which is claimed to be most inclusive because most general (that is, most abstract) that is most skewed by the old errors. And that means that what is supposedly most neutral, disinterested, objective, is most, not least, reflective of past exclusions and their rationalizations and mystifications.* By the time we reach the level of epistemology, what began as a limited particular set of excluding assumptions has been raised to the status of *principles for knowing, of knowledge itself.* Thus, partial definitions of fields are taken up into skewed principles of knowledge, and then those principles are invoked in defense of what is actually their own original partiality.[29]

But, again, we are not stuck: bringing to our teaching the lives and works of those who have been excluded allows us to uncover where and how the knowledge of the dominant tradition has been falsified, not just with regard to particular points, facts, issues, ideas, but with regard to the construction of what we take to be knowledge-itself. Thinking about what it means to "decolonize"[30] our minds, Ruel Tyson notes that "mind" is then revealed as "not simply how we think, but our tastes; not only our cognitive styles and cycles of growth, but . . . the pre-reflective judgments we commonly make about the familiar and the strange; and, finally . . . our desires, the baroque movements of our affections which are as much social as personal; the way we embody spirit; the dances our imaginations perform; the compulsions and elections of our will."[31] "Decolonization" is a necessary step to a healed consciousness, to self-knowledge. The more we know about others, the better we know ourselves. And the more we know about ourselves, the more able we become to comprehend others. It is only when our self-definition is built on exclusions and devaluations of others that those others threaten us, revealing the circular 'reasoning' of prejudice.

The confusion felt by those faced with a to-them-strange new work reveals something about mind; it knows in ways that involve feelings. As Susanne Langer wrote in a striking first sentence, "Feeling, in the broad sense of whatever is felt in any way, as sensory stimulus or inward tension, pain, emotion or intent, is the mark of mentality."[32] The anger with which some defend their 'objective' knowledge reveals something about objective knowledge; it is fraught with emotion and entangled with values that are themselves subjectively felt. "Mind," "reason," "knowledge," have been comprehended by particular people in particular ways that variously reflect, reinforce, question, or transcend the deeply felt reality of the articulated hierarchy of power. There is something to lose in any change in what we take to be knowledge, just as there is something to gain: power is at stake here, including the most basic power of all, the power to define what and who is real, what and who is valuable, what and who *matters*.

Here I cannot help thinking of the familiar saying that academic quarrels are as fierce as they are because they concern things that are so trivial—that the intensity of academic in-fighting varies inversely with the seriousness of the matter contended about. I do not think that is always apt; academic squabbles about highly abstract matters can in fact be concerned with issues that matter a great deal, yet are mystified. In the fierceness of at least some academic in-fighting is revealed once again a level of understanding of the degree to which knowledge reflects and reinforces power. The transcript of the Harvard University faculty meeting (sent to me by a friend) at which Women's Studies was finally recognized is a fascinating, and very telling, document, as are the reports and position papers written at Yale when coeducation was under consideration. Anyone who doubts that gender, power, knowledge, and the sense of self are closely intertwined need only examine such documents.

Explaining or justifying resistance to a reconsideration of one's field (or even to the use of more inclusive language, instead of the mystified, nongeneric "he" and "man") by invoking established notions of knowledge as if those were above and beyond history and culture is not only circular reasoning. It is also the academic equivalent of blaming the victim. It has consequences; it matters. The justification of exclusions that draws on definitions, principles, standards of the exclusive system entails saying (implicitly if not explicitly), "If you were excluded, you deserved to have been excluded." As always, such conceptual errors have high human costs: we teach by what we leave out. If no woman is represented among the philosophers studied, students learn that no woman ever did philosophy, which is untrue even in the narrow sense of 'doing philosophy.' And if nothing is said about the omission, students also pick up, on the preconscious level, another falsehood—that no woman could, and therefore that no woman can, do philosophy. It comes to seem the fault, the failing, of women that we were excluded from the ranks of philosophers. In many senses students learn that a woman philosopher is anomalous, a strange kind of beast.

On the other hand, if a teacher, intending to be inclusive, claims that the "he" and "man" in works taught are generic when in fact the author thought only of males, we still have a problem. A nongeneric "he," proclaimed after the fact to be generic, does not make the thinking built around "him" inclusive; it simply masks the exclusivity. An untruthful claim that "he" is generic is also, in my experience, often used to trivialize, even to ridicule, the idea that *it matters* whether or not an author excluded well over half the human race. "We can't read our own views back into history," a teacher explains. "People then didn't say 'he or she,' so we'll just read 'he' as generic." That, of course, more than suggests that it is silly to pursue the matter. But if an important work was written by someone who used "he" as it has been used throughout most of the dominant tradition—to refer to males, usually a particular group of them, who are being thought about as if they were the inclusive term, the norm, and the ideal for all—that matters. Theories of the state generated from consideration only of men, and a particular group of them at that, ought not to be studied as if they were indeed inclusive. And if it is admitted that they *were* exclusive, but that exclusivity is dismissed ("That's the way things were then; we can't expect Hobbes to have our sensibilities"), students learn that *the exclusion and devaluation of well over half of humankind does not matter ethically, politically, or intellectually.* But can Rousseau be understood if we generously ignore, or pass off as irrelevant, or smile with benign superiority about, his views concerning half of humankind? That, surely, is culpably sloppy scholarship, analysis, teaching— and it is ethically culpable as well.

We cannot now, by a fiat from the present, either ignore ex- clusivity or transmute it into inclusiveness. The 'simple' matter of pronouns contains the whole of our problem, and there is no short- cut to fixing it. Every time we stumble over a pronoun, we stumble over the root problem that entangles the dominant tradition in its own old errors.

‗ In a sense we have here come full circle: when we unwind the apparently simple observation that "he" is not genuinely inclusive, we find the same problems, the same deep and old errors, that are revealed by the most sophisticated epistemological analysis of what we take to be knowledge. Knowledge of, by, and for a part of humankind that claims to be of the whole is partial in both senses of the term. And the spiral of errors that began with an exclusive focus on the few continues even in the most abstract thinking, even in epistemology. Systems of thought about thought as they have been constituted cannot provide us with an Archimedean place to stand from which we can move the world. Such a place remains to be found and may, indeed, never be—no one place is large enough, or strong enough, for us all, and knowledge about our world, about our selves, should, perhaps, come from within and not from with- out the human world. What we know now is that, in coming to know all that has been excluded for so long, we are circling the globe as well as exploring our world's center. If we would have transformation, and not merely a palace coup or a revolution that simply effects yet another turning-upside-down, we need no less.

V

Back to Basics

Despite the fact that I have indulged in raising some of the more complex epistemological questions (because I find them irresistibly interesting, and because I do not think it responsible to avoid them), there are really only a few basic realizations here. They are both easily stated and enormously complex in their implications. Let me reiterate them so they will not be lost in the variations I have allowed myself to play, and hope I have invited others to play, on the intriguing questions they surface.

There is a *root problem* at the base of the dominant meaning system that informs our curricula—a tangle that results from taking the few to be the inclusive term, the norm, and the ideal for all. That problem, which can be considered in part as one of *faulty generalization*, even universalization, is compounded by the (not surprising) consequence of privileging central *singular* terms, notably "man" and "mankind," which lead directly to such singular abstract notions—and ideals—as "the citizen," "the philosopher," "the poet." Such singularity makes thinking of plurality, let alone diversity, very difficult indeed, and, in its idealizing aspects, promotes circular meaning. Together, faulty universalization, an emphasis on singularity, and circularity tend strongly and stubbornly to make considerations of time and space, of history and place, difficult to include in knowledge and meaning constructions: the universal, singular, normative Man appears to have no particular contexts at all. Thus, Man, with other foundational concepts, is *mystified*, made to appear what it is not, and whole systems of knowledge built around such concepts come to appear to have neither contexts nor consequences that should be considered to be central (rather than peripheral) to their truth and meaning. The result is *partial knowledge* masquerading as general, even universal.

Again, what we know reveals itself to contain errors of (1) faulty generalization (generalizing too far from too few without recognizing it), and (2) circularity of reasoning (drawing on definitions, principles, standards derived from faulty generalizations to explain and justify the continuing exclusion and devaluation of all that was held out of the initial inquiry). The confusions that result underlie and perpetuate the creation of (3) mystified concepts (in which the partial origins of the hierarchically invidious tradition are hidden but continue to have effect), so that (4) partial modes of knowing and knowledge systems, considered without analysis that reveals their contexts and consequences, produce ways of thinking about knowledge that, rather than providing perspective on those modes and systems, perpetuate and justify the original exclusions.

Furthermore, because the few not only were taken to be the inclusive term, the norm, and the ideal, but were defined and came to know themselves *in contradistinction* to all others, deuniversalizing everything in our knowledge and meaning systems is not, by itself, enough.

If we did no more than particularize what has been considered general, or even universal, the hegemonic few would then appear as one set of particulars among others—as if all we needed to do were to add "and she" to all references to "he," and/or give the few their 'markers' by saying, for example, "the privileged Euro-American male heterosexual philosopher," or, more startlingly in today's virulently homophobic society, "the great male Athenian homosexual philosopher, Plato." (Using the latter 'marker' would open up another huge tangle in the dominant tradition, which includes in its canon of Great Books many by men who would today be labeled, and very likely persecuted as, "homosexuals," as they would not have been earlier.) It is indeed helpful to particularize, but while undoing universals derived from faulty abstractions does clear the space and unblock the light we need to see those who are present mostly as absences, or Others, lesser beings, or victims, we must also recognize *how* the dominant few have been particular. Their particularity has been and is different from that of other groups: they have been only one group among many, but they have been so as a defining, power-wielding few. They have been particular in the mode of false universality; of being the definers for others who were the defined; of being the subjects who 'knew' the others as their objects, claiming that only their own standpoints transcended 'mere' subjectivity. They have been, in many senses, the colonizers.

As we work to particularize this group without mystifying it yet again by overlooking the fact that it has been "more equal than others" (to borrow Orwell's classic phrase), we need also to work with the observation that the defined were for the most part not positively but, rather, negatively defined. We cannot, with a few qualifiers added after the fact, arrive at equalized plurality. Many of us have been present only as absences, as that from which 'real' people separated and distinguished themselves. That is why democratic pluralism, on the face of it a fine position, cannot be espoused in today's world as if all we had to do was *choose* it. To achieve a truly egalitarian pluralism conceptually and politically, it is necessary for all groups to achieve self-knowledge, developed from within rather than imposed from without; for that knowledge to be fully and equally taken into account in any general concepts, theories, laws, principles, organizations, polities; and for provision to be made for the long transition period we face before the hierarchically invidious monism that is expressed in almost all dominant structures is truly transformed.

When people say to me, "But isn't the point to be able to speak of *humankind?* Shouldn't we drop all the emphasis on women, on different groups of women, on all the 'kinds' of men, and get on with learning about and caring for *humans?*" I say, "That may be a goal, but if we act now as if we have already achieved it, as if all we need do is assert our gender-, race-, or class-blindness, the awful weight of an old, fully developed, very powerful meaning and power system will ensure that in critical ways 'human' will continue to be conflated with 'man,' and 'man' with a particular group of males. *Saying* we are now inclusive cannot make it so. It will take a while to transform what has been developing for millennia."

Those who like to pretend that the fragile transitional measures and protections we have just barely established are instances of "reverse discrimination" are trying to have it both ways. They want Man to continue to be universal so they can pretend that their privilege comes from a neutral, disinterested assessment of their own personal merit, but when tiny pockets of consideration are designed to compensate others for the inequities of that mystified hegemonic status, they rush to proclaim themselves just one group among many and hence entitled to the 'special' provisions too. We cannot pretend *either* that we are able to think well about humans *or* that giving us all equally particular prefixes or group identifications fixes the problem.

Furthermore, the self-knowledge of all nonuniversalized groups must also take into account the ways in which those primarily defined in contradistinction to the hegemonic few have also been defined against each other. There has been a hierarchy among Others, too; Black women and white women have been defined-against as well as defined-with each other as white women have participated in race and (often associated) class privileges denied Black women. Some Black men have claimed the rights due their 'manhood' not only from white men but in opposition to the equal rights (personal as well as political) of Black women.

We are aided, not impeded, in holding onto these simple/complex realizations by the fact that we stumble into them almost every time we open our mouths, and we can hardly complete a statement without rediscovering just how used we are to the singular, universal "he," the long string of prefixes carried by all who do not belong to the single group that is itself rarely if ever prefixed. Such utterly nontrivial language difficulties confront us with the magnitude of our task; we cannot even speak to each other in the course of our daily affairs without encountering it, nor can we avoid it at the highest levels of abstraction.

To repeat: we cannot just tack on discrepant ideas; we cannot add the idea that the earth is round to the idea that it is flat. In our case, (1) we cannot add ourselves to a part that has claimed to be the whole, nor (2) can we reduce the hegemonic part to one-among-others by simple intellectual fiat. We must deal directly, stubbornly, consistently, at all levels with the realization that there is one part that has claimed to be the whole, the norm, and the ideal—and has held the power necessary to enforce that contradictory status. It is certainly not crystalline clarity, nor consistency, nor avoidance of contradictions that has held the dominant system in its place for so long; power, exercised and suffered directly through acts of exclusion, internalized in a sense of entitlement in some, in a sense of vulnerability or inadequacy in many others, is at play here.

But let us be clear: our goal is not necessarily to undo all universals and the very idea of universals. It is to particularize accurately, to demystify the functions of power and hierarchy. It is not, after all, universalization itself, or abstraction itself, that is necessarily harmful; it is *false* universals, faulty and mystified abstractions, that concern us. And they concern us precisely because they mask the possibility of approaching, at least, visions and concepts and commitments that could inspire us all.[1]

We are by no means concerned only with destruction, as I have noted, nor do we adopt a purely "us against them" position when we undertake the work of transforming the dominant tradition. We admit our participation (to varying degrees that must be honestly recognized) in that which we are struggling to change, recognizing that the errors are so complex and all-pervasive that few are utterly free of their effects, and that changed thinking does not begin, or create, *de novo*. And that is not all bad; there are moments of great inspiration as well as examples of a rich diversity and of liberatory thinking within the dominant tradition. We can find much that is of help to us, much that can inspire our work, in the tradition as well as outside it when we stop ignoring or blithely explaining away its errors and exclusions. Thus, in the classroom, we invite students to join us in approaching what has come down to us in a spirit of inquiry that will help us all think well and freely about what they will, in turn, critique, create, pass on. We try to inform quests for knowledge, explorations of modes of knowing, with a sense of responsibility for the human world. We admit, then, that it *matters* that Aristotle's modes of thinking allowed him to support his culture's justifications of slavery and the subordination of women. Having done so, we can also then notice and take very seriously the fact that Plato's method took him on occasion beyond his times, as when he observed that sex is not an appropriate criterion in the selection of philosopher–leaders. We can then begin to locate and focus on other striking instances of liberatory thinking within the tradition itself. After all, what is more fascinating and more important than discovering how even the privileged have on occasion thought themselves free? We do not pay the dominant tradition a compliment when we think we must pass quickly over or excuse its errors—quite the contrary. In doing so we risk trivializing some of its moments of lasting greatness, and the lessons we can learn from them.

At the same time, we need to explore a much richer range of materials, lives, voices, visions, and achievements, to learn the stories and modes of thought and creation of others. As we do so, we engage students by recognizing their diverse as well as common connections to our shared world, working with them to approach an education that might be, in the rich meaning of the terms, both humane and liberal in the sense of liberatory, compatible with freedom.

THOUGHT AND ACTION

I have used one of my favorite philosophers to provide an example of a great mind that was nevertheless skewed by the old errors. Let me, then, also cite Kant in a different spirit: here is his call to an understanding of the humanities that could help us transcend the limitations of the tradition:

> The propaedeutic does not consist in following precepts, but in culti-vating our mental powers by exposing ourselves . . . to what we call *humaninora* (or: the Humanities); they are called that presumably because *humanity* (Humanitat) means both the universal *feeling of sympathy,* and the ability to engage universally in very intimate *com-munication.* When these two qualities are combined, they constitute the sociability that befits humanity.[2]

Here there is a recognition of the responsibility of the quest for knowledge to be open to all humankind in a way that might make possible an approach to (never an arrival at) communication that is *both* intimate *and* universal. To insist on both intimacy and univer-sality, understood as regulative ideals rather than possible achieve-ments, is to insist on openness to the individual, to the particular, as well as to the general, the universal. Intimacy is a mode of relation that refuses generalizations: to be intimate means to break through *what* someone is in order to become open to *who* s/he is, to experi-ence *this* person as she is herself, not as she seems to be when filtered through pre-judgments about the category Woman. Great literature gives us such moments of comprehension and, in so doing, suggests that the intimate and the universal are not opposites after all. Universality is a creation of thought that moves through all limitations, all particular definition, in recognition of profound con-nectedness. It need not come only or primarily or most convincingly through an abstraction that creates utterly context-free symbols such as numbers. It can emerge from immersion in the particular, the individual, as well (as in stories). Between these ideas that call us to commune with each thing, each person, each moment, with full attentiveness, and to reach, also, for visions of connections within a whole beyond any particular, lie the richly complex social and political realms in which we struggle to live with each other. The intimate and the universal both remove us temporarily from the tension of the plural, active public realm, but we need always to return to it as well.

Arendt wrote, "We are all the same, that is, human, in such a way that nobody is ever the same as anyone who ever lived, lives or will live."[3] She insisted on our sameness in the apparently paradoxical mode of uniqueness (which makes the old errors impossible, if we can succeed in understanding and honoring it) in the context of discussing action, the political. "Plurality," which is uniqueness recognized in public, where we can see and experience that we are each unique, "is the condition of human action."[4] Plurality is also a result, a gift, of action. Without action in a public realm held open to all by guarantees of equality, it is all too easy to think of uniqueness as a special quality of the privileged few—there are the individuals who appear before us, revealing themselves through what they say and do, and then there are "the masses," "the common people." To be denied freedom of action, to be denied equality, is to be denied the opportunity to reveal and experience one's uniqueness, the opportunity to recognize that we are *all* unique.

Undoing *false* universals that have given only a few the privilege of being both unique and universal is not the same as undoing the idea of universality itself. "We are all the same" can be a highly ethical and politically sensitive claim, one that calls on us to remember human connectedness, and to value it. It is dangerous when we misconstrue sameness, as I have noted before, but that does not mean that we must or should give up our belief in our deepest connections. "The brotherhood of mankind" may be a notion we wish to undo, but that is because it is cast in partial terms, and false universals divide us; they do not connect us. In fact, they make it impossible to think universally because they have universalized falsely, inflated a part into the whole.

I am suggesting that, in addition to our conceptual critique, we can learn to see the partiality of past universals when we stop severing the quest for knowledge from genuine experience of action. The life of the mind and the life of action may be two different modes of human life, but that does not mean they are radically discontinuous. Both were restricted for too long to privileged men;

the meanings of both have been misconstrued as a result. Consider: you have heard of "the man of action." Have you ever heard of "the woman of action"? Or, even more strikingly: news commentators and political pundits like to speak of "the man in the street." But the only parallel for women is "a woman of the streets." Man, outside in public, is political; Woman in the same place is sexual. Our understandings of action and of politics are as skewed as our understanding of the life of the mind, and for the same reasons.

What we need to comprehend is and will be related to what we need to do; what we need to do is related to what we need to comprehend. Knowledge, untransformed, is irrelevant to citizenship, to action, not because it is about 'higher' things than politics, not because knowledge is 'purer' than action, but because what we have known and the modes of knowing behind it are locked into universals derived from partial, faulty, hierarchically arranged abstractions that cannot be found in or illuminate real, existent, particulars, or develop a feeling of universal egalitarian connectedness, or help us learn to think in the place of many others. A transforming vision of knowledge expresses our realization that humans are natal as well as mortal, that the human condition of plurality is made visible in a free public life, that we *need* that plurality for knowledge that approaches comprehensiveness, and hence that knowing is related to acting as knowledge is related to politics.

FROM ERRORS TO VISIONS

Visions of where we may go emerge from critique of where we are and have been.

When we recognize that our predecessors generalized too far from too few, and too often not only generalized but universalized with only the few in mind, we open ourselves to diversity that can be arrayed before us in all its challenge to our minds, our imaginations, our hearts, our dreams with and for humankind. In particularizing what was universal, we make it possible to cease turning difference into deviance; we stop confusing equality with sameness; we learn to think much more subtly and to live and work with more complexity and fineness of feeling and comprehension, taste and judgment. We begin again to create ways of thinking that support democracy rather than undermining it, as the old hierarchically invidious monism has done for so long.

When we recognize that we have been trapped in circular definitions, using definitions, key concepts, and standards to justify the very systems of meaning—and living—from which they were derived, we can stop accepting hierarchical ordering that continues the dominance of the few. We are challenged to immerse ourselves again in what we are studying, to suspend judgment for a while, to learn to hear new voices, and hence to emerge with new definitions and concepts and judgments that are, again, finer, more complex, more subtle, and much more adequate to the interrelated world in which we must, now, live. We can stop pitting excellence against equity as we come to realize that without equity, we necessarily confuse excellence with exclusivity. We become able to see art in quilts as well as on canvas; to feel respect for those we may not yet understand; to admire thinking in entirely different systems of logic and meaning; to find spiritual wisdom in forms of worship unlike the dominant Western forms; to hear the poetry in spirituals and the literature in diaries and letters. We expand the range of human expressiveness and meaning from which all can and should learn.

When we give up mystified concepts, we become able to create new concepts that, like touchstones, help us find important knowledge where before we did not even look. We can give up, for example, the depressing notion that we all derive from Man the Hunter, and remember that we also come from Woman the Gatherer—and from societies in which the one was not more important than the other. We can remember that Economic Man, the great rational decision-maker whose 'rationality' is measured by how well he plans to "maximize profits" in a capitalist economic system, is by no means universal even within capitalist systems. Then we can not only study but learn from others, from those who make decisions about resources out of concern for ancestors, or children, or respect for the land, or the collective good of all, rather than narrowly construed, competitively sought self-interest. We become open to noticing that some people make moral decisions by considering the needs and values of particular individuals in the contexts of real lives that preceded and will continue after the decision, rather than by invoking supposedly timeless, falsely abstracted moral principles that cannot adequately connect with the interdependent particularity of the world in which we must, after all, strive to be moral.

If we uncover in order to discard or correct partial yet self-justifying epistemologies, in as well as across fields, we become better able to comprehend many modes of knowing and knowledge systems. For example, if we relinquish the notion that we 'cover' the subject matter our fields name, and remember that we teach what has been agreed on by those who won out in intellectual and professional battles already restricted to the few—battles whose outcome often depended on availability of money, prestige, and access to intellectual community—we become able to teach our subjects as human constructs that are both defined and open to redefinition. We become able to live up to our own best promises, to see again that philosophy is not a list of texts or familiar problems from one tradition, but a quest for wisdom, an effort to find meanings as well as truths, and to think about what that effort itself means, and might be; that history is not the story only of the hegemonic few, the record-keepers and those the record-keepers recognized, but constructed human stories that shape the life-conditions of all of us; that literature is not a particular collection of canonical works, falling into a few schools and periods that are in conversation only with each other, but the effort of human minds and spirits to shape experience and feeling and thought into imaginative forms that speak across the boundaries that both relate and divide us.

With these realizations, new questions, emergent revelatory tools and methods, and the vast resource of all that has been excluded, we begin again the quest for knowledge, for self-knowledge. We recognize some things so obvious once seen that, like the child who said, "But the Emperor is naked!" we make others uncomfortable—because it is dangerous to see power unclothed rather than accept it so thoroughly on its own dictated terms that we actually skew our perceptions. (I have always thought that the realistic end to that story would have the child shushed and sent to bed without supper, and the parents suddenly suspect in their community as humorless trouble-makers.) We insist on paying very serious attention to phenomena long 'explained' as "natural," especially one of the most obvious and all-permeating facts of almost every society, the mutually implicated construction of sex and gender that gives men power over themselves and over women that women do not have. Gender becomes a subject matter, a key to significations otherwise locked, a primary critical and revelatory tool of resistance and re-creation.

In the long-familiar list of givens about Mankind, we find Man identified as the creature with speech, the creature with rationality, the political animal, and, looming large, the being who is aware of his mortality. All these categories are limited without consideration of all of us, of how gender is shaped by and shapes them differently at different times and across cultures, but shapes them. All these, and more, can be reconsidered, transformed, when we open to understanding not hobbled, blinded, by lack of recognition of gender, race, and class, of real historical and cultural meaning/power contexts and constructs. What speech has meant and means to women, to men of nonprivileged groups, in different cultures, becomes available to us to study and learn from. What reason can mean is expanded, enriched. What is political can be more accurately defined so we see the pervasive workings of power and its multiple meanings. And mortality is placed back in its context in the fabric of continuing, interrelated human life, where those in some other cultures, and those who think equally of natality, know it to belong.

═ Knowledge falsely abstracted from its context, locked into circular self-validation, built around mystified concepts, and taught out of its own context as a human endeavor lacks the richness of the full human drama. Such knowledge, untransformed, remains curiously abstract, removed from the realities of our students' as of our own worlds, reducing teachers far too often to all kinds of rhetorical tricks to engage the interest of students who feel, even if they do not recognize, either that they are excluded, which is painful, or (if they are of the privileged few) that too much is being claimed for them, which is frightening. Such knowledge and modes of knowing cannot adequately prepare us or our students to envision the kind of universality of communication—never actual, but a horizon that holds what is actual in perspective—to which the virtues of a transformed knowledge can call us.

Those who have been excluded are not, after all, the enemies of civilization. We are, as we have always been, essential to its very possibility: the world needs to hear all our voices. Transformed knowledge should help us all envision and actually experience moments in which the *possibility* of the intimate, universal communication that is the transforming heart of publicly responsible learning comes alive.

ANOTHER VIEW OF BEGINNINGS

In the realm of thinking, as in that of action, nothing is ever finally settled. Whenever thinking seems to reach a conclusion, another thought, another question, another voice, emerges. There is always

another way to turn an idea, another perspective on a phenomenon, a different conceptual approach to explore, a fresh and startlingly suggestive example to be taken into account. What seems
settled one moment is unsettled again the next. I presume, then,
that if you have been thinking with me and all the others whose
voices I have invited into our conversation, you have at least as
many unsettled questions now as you did at the beginning. Perhaps
you even have more.

If so, I am pleased. While others are doing the invaluable work of
detailed research that answers important specific questions, I want
to join in thinking about what those questions and findings might
mean for us. And while still others, more systematically minded,
work to explore, re-create, and create theoretical frameworks to
give conceptual contexts for facts, descriptions, interpretations,
explanations, I cannot help stepping back and trying to think about
those theories, too. I do not want there to be one "feminist theory,"
or "theory of feminism." I want there to be many, so that, on that
level too, we are called back into thought by the multiplicity of
possible ways of knowing. All of this work is important; there can
be no sound theories without careful research to uncover and to
create facts, facts require theory to help us make sense of them, and
facts and theories should, I believe, be constantly considered to see
what they *mean*, what difference they make. To act aimlessly and
always only in response to the immediate situation because there is
no theoretical framework is a problem for action, as is the turning of
theory into rigid ideology. The adoption of a theory can be a critical
turning point for action, for good and for ill. It matters.

And when we ask ourselves, What does this *mean?* we are calling
on our ability to think alone and together in a way that prepares us
to make judgments, to make choices, to take responsibility in the
world of action we share with others.

I say all this to bring my book to a close with the recognition that I
have not dealt with strategies for change, but I hope I have joined
many others in helping to prepare the ground for a whole different
set of conversations that are directed expressly at action informed
by the on-going effort of conceptual critique and reflexive thinking.
I am aware that the open-endedness of thinking and the 'negativity'
of critique seem, to some, to make action more difficult. Over the
years I have been asked many times if I do not think some kind of
utopian vision, rather than critique, is necessary for real change,
and why I do not get on with envisioning alternatives. I have

several responses. First, there are others whose gifts lie in imagining alternatives.[5] We could not do without them, and there is no reason why I should try to do what they do so well. Second, I worry about 'new' visions emerging without an on-going critique, since I have a great respect for the power of unanalyzed assumptions and error to continue to affect us without our wishing them to. Third, I find a great deal of positive and creative vision within critique. To begin to uncover what is wrong is to begin to be able to see what could be right, and to do so by concentrating on what *is*, not what *ought to be*. It sometimes seems to me that we are more likely to be able to change what is if we understand it very well than if we turn from it, imagine something quite different, and then have to begin afresh to figure out how to get there from here. Furthermore, I am always worried by efforts to 'get there from here' when the 'there' toward which we act is too clear to us, too developed. Such visions turn far too easily into prescriptive ends, in view of which present pressing realities—and too often real people—turn into no more than means.

And, finally, I believe, as I have said, that thinking reflexively is one of the grounds of human freedom, in part because it reveals to us that we are always both subject and object of our own knowing, of our culture, of our world. We are not just products, objects, of our world, nor are we just subjects existing in a void. We are free subjects whose freedom is conditioned—not determined—by a world not of our making but in many ways open to the effects of our actions. If nothing else, then, I believe in the educational importance of thinking and of critique as preparations for a kind of action that engages with others, and with the world, rather than submitting to it or trying to 'master' it.

Action is, of course, necessary. Along with the thinking I have done with educators all over the country, I have also consulted on institutional change and related political strategizing. In those sessions, I do not begin with philosophical reflections about the dominant meaning system, or the curriculum. I begin by trying to find out what the particular situation is in which change is desired, what the resources and obstacles to change *here* and *now* may be. We consider possible allies, effective rhetoric, untapped sources of funding, specific histories, powerful individuals. But if I were to go into any kind of detail about institutional change, and/or changes that are possible within specific disciplines, and/or changes in particular courses, I would be writing another book. Allow me, then, to suggest that change comes when thinking is released from old tangles of errors that have locked it into the past *and* when we learn to analyze the potential for real change in our very specific contexts. In that movement from the conceptual to the concrete, and from the concrete to the conceptual, is one of the most important conversations of all, the one that returns thinking to the world it helps illuminate, and, in turn, challenges that thinking to take account of particulars, individuals, specific situations.

For these deeply related efforts, we need realism and hope, philosophy and strategies, flexibility and stubbornness, honesty and imagination. Most of all, perhaps, we each need to find out how we work best, and to figure out how we can contribute, drawing on our own strengths, interests, and pleasures. It does little good to decide what ought to be done and how it ought to be effected with no reference to the specific people who will have to do the work. People who do what they are sure is 'right' in a way that goes against their grain can rarely keep up the effort very long, and they run the risk of becoming dogmatic, unhappy, and even dangerous. Those who work for what they believe in, in ways that suit them and their own particular strengths, can keep going longer while continuing to grow through their work.

If both thinking and acting are essential to freedom, as freedom is essential to them, then they are to be enjoyed for their own sake as well as for what they may lead us toward. The effort to think ourselves free does not suffice to make us free—by no means. But it does give us a profound experience of freedom as we do it. I suppose that is one of the reasons why, when people have asked me and others how we can stand to spend so much time thinking about how overwhelming, and unjust, the dominant systems are, I usually find myself saying, "Because I enjoy thinking, and I love the people with whom I have been privileged to do it."

Although the quotation from Anna Julia Cooper with which I opened this book may seem to imply, wrongly, that *everyone* will greet the newly re-emerging multicultural scholarships with great pleasure, she is certainly not wrong about how some of us have felt: "The darkened eye restored, every member rejoices with it."

But such moments do not last, and without institutional and political changes that are designed to open the structures and privileges of the few to the whole, they can become no more than the secret pleasures of yet another closed group. That is why it is important that we continue to reach out to others, to explain what we are thinking and doing, to open ourselves to responses, questions, challenges. Every such conversation is, for all engaged in it, a new beginning and, indeed, an enactment of the ends we seek.

> Surely it is time for the true grace of women
> Emerging, in their lives' colors, from the rooms, from the harvests,
> From the delicate prisons, to speak their promises.
> The spirit's dreaming delight and the fluid senses'
> Involvement in the world. Surely the day's beginning
> In midnight, in time of war, flickers upon the wind.
>
> O on the wasted midnight of our pain
> Remember the wasted ones, lost as surely as soldiers
> Surrendered to the barbarians, gone down under centuries
> Of the starved spirit, in desperate mortal midnight
> With the pure throats and cries of blessing, the clearest
> Fountains of mercy and continual love.
> These years know separation. O the future shining
> In far countries or suddenly at home in a look, in a season,
> In music freeing a new myth among the male
> Steep landscapes, the familiar cliffs, trees, towers
> That stand and assert the earth, saying: "Come here, come to me.
> Here are your children." Not as traditional man
> But love's great insight—"your children and your song."
>
> Coming close to the source of belief, these have created
> Resistance, the flowering fire of memory,
> Given the bread and the dance and the breathing midnight.
> Nothing has been begun. No peace, no word of marvelous
> Possible hillsides, the warm lips of the living
> Who fought for the spirit's grace among despair,
> Beginning with signs of belief, offered in time of war,
> As I now send you, for a beginning, praise.

> —Muriel Rukeyser, "Letter to the Front: X"[6]

Notes

NOTES

The following notes give the usual information on sources of direct quotations, and I have also used them to suggest further readings in some areas. Still, the scope of this book made it impossible to approach adequacy, let alone completeness, with such suggestions. Given that it is a serious thing to omit mention of important works when some *are* mentioned, it might have been better not to have gone beyond direct citations, but I did not want to do that. I have settled for scattering hints along the trail, as it were, trusting that anyone interested will continue the quest far beyond the works cited here. There are many to be found, including some of my favorites that I profoundly regret having left out.

Excellent help in locating the literature can be found in bibliographic and source books by Patricia Ballou, Susan Searing, and Betty Schmitz, among others, as well as in such on-going publications as *Signs, Feminist Studies, Sage, Frontiers, Women's Studies Quarterly,* the *Women's Review of Books, Off Our Backs, New Directions for Women,* and newsletters from the Project on the Status and Education of Women (Association of American Colleges) and many other organizations. Special projects and publications of the various academic professional associations are also available and very helpful (e.g., the collections of syllabi and bibliographies undertaken by the Organization of American Historians). The various centers for research on women can also be very helpful; they can be located through the National Council of Centers for Research on Women, Sara Delano Roosevelt Memorial House, 47–49 East 65th Street, New York, NY 10021.

Above all, it is helpful to recognize that there are at least a few people on every campus who are knowledgeable in the area of feminist scholarship. Most are delighted to be of help to friends and colleagues who are willing to ask for it.

I. A VIEW OF BEGINNINGS

1. Ann J. Lane, "Mary Ritter Beard: Woman As Force," in Dale Spender, ed., *Feminist Theorists: Three Centuries of Key Women Thinkers* (New York: Random House, 1983), p. 347.

2. Joan Kelly, *Women, History, and Theory* (Chicago: University of Chicago Press, 1984), p. 66.

3. Paula Giddings, *When and Where I Enter . . . : The Impact of Black Women on Race and Sex in America* (New York: William Morrow, 1984), p. 5.

4. Anna Julia Cooper, *A Voice from the South* (New York: Oxford University Press, 1988), pp. 121–23.

5. Jeffner Allen, *Lesbian Philosophy: Explorations* (Palo Alto, Calif.: Institute of Lesbian Studies, 1986), p. 13.

6. Linda Gordon, "What's New in Women's History," in Teresa de Lauretis, ed., *Feminist Studies: Critical Studies* (Bloomington: Indiana University Press, 1986), p. 21.

7. For other reflections on the effects of terminology in this area, see Peggy McIntosh, "A Note on Terminology," *Women's Studies Quarterly* 11 (Summer 1983): 29–30.

8. Teresa de Lauretis, "Feminist Studies/Critical Studies: Issues, Terms and Contexts," in de Lauretis, ed., *Feminist Studies: Critical Studies*, p. 3.

9. Ibid., p. 7. See also Elizabeth Minnich, *Toward a Feminist Transformation of the Curriculum,* Proceedings of the 5th Annual GLCA Women's Studies Conference (Ann Arbor: GLCA, 1979).

II. CONTEXTUAL APPROACHES: THINKING ABOUT

1. Frederick Rudolph, *Curriculum: A History of the American Undergraduate Course of Study since 1636* (San Francisco: Jossey-Bass, 1977), pp. 168, 169.

2. Ibid., p. 169.

3. Patricia Palmieri, "From Republican Motherhood to Race Suicide: Arguments on the Higher Education of Women in the United States, 1820–1920)," in Carol Lasser, ed., *Educating Men and Women Together* (Chicago: University of Illinois Press, 1987).

4. Linda Kerber, *Women of the Republic: Intellect and Ideology in Revolutionary America* (Chapel Hill: University of North Carolina Press, 1980), p. 10.

5. Paula Giddings, *When and Where I Enter . . . : The Impact of Black Women on Race and Sex in America* (New York: William Morrow, 1984), pp. 104–5.

6. For an excellent feminist analysis of the dominant tradition of thought about education, see Jane Roland Martin, *Reclaiming a Conversation: The Ideal of the Educated Woman* (New Haven: Yale University Press, 1985). For sup-

portive analyses of the role of education and how it might be reconceived and practiced, see, for example, Paulo Freire, *Pedagogy of the Oppressed*, trans. Myra Bergman Ramos (New York: Seabury Press, 1970); Henry A. Giroux, *Ideology, Culture, and the Process of Schooling* (Philadelphia: Temple University Press, 1981); Ira Shor and Paulo Freire, *A Pedagogy for Liberation: Dialogues on Transforming Education* (South Hadley, Mass.: Bergin and Garvey, 1987).

7. See, for example, Barbara Christian, "The Race for Theory," in *Feminist Studies* 14 (Spring 1988): 67–79.

8. I have here drawn heavily, and with gratitude, on Sara Evans, *Personal Politics* (New York: Random House/Vintage Books, 1979).

9. For more work on the 1960s and 1970s movements, see also, for example, James Miller, *Democracy Is in the Streets: From Port Huron to the Siege of Chicago* (New York: Simon and Schuster, 1987); Clayborne Carson, *In Struggle: SNCC and the Black Awakening of the Nineteen Sixties* (Cambridge: Harvard University Press, 1981); Todd Gitlin, *The Sixties: Years of Hope, Days of Rage* (New York: Bantam Books, 1987); Wini Breines, *Community and Organization in the New Left: 1962–1968* (New York: Praeger Publishers, 1982); Sohnya Sayres et al., eds., *The 60's Without Apology* (Minneapolis: University of Minnesota Press, in cooperation with Social Text, 1984).

10. "A Kind of Memo from Casey Hayden and Mary King to a Number of Other Women in the Peace and Freedom Movements, November 18, 1965," in Evans, *Personal Politics,* p. 235.

11. Cynthia Washington, "We Started from Different Ends of the Spectrum," ibid., pp. 238–40. See also Alice Walker, *Meridian,* a complex and fascinating novel about the Civil Rights Movement.

12. See, for example, the fine study by Harry C. Boyte, *The Backyard Revolution: Understanding the New Citizen Movement* (Philadelphia: Temple University Press, 1980).

13. See, for example, Evans, *Personal Politics;* Bell Hooks, *Ain't I a Woman: Black Women and Feminism* (Boston: South End Press, 1981), and *Feminist Theory: From Margin to Center* (Boston: South End Press, 1984); Giddings, *When and Where I Enter;* Elly Bulkin, Minnie Bruce Pratt, and Barbara Smith, *Yours in Struggle: Three Feminist Perspectives on Anti-Semitism and Racism* (New York: Long Haul Press, 1984); Johnella Butler, "Minority Studies and Women's Studies: Do We Want to Kill A Dream?" *Women's Studies International Forum* 7, no. 3 (1984): 135–38.

14. See also Audre Lorde, "An Open Letter to Mary Daly," and other essays in Cherrie Moraga and Gloria Anzaldua, eds., *This Bridge Called My Back: Writings by Radical Women of Color* (Watertown, Mass.: Persephone Press, 1981); Barbara Smith, ed., *Home Girls: A Black Feminist Anthology* (New York: Kitchen Table: Women of Color Press, 1983); Florence Howe, *Myths of Coeducation: Selected Essays, 1964–1983* (Bloomington: Indiana University Press, 1984); Robin Morgan, ed., *Sisterhood Is Powerful: An Anthology*

of Writings from the Women's Liberation Movement (New York: Random House, 1970).

15. For some interesting thinking on a few of the early efforts to bring change to the Academy, see Charlotte Bunch and Sandra Rubaii, eds., *Learning Our Way: Essays in Feminist Education* (Trumansburg, N.Y.: Crossing Press, 1983), and Howe, *Myths of Coeducation;* see also the informal publications (by the Barnard College Women's Center) of proceedings of The Scholar and The Feminist Conferences. For an on-going record of efforts at institutional equity, see the publications of the Project on the Status and Education of Women headed by Bernice Sandler of the Association of American Colleges, 1818 R Street, N.W., Washington, DC 20009, and the American Council on Education's Offices of Women and of Minority Affairs, One Dupont Circle, Washington, DC 20036. For accounts of the development of Women's Studies courses and programs in the United States, see back issues of the *Women's Studies Quarterly* (Old Waterbury, N.Y.: Feminist Press); Elizabeth Minnich, Jean O'Barr, and Rachel Rosenfeld, eds., *Reconstructing the Academy: Women's Education and Women's Studies* (Chicago: University of Chicago Press, 1988), and Carol Pearson, Donna Shavlik, and Judith Touchton, eds., *Educating the Majority: Women Challenge Tradition in Higher Education* (New York: Macmillan, 1987), among other works.

16. See also Sandra Coyner, "The Ideas of Mainstreaming: Women's Studies and the Disciplines," in *Frontiers,* tenth anniversary issue: *A Decade of Women's Studies Inside the Academy* 8, no. 3 (1986): 87–96; and Marilyn R. Schuster and Susan R. Van Dyne, *Women's Place in the Academy: Transforming the Liberal Arts Curriculum* (Totowa, N.J.: Rowan and Allenheld, 1985), among others.

17. See also the report of the Association of American Colleges, *Liberal Education and the New Scholarship on Women: Issues and Constraints in Institutional Change,* from the Wingspread Conference, Racine, Wisc., 22–24 October 1981, and Elizabeth Kamarck Minnich, "Education for the Free Man?" in *Liberal Education* 68, no. 4 (1982): 311–21.

18. Linda Nochlin, "Why Are There No Great Women Artists?" in *Art News* 69 (1971): 22–39, 67–71; cf. also Ann Sutherland Harris and Linda Nochlin, *Women Artists: 1550–1950* (New York: Alfred A. Knopf, 1981).

19. This line has been quoted frequently among those involved with Women's Studies, spreading primarily through conversation rather than circulation of a text. However, we now have Charlotte Bunch's collected essays, *Passionate Politics: Essays 1968–1986—Feminist Theory in Action* (New York: St. Martin's Press, 1987); see p. 140. When asked, Bunch said that the idea cited here was developed in conversations with Mary E. Hunt.

20. Many people have found Thomas Kuhn's work on "paradigm shifts" helpful here: Thomas S. Kuhn, "The Structure of Scientific Revolutions," in *The International Encyclopedia of Unified Science,* vol. 2, no. 2, 2d ed. (Chicago:

University of Chicago Press, 1962); see also Kuhn's *The Structure of Scientific Revolutions*, 2d ed. (Chicago: University of Chicago Press, 1970).

21. The idea that we need to rethink the story of the "conquest" of the West struck me first, I think, when I noticed a classic example of the root error in some popular magazine. The phrasing, all too familiar, went something like this: "The early pioneers followed their dreams West, taking with them all their worldly goods, their wives and children." "Pioneers," then, did/does *not* include women, who remain in the old stories on the level of worldly goods, a kind of baggage to be taken along by the 'real' pioneers. Once we have realized that, we can raise basic questions about what the women were doing and undergoing, and those questions immediately suggest that we consider the kinds of issues I have touched on here. Some of the scholars who have worked in this area include John Farragher, Elizabeth Hampsten, Glenda Riley, and Lillian Schlissel; for a compatible approach from the angle of communitarian and/or ecological analyses, see, for example, work by Wendall Berry, Wes Jackson, Aldo Leopold, and John Tallmadge. Books dealing with different subjects that demonstrate how rethinking and re-envisioning women results in basic reconceptualizations and not merely additional information include Linda Gordon, *Woman's Body, Woman's Right: Birth Control in America* (New York: Penguin, 1977); John Berger, *Ways of Seeing* (London: Penguin, 1972); Jesse Bernard, *The Future of Marriage* (New York: World Publishing Co., 1972); and most of the other books and articles I cite throughout.

22. I was struck, and moved, by the Reverend Jesse Jackson's use of the image of a quilt (rather than the old "melting pot") to express the persistent and *not* undesirable patterned diversity of the peoples and cultures of the United States in his speech to the National Democratic Convention in Atlanta in the summer of 1988.

III. CONCEPTUAL APPROACHES: THINKING THROUGH

1. Simone de Beauvoir, *The Second Sex*, trans. and ed., H. M. Parshley (New York: Random House/Vintage Books, 1974), p. xix.

2. For example, I am *not* referring specifically or solely to H. W. Janson's classic *History of Art*, 3d ed. (New York: Harry N. Abram, 1986), in my first curricular example. The title I made up, *The History of Art*, is intended to evoke all the Art History textbooks required through the years, none of which genuinely included women.

3. I thank Patricial Rife for introducing me to the story of Lise Meitner.

4. Werner Jaeger, *Paideia: The Ideals of Greek Culture*, vol. 1, trans. Gilbert Highet, 2d ed. (New York: Oxford University Press, 1965), p. xiv.

5. Ibid., p. xxiv.

6. Walter J. Ong, "Latin Language Study as a Renaissance Puberty Rite," *Studies in Philology* 56, no. 2 (April 1959): 103–24, and see also Elizabeth Minnich, "Institutional and Civic Responsibilities," in *Forum for Higher Education* (Raleigh: NCACU, 1987).

7. Lawrence Cremin, quoted in Merrill D. Peterson et al., eds., *The Humanities and the American Promise: Report of the Colloquium on the Humanities and the American People* (Austin, Tex.: Committee for the Humanities, 1987), p. 11.

8. Walt Whitman, quoted ibid., pp. 9–10.

9. Ibid., p. 11.

10. Frederick Douglass, quoted ibid., p. 11.

11. Gunnar Myrdal, quoted ibid., p. 7.

IV. ERRORS BASIC TO THE DOMINANT TRADITION

Faulty Generalizations

1. Cf. Rayna Rapp Reiter, ed., *Toward an Anthropology of Women* (New York: Monthly Review Press, 1975); Michelle Z. Rosaldo and Louise Lamphere, *Woman, Culture, and Society* (Stanford, Calif.: Stanford University Press, 1974).

2. I have not drawn on any of the often-used labels for different sorts of feminist thought—for example, "liberal feminist," "cultural feminist," "French feminist"—because I am interested in exploring variously overlapping ways of thinking, not in categorizing. For good discussions that *do* categorize, see the works of Alison Jaggar and Paula Rothenberg Struhl, and Hester Eisenstein, among others.

3. Gerda Lerner, *Women and History: The Creation of Patriarchy,* vol. 1 (New York: Oxford University Press, 1966), p. 274; here and elsewhere in her thinking, Lerner uses the differences between the expectations of sisters and brothers as a key to open up the very basic particularities of gender. The actual source for my reference to the idea is conversation with Lerner.

4. Adrienne Rich, "Compulsory Heterosexuality and Lesbian Existence," in *Signs* 5 (1980): 657.

5. Eve Sedgwick, *Between Men: English Literature and Male Homosocial Desire* (New York: Columbia University Press, 1985), pp. 1–2.

6. Alice Kessler-Harris, *Out to Work: A History of Wage-Earning Women in the United States* (New York: Oxford University Press, 1982), pp. 315–16.

7. Angela Y. Davis, *Women, Race and Class* (New York: Random House/ Vintage Books, 1983), p. 94.

8. Carol B. Stack, *All Our Kin: Strategies for Survival in a Black Community* (New York: Harper & Row, 1974), pp. 45–46.

9. For a fine discussion of "woman-as-victim," see Ellen Carol Dubois, Gail Paradise Kelly, Elizabeth Lapovsky Kennedy, Carolyn W. Korsmeyer, and Lillian S. Robinson, *Feminist Scholarship: Kindling in the Groves of Academe* (Chicago: University of Illinois Press, 1985).

10. Gerda Lerner, ed., *The Female Experience: An American Documentary* (New York: Bobbs-Merrill, 1977), pp. xxvi–xxvii.

11. See also Gloria T. Hull, Patricia Bell Scott, and Barbara Smith, eds., *All the Women Are White, All the Blacks Are Men, but Some of Us Are Brave* (Old Westbury, N.Y.: Feminist Press, 1982), as well as collections of short stories edited by Mary Helen Washington, and Gerda Lerner, ed., *Black Women in White America: A Documentary History* (New York: Random House, 1973); also the classic poems and novels by Margaret Alexander Walker, especially the novel *Jubilee* (Boston: Houghton Mifflin, 1967). Others include Filomina Chioma Steady, *The Black Woman Cross-Culturally* (Cambridge, Mass.: Schenkman, 1981), and Robert Farris Thompson, *Flash of the Spirit: African and Afro-American Art and Philosophy* (New York: Vintage Books, 1984). The literature here is extensive; these are, as always, merely hints for beginnings.

12. Immanuel Kant, *Observations on the Feeling of the Beautiful and Sublime* (Berkeley: University of California Press, 1960), p. 109.

13. Ibid., p. 81.

14. Quoted in Vincent Harding, "Black Creativity and American Attitudes," in *There Is a River: The Black Struggle for Freedom in America* (New York: Harcourt Brace Jovanovich, 1981), p. 145.

15. For telling analyses of the ways in which we learn the deepest presuppositions of our culture and the effects of that learning not only on how we conduct our daily lives but on the judgments we make of others, see the works of Edward Hall: for example, *Beyond Culture, The Dance of Life,* and *The Silent Language.*

16. Alfred North Whitehead, quoted in Mary Daly, *Beyond God the Father* (Boston: Beacon Press, 1973), p. 1.

Circular Reasoning

1. Michael Quinn Patton, *Qualitative Evaluation Methods* (Newbury Park, Calif.: Sage, 1980), p. 21.

2. Joan Kelly, *Women, History and Theory* (Chicago: University of Chicago Press, 1984), p. 1.

3. It is striking, for example, that Elaine Scarry's *The Body in Pain: The Making and Unmaking of the World* (New York: Oxford University Press, 1985) emerged from the field of Literature. Scarry's thinking is a powerful example of the breaking of discipline-bound circularity.

4. Frank Newman, "American Education in a Competitive World," in *Forum for Higher Education:* Proceedings of the 67th Annual Conference of

the North Carolina Association of Colleges and Universities, October 1987 (Raleigh, N.C.: NCACU, 1987). The remark is given here as I remember it from the conference and conversations with Frank Newman.

5. Merrill D. Peterson, et al., *The Humanities and the American Promise: Report of the Colloquium on the Humanities and the American People* (Austin, Tex.: Committee for the Humanities, 1987), p. 2.

6. Ibid., p. 16.

Mystified Concepts

1. The quotation is from a talk I heard Allan Bloom give at the Claremont Colleges in California, March 21, 1988; cf. his book, *The Closing of the American Mind* (New York: Simon and Schuster, 1987).

2. I am thinking here (and by no means only here) in conversation with Peggy McIntosh, with whom I have had a running discussion about judgment for several years. She makes a persuasive case that even the word "judgment" is so fraught with negative experiences for many of us that I should not use it. I persist, however, perhaps out of pigheadedness but also because I believe the word and concept need to be rescued from their misuse. I believe the intellectual act of judgment to be basic to action and hence to freedom; it is its replacement by other modes of thought (such as deduction) that I, too, fear. See my essay, "To Judge in Freedom: Hannah Arendt on the Relation of Thinking and Morality," in Gisela T. Kaplan and Clive Kessler, eds., *Hannah Arendt: Thinking, Judging, Freedom* (Australia: Allen & Unwin, 1989).

3. Merrill D. Peterson et al., *The Humanities and the American Promise: Report of the Colloquium on the Humanities and the American People* (Austin, Tex.: Committee for the Humanities, 1987), p. 13.

4. Reported to me by Peggy McIntosh, from conversations she had with Susan Van Dyne.

5. I am drawing on Kant's discussion of judgment in *The Critique of Judgment;* Hannah Arendt's lectures, seminars and discussions of judgment (published and unpublished—I was Arendt's student and teaching assistant and worked with her for many years during and after my doctoral coursework); conversations with Ruel Tyson (especially about Kant and Polanyi, as well as his own work) and with the "Judging Judgment" discussion group of the Society for Values in Higher Education; and on work in which I have had some share at the Kettering Foundation on the concept of the civic arts and, particularly, judgment; cf. Elizabeth K. Minnich, "Some Reflections on Civic Education and the Curriculum," in *Kettering Review* XX (Summer 1988): 35–36. I believe most of John Dewey's work is relevant to these concerns, but I might mention specifically *Quest for Certainty: A Study of the Relation of Knowledge and Action* (New York: G. P. Putnam's Sons, 1960). For Michael Polanyi, see *Personal Knowledge: Toward a Post-Critical Philosophy* (Chicago: University of Chicago Press, 1962).

6. Hannah Arendt, "Introduction," in Walter Benjamin, *Illuminations,* trans. Harry Zohn (New York: Schocken Books, 1969), pp. 50–51.

7. For an interesting effort to understand equal rights as the notion is challenged by comparable worth, see the work of Sara Evans and Barbara Nelson in *Wage Justice: Comparable Worth and the Paradox of Technocratic Reform* (Chicago: University of Chicago Press, 1989). Catharine MacKinnon also does a superb analysis of why and how 'equal rights' is distorted as concept and reality in the present dominant system: see *Feminism Unmodified: Discourses on Life and Law* (Cambridge: Harvard University Press, 1987).

8. Jane Roland Martin, "Excluding Women from the Educational Realm," in Sharon Lee Rich and Ariel Phillips, eds., *Women's Experience and Education,* Harvard Educational Review Reprint Series, no. 17 (Boston: Harvard Educational Review, 1985), p. 172.

9. I am not discussing feminist pedagogy in any general sense here, but I hope the few examples I have included of ways I have learned something about the dominant meaning system by varying what I do in class will at least suggest the importance of the subject. For more on feminist pedagogy, see, for example, Margo Culley, ed., *Gendered Subjects: The Dynamics of Feminist Teaching* (Boston: Routledge & Kegan Paul, 1985). See also *The Radical Teacher,* a journal; reports in the various publications of the National Women's Studies Association; and Bernice R. Sandler et al., reports from the Association of American Colleges' Project on the Status and Education of Women, especially the invaluable report by Roberta N. Hall, with Bernice R. Sandler, "The Classroom Climate: A Chilly One for Women?" (Washington, 1982). I continue to be particularly engaged by the work of Sylvia Ashton Warner; see *Spinster* (New York: Simon and Schuster, 1986), and *Teacher* (New York: Simon and Schuster, 1986).

10. Leonard Harris, *Philosophy Born of Struggle: Anthology of Afro-American Philosophy from 1917* (Dubuque, Iowa: Kendall/Hunt, 1983), p. ix.

11. Kathryn Pyne Parsons, "Moral Revolution," in Julia A. Sherman and Evelyn Torton Beck, eds., *The Prism of Sex: Essays in the Sociology of Knowledge* (Madison: University of Wisconsin Press, 1979), p. 190.

12. Ibid., p. 190.

13. A. L. Basham, *The Wonder That Was India,* 12th ed. (New York: Grove Press, 1954), p. 502.

14. Sara Ruddick, *Maternal Thinking: Toward a Politics of Peace* (Boston: Beacon Press, 1989).

15. For further discussion of logic in its strict technical sense as well as of reason in the Western tradition, see Sandra Harding and Merrill B. Hintikka, eds., *Discovering Reality: Feminist Perspectives on Epistemology, Metaphysics, Methodology, and Philosophy of Science* (Boston: D. Reidel, 1983).

16. Harris, *Philosophy Born of Struggle,* p. ix.

17. Cf. Martin, "Excluding Women."

18. See works by Judith Arcana, Jane Lazarre, and Adrienne Rich among

others, and the special issue of *Sage*, "Mothers and Daughters" 1, no. 2 (Fall 1984).

19. Frederick Rudolph, *Curriculum: A History of the American Undergraduate Course of Study Since 1636* (San Francisco: Jossey-Bass, 1977), pp. 29–30; note that "men of action" does not include "men who work with their hands."

20. Ibid., p. 33.

21. Cf. Benedict de Spinoza, *Ethics*.

22. French feminist writing (including the earlier work of de Beauvoir and work in the United States inspired and informed by the French feminists) speaks particularly effectively about the shaping absence of Woman; see, among others, Luce Irigaray, "This Sex Which Is Not One," in Elaine Marks and Isabelle de Courtivron, eds., *New French Feminisms* (New York: Schocken Books, 1981); Monique Wittig, *Les Guerillieres*, trans. David Le Vay (Boston: Beacon Press, 1985); and Toril Moi, ed., *The Kristeva Reader* (New York: Columbia University Press, 1986).

23. The entry for "woman," by Dennis Baron in Cheris Kramarae and Paula A. Treichler, eds., *A Feminist Dictionary* (London: Pandora Press, 1985), p. 491. For complex multiple meanings of "woman" beyond those covered in English-language dictionaries, some sources can be found, and traced, through publications of Zed Books (formerly the Zed Press); see, for example, Ifi Amadidune, *Male Daughters, Female Husbands: Gender and Sex in an African Society*, and Khawar Mumtaz and Farida Shaheed, *Women of Pakistan*; see also Robin Morgan, *Sisterhood Is Global: The First Anthology of Writings from the International Women's Movement* (New York: Doubleday, 1984); Zed Books and the Morgan anthology can provide starting points for locating many more, including works by women not schooled and/or living in the United States.

24. Sherri Ortner, "Is Woman to Nature As Man Is to Culture?" in Michelle Z. Rosaldo and Louise Lamphere, eds., *Woman, Culture, and Society* (Stanford, Calif.: Stanford University Press, 1974).

25. Cf. Suzanne J. Kessler and Wendy McKenna, *Gender: An Ethnomethodological Approach* (New York: John Wiley and Sons, 1978), and, for a different approach, Gerda Lerner, *The Creation of Patriarchy* (New York: Oxford University Press, 1986).

26. Chandra Talpade Mohanty, "Feminist Encounters: Locating the Politics of Experience," *Copyright* 1 (Fall 1987): 39. (*Copyright* is published by MIT Press in Cambridge, Mass.).

27. For work in this general area, see Ruth Hubbard, Mary Sue Henifin, and Barbara Fried, eds., *Women Look at Biology Looking at Woman* (Cambridge, Mass.: Schenkman, 1979); Ruth Hubbard, "Science, Facts and Feminism," *Hypatia* 3 (Spring 1988): 5–17; Ruth Bleier, *Science and Gender: A Critique of Biology and Its Theories on Women* (New York: Pergamon Press, 1984); Sue Rosser, *Feminism Within the Science and Health Care Professions:*

Overcoming Resistance (New York: Pergamon Press, 1988); Mariette Nowak, *Eve's Rib: A Revolutionary New View of the Female* (New York: St. Martin's Press, 1980). Starhawk's *Dreaming the Dark: Magic, Sex and Politics* (Boston: Beacon Press, 1982), also gives an engaging overview of feminist approaches to the treatment of Nature by male-centered scholarship and science.

28. In this area, see, among others, Gena Correa, *The Mother Machine: Reproductive Technologies from Artificial Insemination to Artificial Wombs* (New York: Harper & Row, 1985); Rita Arditti, Renate Duelli-Klein, and Shelley Minden, eds., *Test-Tube Women: What Future for Motherhood?* (Boston: Pandora Press, 1984); Michelle Stanworth, ed., *Reproductive Technologies: Gender, Motherhood, and Medicine* (Minneapolis: University of Minnesota Press, 1987).

29. See publications from Columbia University's Maison Française Colloquium on Simone de Beauvoir, April 1985, New York; Carol Ascher, *Simone de Beauvoir: A Life of Freedom* (Boston: Beacon Press, 1981); and Margaret Simon, "The Moral Philosophy of Simone de Beauvoir," paper delivered at the American Philosophical Association, inaugural meeting of the Society for the Study of Women Philosophers, New York, December 1987 (I understand that this work is part of a book-in-progress). It is not uncommon to suggest that de Beauvoir did not herself see much of serious worth in what I will call, for brevity's sake, women's culture. For her, women leading 'women's lives' were 'mired' in immanence, while 'men's lives' made transcendence at least possible.

30. The phenomenon that I note here is discussed in psychodynamic terms by Nancy Chodorow in *Reproduction of Mothering: Psychoanalysis and the Sociology of Gender* (Berkeley: University of California Press, 1978), and by other theorists such as Jane Flax (e.g., in "Political Philosophy and the Patriarchal Unconscious: A Psychoanalytic Perspective on Epistemology and Metaphysics," in Harding and Hintikka, *Discovering Reality*) and Lillian Rubin (in *Intimate Strangers: Men and Women Together* [New York: Harper & Row, 1983]). See also Juliet Mitchell's groundbreaking *Psychoanalysis and Feminism* (New York: Random House/Vintage Books, 1974). For historical observations and analyses of particular developments of "women's culture," see Carroll Smith-Rosenberg, "The Female World of Love and Ritual: Relations Between Women in Nineteenth Century America," in Smith-Rosenberg's *Disorderly Conduct* (New York: Oxford University Press, 1985).

31. Jessica Benjamin, "Master and Slave: The Fantasy of Erotic Domination," in Ann Snitow, Christine Stansell, and Sharon Thompson, eds., *The Power of Desire: The Politics of Sexuality* (New York: Monthly Review Press, 1983), p. 280.

32. Eve Sedgwick, *Between Men: English Literature and Male Homosocial Desire* (New York: Columbia University Press, 1985), p. 11.

33. See, for example, Michel Foucault, *The History of Sexuality,* vol. 1,

trans. Robert Hurley (New York: Random House/Vintage Books, 1978); Susan Griffin, *Woman and Nature: The Roaring Inside Her* (New York: Harper & Row, 1978).

34. I find that Foucault's *History of Sexuality* makes a related point and very helpfully illuminates how the construction of sexuality is a construction of power—as, of course, is the construction of Man.

35. J. Glenn Gray, *The Warriors: Reflections on Men in Battle* (New York: Harper & Row, 1959), p. 134.

36. Hannah Arendt, *The Human Condition* (Chicago: University of Chicago Press, 1958), p. 176.

37. Arendt develops her views on the grounding of the capacity to act in the human condition of natality primarily in *The Human Condition*.

38. The remark cited from Gerda Lerner was made during discussion at The Wingspread Conference, "Liberal Education and the New Scholarship on Women," December 1981; for extended feminist analyses of war, see Cynthia Enloe, *Does Khaki Become You? The Militarization of Women's Lives* (Boston: South End Press, 1983); Judith H. Stiehm, *Arms and the Enlisted Woman* (Philadelphia: Temple University Press, 1989); the film *The Life and Times of Rosie the Riveter*, Connie Field, producer/director (Franklin Lakes, N.J.: Clarity Educational Productions, 1980); and the "war novels" of feminists such as Marge Piercy, *Gone to Soldiers* (New York: Summit Books, 1987); Valerie Miner, *Blood Sisters* (New York: St. Martin's Press, 1981); and Susan Daitch, *L.C.* (San Diego, Calif.: Harcourt, Brace, Jovanovich, 1987). I might also mention Joan V. Bondurant, *Conquest of Violence: The Gandhian Philosophy of Conflict* (Berkeley: University of California Press, 1965), for its fine analysis of the Gandhian reformulation of methods for resolving conflict.

39. Cf. Carol Cohn's "Sex and Death in the Rational World of Defense Intellectuals," in *Signs* 12 (1987), on the curious adoption of images of creation and birth by men describing their reactions to the atomic bomb, and as-yet-unpublished work by Helena Meyer-Knapp on "nuclear siege war."

40. Muriel Rukeyser, "Myth," in Sandra M. Gilbert and Susan Gubar, eds., *The Norton Anthology of Literature by Women* (New York: W. W. Norton, 1985), pp. 1787–88.

41. I have drawn on the work, published and unpublished, of Chandra Talpade Mohanty for thinking about strategic concepts (we have exchanged work and had several invaluable—to me, at least—conversations over the years).

42. Sandra Harding, "Why Has the Sex/Gender System Become Visible Only Now?" in Harding and Hintikka, *Discovering Reality*, p. 312.

43. Heidi Hartmann, "The Unhappy Marriage of Marxism and Feminism: Toward a More Progressive Union," in Lydia Sargent, ed., *Women and Revolution: The Unhappy Marriage of Marxism and Feminism* (Boston: South End Press, 1981), p. 14.

44. Joan Scott, "Gender: A Useful Category of History Analysis," *American Historical Review* 91 (1986): 1067.

45. Ibid., p. 1073.

46. Gayle Rubin, "The Traffic in Women: Notes on the 'Political Economy' of Sex," in Rayna R. Reiter, ed., *Toward an Anthropology of Women* (New York: Monthly Review Press, 1975), pp. 176–77.

47. Ibid., pp. 148–50.

48. Quoted in Steven A. Channing, *Crisis of Fear: Secession in South Carolina* (New York: W. W. Norton, 1970), p. 287.

49. Cf. Kessler and McKenna, *Gender: An Ethnomethodological Approach*, and works by Mary Daly (e.g., *Gyn/Ecology: The Metaethics of Radical Feminism* [Boston: Beacon Press, 1979]); MacKinnon, *Feminism Unmodified;* books by Andrea Dworkin (e.g., *Woman-Hating: A Radical Look at Sexuality* [New York: E. P. Dutton, 1976]); as well as works such as those cited above by Joan Scott, Gayle Rubin, Heidi Hartmann, and Mary O'Brien.

50. Cf. Jean-Paul Sartre, *Being and Nothingness: An Essay on Phenomenological Ontology,* trans. Hazel E. Barnes (London: Methuen Press, 1957), on being in-itself, being for-itself, and being in-and-for-itself. This aspect of Sartre's work is often drawn on by existential psychologists as well.

51. Teresa de Lauretis, "Feminist Studies/Critical Studies: Issues, Terms, and Contexts," in *Feminist Studies: Critical Studies* (Bloomington: Indiana University Press, 1986), pp. 9–10.

52. Among my favorite feminist humorists are Nicole Hollander (e.g., *Mercy, It's the Revolution and I'm in My Bathrobe* [New York: St. Martin's Press, 1982], and her other cartoon books featuring Sylvia), and Jane Wagner, *The Search for Signs of Intelligent Life in the Universe* (New York: Harper & Row, 1986), which was also the text for a one-woman show by the superb feminist comic Lily Tomlin.

Partial Knowledge

1. Translator's Preface in Jacques Derrida, *Dissemination,* trans. Barbara Johnson (Chicago: University of Chicago Press, 1981), p. xiv.

2. Alice A. Jardine, *Gynesis: Configurations of Woman and Modernity* (Ithaca, N.Y.: Cornell University Press, 1985), p. 24.

3. Michel Foucault, "What Is an Author?" in Paul Rabinow, ed., *The Foucault Reader* (New York: Pantheon Books, 1984), p. 101.

4. Ibid., p. 120.

5. Ibid., pp. 107–8.

6. The dominant culture has called animal behavior that seems to reflect understanding "instinct" and, in a similar move, calls apt perceptions and understanding on the part of women "intuition."

7. Michel Foucault, *The Order of Things: An Archaeology of the Human Sciences* (New York: Random House/Vintage Books, 1973), p. xxiv.

8. Henry Louis Gates, Jr., quoted in a review of his *Schomburg Library of Nineteenth-Century Black Women Writers* (New York: Oxford University Press, 1988), by Marilyn E. Mobley, *Women's Review of Books* 5 (July 1988).

9. Frederic Jameson, *The Political Unconsicous: Narrative As a Socially Symbolic Act* (Ithaca, N.Y.: Cornell University Press, 1981), pp. 9–10.

10. Gayatri Spivak, *In Other Worlds: Essays in Cultural Politics* (New York: Methuen Press, 1987), p. 15.

11. In "Postmodernism and Gender Relations in Feminist Theory," *Signs* 12 (1987): 621ff., Jane Flax suggests that feminist theory is, or should be, contained within (rather than provide a critical perspective on) other schools of thought. Her idea is nevertheless in some important ways compatible with the position I am taking here. The title of Flax's article, which locates postmodernism with gender relations theory *within* the apparently more inclusive category "feminist theory" belies Flax's own stated point that feminist theory is an aspect of postmodernism and social relations theory.

12. Ibid., p. 643.

13. Jane Flax, "Political Philosophy and the Patriarchal Unconscious: A Psychoanalytic Perspective on Epistemology and Metaphysics," in Sandra Harding and Merrill B. Hintikka, eds., *Discovering Reality: Feminist Perspectives on Epistemology, Metaphysics, Methodology, and Philosophy of Science* (Boston: D. Reidel, 1983), p. 269.

14. Robert Coles, *Children of Crisis* (New York: Dell, 1964); see also the work of such anticolonialist thinkers as Franz Fanon.

15. Elliot Jurist, in the *Owl of Minerva* 19 (Fall 1987): 11. (The *Owl of Minerva* is published by the Department of Philosophy, Villanova University, Villanova, Pa.)

16. Susanne Langer, *Mind: An Essay on Human Feeling*, abridged ed. (Baltimore: Johns Hopkins University Press, 1988), pp. 63–65.

17. Sandra Harding, *The Science Question in Feminism* (Ithaca, N.Y.: Cornell University Press, 1986), pp. 250–51.

18. Hannah Arendt, *The Human Condition* (Chicago: University of Chicago Press, 1958), p. 324.

19. Cf. John A. Allen, ed., *Hero's Way: Contemporary Poems in the Mythic Tradition* (Englewood Cliffs, N.J.: Prentice Hall, 1971); the various works of Joseph Campbell; Carol S. Pearson, *The Hero Within: Six Archetypes for the Way We Live* (New York: Harper & Row, 1986).

20. Maurice Merleau-Ponty, "From Mauss to Claude Levi-Strauss," in *Signs*, trans. Richard C. McCleary (Evanston, Ill.: Northwestern University Press, 1964), p. 120.

21. Chandra Talpade Mohanty, "Feminist Encounters: Locating the Politics of Experience," *Copyright* 1 (Fall 1987): 42.

22. Alfred North Whitehead suggested that we use the idea of "actual occasions" or "events" to replace atomistic, unrelated, static entities/things

as the basic 'parts' of the world; cf. *Process and Reality* (New York: Macmillan, 1929).

23. Cf. Carol Gilligan, *In a Different Voice* (Cambridge: Harvard University Press, 1982); Mary Field Belenky, Blythe McVicker Clinchy, Nancy Rule Goldberger, and Jill Mattuck Tarule, *Women's Ways of Knowing* (New York: Basic Books, 1986); Barbara Hilkert Andolsen et al., eds., *Women's Consciousness, Women's Conscience* (San Francisco: Harper & Row, 1985); Nell Noddings, *Caring: A Feminine Approach to Ethics and Moral Education* (Berkeley: University of California Press, 1984); Sara Ruddick, "Maternal Thinking," *Feminist Studies* 6 (Summer 1980), and her 1989 book, *Maternal Thinking: Toward a Politics of Peace* (Boston: Beacon Press).

24. See the work of John Dewey.

25. Cf. critiques of Betty Friedan's emphasis on the white, middle-class housewife: for example, Catharine R. Stimpson, in *Ms.* 10 (December 1981): 161; Arlene Avakian et al., "Women Critique Racism Conference," letter to National Women's Studies Coordinating Council and *Off Our Backs*, March 1982, p. 25; Bettina Aptheker, "Strong Is What We Make Each Other: Unlearning Racism in Women's Studies," *Women's Studies Quarterly* 9 (Winter 1981): 13–16; "Black Studies and Women Studies: Search for a Long Overdue Partnership—A Panel Presented at the Sixth Annual Conference of the National Council for Black Studies," *Women's Studies Quarterly* 10 (Summer 1982).

26. See Lorraine Hansberry, *To Be Young, Gifted and Black* (New York: Signet/New American Library, 1970).

27. See the work of Gerald Graf. I am thinking particularly of the presentation he made on a panel I shared with him at a Duke University and University of North Carolina/Chapel Hill Conference in the fall of 1988, the proceedings of which are published in *South Atlantic Quarterly* 89, no. 1 (Winter 1989); the *South Atlantic Quarterly* is published by Duke University Press.

28. For work by feminist scholars showing how 'even' science yields to a feminist critique, see Diana Long Hall, "The Social Implications of the Scientific Study of Sex," in *The Scholar and the Feminist IV: Connecting Theory, Practice, and Values*, proceedings of a conference sponsored by the Barnard College Women's Center (New York: Barnard College, 1977); Evelyn Fox Keller, *Reflections on Gender and Science* (New Haven: Yale University Press, 1985); as well as works previously cited by Ruth Bleier, Ruth Hubbard, Sue Rosser, and others.

29. For an intriguing discussion of current logical approaches to language, see Jaakko Hintikka and Merrill B. Hintikka, "How Can Language Be Sexist?" in Harding and Hintikka, *Discovering Reality*, p. 146. The Hintikkas find what they consider a male emphasis on "discrete individuals whose identity from one model (world) to another is unproblematic," thereby adding considerations from language philosophy and logic to anal-

yses of objectivity as a *desideratum* shaped by male patterns of individuation.

30. Cf. the works of Freire, Fanon, and Cabral.

31. Ruel W. Tyson, "Live by Comparisons: A New Home for Reason in the University?" the Sixth Annual Memorial Lecture, Society for Values in Higher Education, August 1987, published by *Soundings: An Interdisciplinary Journal* (Knoxville, Tenn., 1988).

32. Langer, *Mind*, p. 3.

V. BACK TO BASICS

1. I am grateful here for an exchange of letters with Carl Schorske following the "History And . . ." Conference at Scripps College in the spring of 1988, which led me to think further about the role and importance of universals.

2. Immanuel Kant, *The Critique of Judgment*, trans. Werner S. Pluher (Indianapolis, Ind.: Hackett, 1986), no. 60, p. 231.

3. Arendt, *The Human Condition*, p. 8.

4. Ibid., p. 8.

5. See, for example, works by Ursula K. LeGuin, Marge Piercy, and Charlotte Perkins Gilman.

6. From *The Collected Poems of Muriel Rukeyser* (New York: McGraw-Hill, 1978), p. 242; originally published in her *Beast in View* of 1944. © 1944. The poem is reprinted here by permission of International Creative Management.